ma and Society Series
eral Editor: Jeffrey Richards

lished and forthcoming:

anned in the USA': British Films in the United States and their Censorship, 1933–1960
Anthony Slide

Best of British: Cinema and Society from 1930 to the Present
Anthony Aldgate & Jeffrey Richards
Revised Edition

The British at War: Cinema, State and Propaganda, 1939–1945
James Chapman

British Cinema and the Cold War
Tony Shaw

British Film Noir: Shadows are my Friends
Robert Murphy

The Crowded Prairie: American National Identity in the Hollywood Western
Michael Coyne

Distorted Images: British National Identity and Film in the 1920s
Kenton Bamford

Film Propaganda: Soviet Russia and Nazi Germany
Richard Taylor
Revised Edition

Licence to Thrill: A Cultural History of James Bond Films
James Chapman

Spaghetti Western: Cowboys and Europeans from Karl May to Sergio Leone
Christopher Frayling
Revised Edition

The Unknown 1930s: An Alternative History of the British Cinema, 1929–1939
Edited by Jeffrey Richards

Cine
Gen

Pu

Christmas at the Movies

CHRISTMAS AT THE MOVIES

Images of Christmas in American, British and European Cinema

Edited by

Mark Connelly

I.B.Tauris *Publishers*
LONDON • NEW YORK

Published in 2000 by I.B.Tauris & Co Ltd
Victoria House, Bloomsbury Square, London WC1B 4DZ
175 Fifth Avenue, New York NY 10010

In the United States and Canada distributed by St. Martin's Press
175 Fifth Avenue, New York NY 10010

ISBN 1-86064-397-3

A full CIP record of this book is available from the British Library
A full CIP record of this book is available from the Library of Congress

Library of Congress catalog card: available

Typeset in Garamond 11 on 12 by The Midlands Book Typesetting Company, Loughborough
Printed and Bound in Great Britain by MPG Books Ltd, Bodmin, Cornwall

Contents

Illustrations

Scrooge (Alastair Sim) and Bob Cratchit (Mervyn Johns), *Scrooge* (1951).

George Bailey (James Stewart) and Clarence Odbody (Henry Travers), *It's a Wonderful Life* (1946); George Bailey, Clarence Odbody and Mary Hatch (Donna Reed), *It's a Wonderful Life* (1946).

Christmas in a tube shelter. *Christmas Under Fire* (1940).

Rose Adair (Dorothy Hyson), Edwin Stott (Robertson Hare), David Winterton (Ralph Lynn) and Ernestine Stott (Norma Varden), *Turkey Time* (1933); Jenny Gregory (Celia Johnson) and David Patterson (John Gregson), *The Holly and the Ivy* (1952).

A Christmas Story (1983)

Guy (Nino Castelnuevo) and his wife and son in *Les Parapluies de Cherbourg* (1964).

Carnival Night (1956)

Nastia (Elena Shevchenko) with one of her pupils in *The Sympathy Seeker* (1997)

Poster of *Plácido* (1961).

Acknowledgements

This book came out of conversations with Jeffrey Richards and Mark Glancy and so I would like to thank them for encouraging the idea in the first place. I would also like to thank Philippa Brewster of I.B. Tauris for taking on the project and then making many perceptive and helpful comments on the nature and structure of the piece. Big thanks also go out to all the contributors for being so patient with this novice editor who tried his best to learn the skills on the job.

For the illustrations I would like to thank BFI Stills, Posters and Designs. I would also like to thank Tartan Video, Warner Brothers, Twentieth Century Fox, Paramount and Universal. All attempts have been made to locate copyright holders of material used. However in certain cases this has not proved conclusive. If any acknowledgement is missing or wrongly attributed it would be appreciated if contact could be made to ensure that it is rectified.

Guy Austin would like to thank: Maire Cross, Renate Gunther, Martin Hurcombe, Béatrice Le Bihan, Annie Rouxeville, Walter Robinson, Dave Walker and Geraldine Walsh-Harrington, for their valuable suggestions.

Rowana Agajanian extends her thanks to James Chapman.

General Editor's Introduction

During the nineteenth century the family reading of Charles Dickens' *A Christmas Carol* was one of the rituals of Christmas. In the latter part of the twentieth century, the ritual television showing of Frank Capra's film *It's a Wonderful Life* took its place. This is symptomatic of the process by which cinema became an integral part of the celebration of Christmas in the twentieth century. The Christmas season was a major period for the release of the latest Hollywood blockbusters and those films which failed at the box-office were known within the industry as 'Christmas turkeys'. Thanks to Hollywood, Christmas as we know it has become steadily Americanized. More than half the essays in this collection chart the process by which Hollywood has appropriated and colonized Christmas. Even Dickens has been taken over as part of this operation, as James Chapman demonstrates in his exemplary essay.

But this rich mix of essays is full of plums. Almost no facet of the Christmas movie is left unexplored. We can read about the role of the Christmas film in wartime both in Britain and America, the cinematic career of Santa Claus and the rise and rise in popular esteem of *It's a Wonderful Life*. But all is not just joy to the world and peace and goodwill to all men in the cinematic Christmas. There is a darker side, gleefully analyzed by Kim Newman, in which the schmaltz and saccharine conventions of *White Christmas* are undercut by the depredations of a parade of psycho santas and Christmas slashers.

The cinematic Christmas is put into a global context by the inclusion of revealing essays on Christmas movies in France, Spain and the Soviet Union, where the Hollywood version confronts homegrown traditions. What this wide-ranging and stimulating collection of essays reveals is that there is far more to Christmas at the movies than just Dickens and Capra and that the picture is far from straightforward. There are affirmations of and subversions of the family: celebrations and critiques of the commercialization of Christmas; anthems to peace and to violence; there are both angels and demons. The seasonal refrain of all these essays is unquestionably: 'Have yourself a complex little Christmas'.

Jeffrey Richards

Contributors

Rowana Agajanian is a research student at the Open University. She is a contributor to the forthcoming collection *Windows on the Sixties: Exploring Key Texts of Media and Culture*, edited by Anthony Aldgate, James Chapman and Arthur Marwick and is currently researching the work of the Children's Film Foundation.

Guy Austin has just published a book on the films of Claude Chabrol. He is a lecturer in the Department of French, University of Sheffield.

Birgit Beumers is a lecturer in the Department of Russian Studies, University of Bristol. She is the editor of *Russia on Reels: The Russian Ideal in Post-Soviet Cinema*.

James Chapman is Lecturer in Film and Television History at the Open University. He is the author of *The British at War: Cinema, State and Propaganda, 1939–1945* (1998) and *Licence To Thrill: A Cultural History of the James Bond Films* (1999), both published by I. B. Tauris in the 'Cinema and Society' series. He is also co-editor of *Windows on the 'Sixties: Exploring Key Texts of Media and Culture* (2000).

Mark Connelly is author of *Christmas: A Social History* and is the Reuters Lecturer in Media History at the University of Kent.

Peter William Evans is Professor of Hispanic Studies at Queen Mary and Westfield College, London. His cinema books include *The Films of Luis Bunuel: Subjectivity and Desire* and *Spanish Cinema: The Auteurist Tradition*.

H. Mark Glancy is a lecturer in Film History at Queen Mary and Westfield College, London. He has recently published *When Hollywood Loved Britain: The Hollywood 'British' Film 1939–1945*.

Jonathan Munby has an interest in black American cinema and has recently published *Public Enemies, Public Heroes: Screening the Gangster from Little Caesar to Touch of Evil*. He is a lecturer in American Studies at the University of Lancaster.

Kim Newman is a journalist and author and authority on horror movies. His works include the *BFI Companion to Horror* and *Apocalypse Movies: End of the World Cinema*.

Jeffrey Richards is Professor of Popular Culture at the University of Lancaster. He has published on many aspects of cinema and film history, most recently *Film and British National Identity: From Dickens to Dad's Army* and a new edition of *Best of British: Cinema and Society from 1930 to the Present*.

Sarah Street is a lecturer at the University of Bristol and has an interest in the development of the British film industry. She is the author of *British National Cinema*.

Introduction

Mark Connelly

Christmas is now an international festival. It touches nations that do not celebrate Christianity as their main religion. A good example is Japan, for in recent years it has adapted aspects of the season – Santa, decorations, trees – into its calendar.[1] The reason why Christmas is known everywhere is simple – cinema. Cinema has shown people what the festival of Christmas is like, particularly how it is celebrated in America, more than any other medium. Cinema and Christmas are intertwined; but there are hardly any dedicated studies or surveys of these films. This book is a response to that lacuna.

Most people know at least one Christmas movie and most people can recall a childhood visit to the cinema at Christmas, usually to see a festive movie. Perhaps this is at the heart of the connection. Christmas is a holiday time and the cinema has responded to this pool of potential customers with free time. But this causes us to ask how exactly Christmas became a festival of great importance to the world. A few words on the history and gestation of Christmas are needed by way of preface.

The Development of Christmas

Christmas was not at all important to the early church. The festival had very little significance when compared with the real heart of Christianity, the Resurrection. Easter was the key festival, the commemoration of the death, and defeat of death, by the Risen Lord. Christmas came a poor second in the liturgical year. But from the late Dark Ages and into the early Middle Ages the papacy began to show an interest in the mid-winter festival. The Roman Catholic Church managed to melt down many of the pagan and celtic rites marking the heart of winter into the Christian observance of Christmas. Slowly Christmas started to become more important in the Christian year. Specifically written seasonal carols came into the celebration. In Italy, the *praesepio*, or crib, was introduced by St Francis. Across Europe the great flowering of Gothic art saw the annunciation, nativity and adoration by wise men and shepherds interpreted in thousands of stained-glass windows.

Reformation and Renaissance had contradictory effects on Christmas. In Germany Luther quite merrily took on the season and so kept a connection with the Catholics of the Holy Roman Empire. But the more extreme forms of Protestantism seen in some of the Swiss cantons, England and Scotland rejected the festival as a popish, uncanonical extravagance. The irony of the situation is that England, from the late-eighteenth century, became the nation that felt most spiritually and historically connected with the season. The compromise religion of the Church of England, in fact, ensured that Christmas survived the more extreme expressions of the Reformation. But this situation did not look so sure when the monarchy was toppled and a Commonwealth declared in the mid-seventeenth century. Cromwell banned Christmas and punished any celebrations of it. Though this caused Christmas to slip a little it never totally lost its grip on the popular imagination. Indeed Christmas spread through the English-speaking world during this period.

English settlers in the New World took their Christmas traditions with them, where they were to merge into the similar, Northern European traditions of the Dutch settlers. Though Calvinist attempts were made to crush Christmas in the New World, the festival was to show that its emotional hold was just too firm. In a world devoid of electric light, afflicted by pestilence and disease, winter was an extremely frightening, depressing and trying time. The harsh weather of northern Europe and in some of the colonies of the New World ensured that a festival designed to uplift the spirits and drive away gloom retained an inherent popularity. A similar situation held sway in Russia and the lands of the Orthodox churches.

The image we have of Christmas today is one largely distilled from the Anglo-American vision of the season. As noted, the English rediscovered their past Christmas heritage in the late-eighteenth century and into the Victorian period. It is commonly said that the Victorians invented Christmas but that does not appear to be the case. Much of what the Victorians did was simply to reinvigorate, investigate and revive. The nineteenth century therefore saw the carol make its renaissance in England; Christmas trees and decorations reappeared (they were known long before Albert allegedly pioneered them in Britain); presents were given; pantomimes were attended; dining and partying flowered again. The key symbol of this renaissance, but again not its instigator, was Charles Dickens with his Christmas Books, and *A Christmas Carol* (1843) in particular. The USA adopted many of these themes and took Dickens to its heart. With the continual mixing of all the Christmas traditions of immigrants to the USA the Anglo-Saxon Christmas became predominant. The old English Father Christmas was amalgamated with analogous European figures, such as Kris Kringle, Saint Nicholas and Father Frost, resulting in Santa Claus. As the USA overtook Britain to become the principal power of the globe the American Christmas became the key interpretation of the season. But it was a Christmas tree that had grown out of a largely English root.[2]

Christmas and the Birth of Cinema

The idea of Christmas mostly commonly explored in cinema, whether as celebration or critique, is largely based upon the vision that evolved in the nineteenth century. The Victorians took up Christmas and all its trappings and used them to celebrate home, family and charity. Domesticated Christian values predominated. This was the inheritance bequeathed to cinema, an inheritance that was also felt, and continues to be felt, in European and US society today.

Penne Restad, in her excellent examination of Christmas in America, has noted how important Christmas is in Hollywood productions:

> When Christmas is not the central theme nor even a minor one in a film's story line, directors, screenwriters and others have further codified the fragmented reminders of the holiday into highly tele-graphic conditions. A quarter, and perhaps even a majority of top-grossing motion pictures released in recent years at least mention Christmas or have a scene with a Christmas icon – a fleeting cameo of a Christmas tree, or the trailing melody of an oft-hummed carol – regardless of the movie's actual theme. These further circumscribe Christmas in order to convey a potent, highly condensed expression of American faith and values.[3]

So the values of Christmas have become those of America, or vice versa, and Hollywood has thrown its weight behind them. Many of the essays in this collection are an exploration of that connection.

Christmas was such an all-pervasive part of European (but particularly English) and North American life by the late-nineteenth century it is hardly surprising that cinema took to it from the start. Dickens was just too good a target. Silent versions of *A Christmas Carol* proliferated.

Alongside these all manner of Christmas films were produced, sporting such titles as *The Old Folks' Christmas* (1913); *Christmas Day in the Workhouse* (1914) and *One Winter's Night* (1914). But during the 1920s and 1930s there was a lapse in Christmas films, aside from yet more versions of *A Christmas Carol*. The reasons for this are not entirely clear, especially when films that do make mention of Christmas seem to have gone out of their way to do so. A good example is the 1936 MGM version of *A Tale of Two Cities*, in which a Christmas scene is added, having no point of reference with the original text. It seems that Dickens and Christmas had become so intertwined that it was natural to add a festive scene to the film. Cinema's lack of attention was radio's chance. Throughout the 1930s American homes were filled with the tones of Lionel Barrymore as Scrooge radiating from their radios each Christmas. On one occasion Orson Welles's *Mercury Theatre* performed the story with Barrymore in his usual role and Welles as Dickens/narrator.

The Second World War really kick-started the modern Christmas movie. But the wartime Christmases of British and American cinema were very different. Mark Glancy's chapter shows how Hollywood created an idealized vision of Christmas at home. Christmas was presented as a lush fairytale land of plenty and joy, even if a few glitches had to be overcome on the road to Christmas Day, as seen in Preston Sturges's *Remember the Night* (1940). It was a world guaranteed to appeal to lonely, homesick GIs stuck out on Pacific Islands or sitting in training camps in England. It was a world that displaced female war workers could dream of and aspire to. It was a dream of what America would become in the post-war world. By contrast British Christmases seemed stuck in the gritty reality of here and now. Sarah Street reveals how the British literally brought a documentary reality to the Christmas of the blitz of 1940 in the Crown Film Unit production *Christmas Under Fire*. Feature films also concentrated on the way in which wartime conditions affected the celebration of Christmas, as seen in *In Which We Serve* (1942).

For a short period in the immediate aftermath of war, when it appeared that the dreams of many Americans for a stable and prosperous future might not appear, Hollywood changed tack. Jonathan Munby argues that *It's a Wonderful Life* (1946) is not a simplistic, feel-good movie at all. Instead it can be read as a parable of malaise and a warning that America is not all it might be. A similarly dark interpretation can be said to fill Berlanga's understanding of Christmas in Francoist Spain, *Plácido* (1961). The film shows those in need of charity as freaks and strange outcasts, but, as Peter Evans points out, its comic moments are reminiscent of Sturges. Similarly Guy Austin's examination of French Christmas movies shows that though there are indeed celebrations and nostalgic longings for the good old-fashioned Christmas, as seen in *Château de ma mère* (*My*

Mother's Castle 1990), the season could also be used to highlight pain and an element of lingering regret, encapsulated in the final scene of *Les Parapluies de Cherbourg* (*The Umbrellas of Cherbourg* 1964). *Yauara-t-il de la neige à Noël?* (*Will It Snow For Christmas?* 1997) shows a family collapsing into misery and hints at suicide, maintaining the darkness of *It's a Wonderful Life*. Russian cinema too has produced such introspection and grimly awful Christmases: *S novym godom, Moskva* (*Happy New Year, Moscow*, 1993) shows a group of flatmates whose problems are massively exacerbated by the false sense of togetherness the season demands. Christmas at the movies was therefore capable of breaking free from sweet, nicely rounded endings and the other clichés that are often associated with it.

It's a Wonderful Life also reintroduced the supernatural element to Christmas films: as both Munby and Chapman show, the film has distinct elements of *A Christmas Carol*. The wartime Christmases of British and American movies had avoided this angle, preferring the vision of reality and a homely dream respectively. The intervention of Clarence, the angel, in *It's a Wonderful Life* was soon imitated in such films as *The Bishop's Wife* (1947), in which Cary Grant descends to earth in order to bring human warmth and Christmas cheer to a rather dour bishop (David Niven), and *Tenth Avenue Angel* (1948).

Christmas had always been connected with supernatural visitations and Dickens built upon that connection. Cinematic versions of *A Christmas Carol* had been popular since the earliest days of film, as noted. James Chapman shows how Scrooge and the ghosts became men for all seasons insofar as cinematic interpretations have tended to reflect the spirit of their own times. For the Britain of the 1930s *Scrooge* (1935) emphasized the need for national unity in times of stress; for the new welfare state Britain of the fifties *Scrooge* (1951) was a chance to examine properly the bad old days of the Victorian past. Just as the story was updated for American audiences and American conditions in 1947 with *It's a Wonderful Life*, so too was the original redesigned to reflect British interpretations of its past and contemporary society. Chapman's piece further explores how the story has lent itself to harsher and more anarchic versions, such as *Scrooged* (1988) and *The Muppet Christmas Carol* (1992).

Anarchic interpretations of Christmas appear to abound in Russian cinema. The season in Russia has deep connections with magic, spirituality and the supernatural. The Soviet regime tempered certain aspects of this but Birgit Beumers shows how this spirit has re-entered Russian Christmas films with *Eta veselaia planeta* (*This Merry Planet* 1973), a film in which aliens try to abduct a bank manager! There are connections here with the almost glorious *Santa Claus Conquers the Martians* (USA 1964).

In most cases the arrival of a supernatural figure in these films almost always means a guarantee of earthly, material success, provided the mortal takes notice of the visitor. The spiritual world is very firmly connected to that of the secular and acquisitive. Only rarely does such a visitor create a genuine change in family fortunes, as Jeffrey Richards shows in his investigation of *The Cheaters* (1945). But it is also noticeable that Santa Claus only becomes a significant figure in the movies once America truly became an acquisitive and mass-consumerist nation – the years after the Second World War. Prior to *Miracle on 34th Street*'s release in 1947 there are very few screen appearances by Santa. It seems as if it took an all-pervasive shopping culture to bring him to cinematic life.

As Western, and more particularly American, consumer society has reached greater heights its Christmas-time cinematic rendering has tended to increase its element of violence, as protest, as slapstick comedy and for entertainment. Kim Newman reveals not just the dark side of Christmas but its sheer macabre horror as well. Films such as *You Better Watch Out* (1980) show how middle-class Christmases can descend into hellish adventures, while *Silent Night, Deadly Night* (1984) turns Santa Claus into a Herod-like character who is more intent on killing children than giving them presents. Alternatively, Jeffrey Richards shows how English middle-class families have their Christmas and familial ups and downs in a very English way. Complementing the horrific Christmas is Rowana Agajanian's survey of the violent Christmas. She reveals the irony that films such as *Lethal Weapon* (1987) mix Christmas and violence with a total *lack* of irony, despite having a tongue-in-cheek and ironic approach to the action movie genre. On the other hand *Home Alone* (1990) has something of the pantomime and cartoon about it and makes children the instruments of violence. Claude Lévi-Strauss argued that Christmas was similar to North American aboriginal customs of placating the violent spirits of the dead. He saw Christmas present-giving to children in a similar way, a method of controlling unpredictable elements in society.[4] *Home Alone* appears to fit elements of this theory for it is about a child left entirely to his own devices at Christmas – the result is a mayhem of slapstick violence.

The Idea of Christmas and Cinema

Penne Restad has also highlighted the extremely important fact that Christmas often plays a role in films not actually centred on the season.[5] Christmas becomes an emotional shorthand to impart mood and the *mise en scène* to the viewer. Taking a clutch of examples, we can see this at work. Barry Levinson's *Diner* (1982) starts on Christmas night 1959 and concerns events running up to New Year. The trappings of Christmas are everywhere: decorations and songs heard in the diner; a nativity display outside a church; frosty weather. However, the film is not really about

Christmas and mixes Jewish characters with Christian ones. But it is a film about relationships, about problems between older and younger family members, about establishing a place within society. Christmas and its associations are therefore vital in order to create the right milieu. A similar theme can be seen in Rob Reiner's *When Harry Met Sally* (1989). The great bulk of the action takes place during a succession of New York autumns and winters, with the run-up to Christmas being particularly important. At one point Harry (Billy Crystal) states, 'Boy, the holidays are tough. Every year I just try to get from the day before Thanksgiving to the day after New Year's.' The film is unashamedly emotional and nostalgic. The nostalgia is imparted by its music and obsession with season. We therefore see Central Park covered in snow, accompanied by the strains of *Winter Wonderland*. A huge Christmas tree is taken home while Bing Crosby sings *Have Yourself a Merry Little Christmas*. The film is sentimental and so Christmas is vital to it. Both films also reflect the American obsession with the 1950s, a cultural phenomenon that was triggered by *American Graffiti* (1973) and reached new heights in the 1980s. Christmas was, no doubt, more like Christmas in the 1950s. Once again Christmas is important for the conventions it places in the viewer's mind. Such is the significance of Christmas to movies in general.

This book is an eclectic collection, covering many different types of Christmas film, from many countries but leaning towards British and American productions. It is also acknowledged that the collection does not cover everything. Constraints of space have necessarily demanded that many interesting aspects have not been included. European cinema no doubt has more to offer. The strong German and Northern European Christmas traditions must find reflections in the national cinemas of Germany and Scandinavia. It is fascinating to ponder on what Nazi cinema might have made of Christmas given its connections with German history and legend. Swedish cinema has also made its contribution. Probably the best example is Bergman's *Fanny and Alexandra* (1982). Family crises, problems with faith, rites of passage, are all examined via the medium of the celebration of Christmas. Italian cinema too, coming under the strange mixture of Catholic and left-wing influences, must have something to say on the season.

The actual nativity itself is also missing. The birth of Christ has been seen on the screen but it is usually incidental to other tales. There is a glorious nativity scene in *Ben Hur* (1959) and a more sober one in Pasolini's *Il Vangelo Secondo Matteo* (*The Gospel According to St Matthew* 1964) in which there is a particularly brutal Slaughter of the Innocents. But the stark truth is that Christmas films, like much of the modern Christmas itself, are not directly interested in the birth of Christ.

Instead this collection seeks to examine some of the great Christmas films of American and European cinema and some of the lesser-known ones that, nonetheless, make significant points about the way in which Christmas has been perceived, celebrated and presented in American and European society and cinema. To paraphrase Dickens's preface to *A Christmas Carol*: 'We have endeavoured in this book to raise the Ghost of an Idea, which shall not put readers out of humour with themselves, with each other, with the season, or with us. May it haunt their houses pleasantly, and no one wish to lay it.'

Notes

1. Brian Moeran and Lise Skov, 'Cinderella Christmas; Kitsch, Consumerism, and Youth in Japan' in Daniel Miller (ed.), *Unwrapping Christmas* (Oxford: Clarendon Press, 1993), pp 105-33.

2. For further details on the history of Christmas see the following: M. Connelly, *Christmas: A Social History* (London: I.B. Tauris, 1999); P. Davis, *The Lives and Times of Ebenezer Scrooge* (New Haven, Conn., 1990); J.M. Golby and A.W. Purdue, *The Making of the Modern Christmas* (London: B.T. Batsford, 1986); P. Restad, *Christmas in America* (Oxford: Oxford University Press, 1993).

3. Restad, pp 170–1.

4. Claude Lévi-Strauss, 'Father Christmas Executed' in Miller, pp 30–54.

5. Restad, p 171.

1

God Bless Us, Every One: Movie Adaptations of *A Christmas Carol*

James Chapman

Charles Dickens's *A Christmas Carol* was published in December 1843 to immediate popular acclaim. Dickens's contemporary William Thackeray famously described the book as 'a national benefit, and to every man and woman who reads it a personal kindness'.[1] Other reviewers were equally complimentary, to such an extent, indeed, that Dickens himself could tell his brother that '[t]he *Carol* is a prodigious success'.[2] It was equally popular with Dickens's readers, the elegant crimson and gold bound volume, published by Chapman and Hall and illustrated in colour by John Leech of *Punch*, selling some 6000 copies within its first week at the inexpensive price of five shillings apiece. The very embodiment of seasonal good cheer, it was most warmly received and plaudits were heaped upon Dickens for his morally uplifting tale of Ebenezer Scrooge, a miser who mends his ways after being visited on Christmas Eve by a succession of frightening but generally benign ghosts. 'Blessings on your kind heart,' wrote the lawyer and critic Lord Francis Jeffrey to Dickens. 'You should be happy with yourself, for you may be sure you have done more good by this little publication, fostered more kindly feelings, and prompted more positive acts of beneficence, than can be traced to all the pulpits and confessionals in Christendom since Christmas 1842.'[3]

For all its enthusiastic contemporary reception, however, it would be fair to say that *A Christmas Carol* is not generally regarded by literary critics

and Dickensian scholars as being among its author's most important or
accomplished works. In an *oeuvre* that reads like a roll-call of canonical
Victorian literature, this is perhaps understandable. Not only is the *Carol*
significantly shorter than most of Dickens's other works, but the assump-
tion that it is not intended to be taken too seriously is inscribed in the text
itself. Dickens's own preface ('I have endeavoured in this Ghostly little
book, to raise the Ghost of an Idea, which shall not put my readers out of
humour with themselves, with each other, with the season, or with me.
May it haunt their house pleasantly, and no one wish to lay it.') suggests
that it is intended as nothing more than a seasonal *jeu d'esprit*. Dickens had
written it quickly in the autumn of 1843 while also working on *Martin
Chuzzlewit*. 'Never had he worked with such furious energy and enthusiasm, with so much laughter and so many tears, as he did on *A Christmas
Carol*', wrote J.B. Priestley.[4]

The whimsical nature of the *Carol* is surely the main reason why it has
not attracted the same sort of critical attention as so many of Dickens's
other works. For one thing, the prose style of the book is rather more
colloquial than its author's major novels. Its tone is described by critic
Michael Slater as being 'that of a jolly, kind-hearted bachelor uncle seated
across the hearth from his hearers on some festive domestic occasion'.[5] It
is little wonder, then, that it became a favourite Christmas pastime for the
Carol to be read aloud. This tradition persisted long after Dickens's death:
in the 1930s, for example, it was made known that American President
Franklin Roosevelt read the story to his family every Christmas Eve.
Another likely reason why it has been largely neglected in Dickensian
scholarship is the perception that the *Carol* lacks the thematic and artistic
maturity of its author's most celebrated works. It predates the period
which most Dickensian scholars identify as the peak of his career, usually
seen to begin with *Dombey and Son*, serialized between 1846 and 1848, and
extending throughout the 1850s.[6]

While it is not the purpose of this chapter to argue for or against the
merits of the *Carol* as a literary text, there is nevertheless a good case to
suggest that the book deserves more critical consideration than has generally been the case. Most obviously, it exemplifies the social conscience
and sense of moral responsibility that was such a hallmark of Dickens's
work throughout his career. It was very much a product of the 'Hungry
Forties', a decade of agricultural depression and urban poverty. For all the
whimsicality of the story, there is a serious side to the *Carol* which highlights the plight of the poor, particularly children, personified in the
character of Tiny Tim, the crippled son of Scrooge's put-upon but loyal
clerk Bob Cratchit. Scrooge, it may be argued, represents the unfeeling
and selfish elements of the prosperous middle and mercantile classes of
early Victorian Britain. He is indifferent to the plight of the poor, refusing

to give charity on the grounds that he has already paid taxes which go towards the upkeep of the prisons and workhouses ('I don't make merry myself at Christmas, and I can't afford to make idle people merry. I help to support the establishments I have mentioned: they cost enough: and those who are badly off must go there'). Scrooge's sentiments reflect those of many politicians and administrators who worried about the rising cost of poor relief: the rationale behind the controversial Poor Law Amendment Act of 1834 – a measure dubbed by its critics the 'Whig Starvation and Infanticide Act' and which Dickens had attacked in *Oliver Twist* – had been primarily an economic one in that it was intended to reduce the cost of poor relief, and only secondarily a social one. The stigma attached to the workhouse was such that, as the charitable gentlemen in the *Carol* remark, 'many would rather die' than enter one. Scrooge's unfeeling reply ('If they would rather die, they had better do it, and decrease the surplus population') recalls, whether intentionally or not, Thomas Malthus's *Essay on Population* (1798), which had argued that the populace was increasing faster than the capacity to feed it. The population of England and Wales doubled between 1801 and 1851, and by the 1830s there were approximately a million and a half paupers in a population of thirteen million.[7] Later, of course, Scrooge's remarks come back to haunt him. When he asks whether there is any hope for Tiny Tim, the Ghost of Christmas Present reminds him of his earlier sentiments ('If he be like to die, he had better do it, and decrease the surplus population'). When the same spirit opens its robe to reveal a starving boy and girl, representing Ignorance and Want, and Scrooge asks 'Have they no refuge or resource?', the ghost replies again with Scrooge's own words ('Are there no prisons? Are there no workhouses?'). Scrooge's redemption at the end of the book, which sees him make generous provision for the poor, and especially for the Cratchits, affirms Dickens's own faith in the charitable duty and social responsibility expected of the wealthier classes.

The *Carol*, then, exhibits many of the themes which are common to the rest of Dickens's work. A 'ghostly little book' it may have been, but the fantastic content of the story – which may be interpreted literally, in the sense that Scrooge is visited by 'real' ghosts, or as a nightmare in which he sees the error of his ways – does not mean that its observations on the injustices of Victorian society are any less pertinent than, say, *Hard Times* or *Little Dorrit*. It is in its way as damning an indictment of social deprivation as *Oliver Twist*, as pronounced a critique of greed and selfishness as *Martin Chuzzlewit*, and, for Scrooge himself, as much a story of self-discovery as *David Copperfield* or *Great Expectations*.

Nevertheless, it is not for its qualities as a social critique that the *Carol* is best known, but for its evocation of Christmastime. In this sense the *Carol* is an example of one of those works that has acquired a wider cultural significance above and beyond any literary qualities it may or may not possess. Dickens is often credited with having 'invented' the Victorian Christmas. Along with Washington Irving in the United States, Dickens is regarded almost as the 'father' of the modern Christmas. While he was by no means the only Victorian novelist or essayist to write about Christmas, Dickens returned to it more often than most. The *Carol* was neither his first nor his only Christmas story, though it is undoubtedly his most famous and most enduring. He had already written a short story, 'A Christmas Dinner', which was published in his first book, *Sketches By Boz*, in which a mother who disapproves of her daughter's marriage to a poor man is reconciled to her at Christmas; while his first full novel, *The Pickwick Papers*, had included a sequence of Christmas celebrations at Dingley Dell in which Mr Pickwick and his companions rediscover the joys of childhood through their games and feasting. The *Carol* was followed by another four 'Christmas books', *The Chimes*, *The Cricket on the Hearth*, *The Battle of Life* and *The Haunted Man*, with the five stories being published in a single volume in 1852. *The Chimes* is the closest to the *Carol* in content, being a ghost story set on New Year's Eve in which the good-natured Toby Veck is shown the hardships suffered by various characters when he is mesmerized by chiming bells, spirits and elfin creatures. *The Cricket on the Hearth*, which is set during winter though has nothing specifically to do with Christmas, is a story of lovers reunited through the intervention of a speaking faery cricket which provides guidance for John Peerybingle, who wrongly believes his wife to be in love with another man. *The Battle of Life* is another love story following the romantic fortunes of Dr Jeddler's two daughters, and which unlike the other Christmas books has no supernatural plot element. *The Haunted Man* (the full title of which is *The Haunted Man and the Ghost's Bargain*) is a Faustian story about a man who enters into a compact with an evil spirit to ease the suffering he has known by transferring his own troubles to others.

The significance of Dickens's Christmas stories is to be found less in their quality as literature than in the role they have played in the social and cultural construction of Christmas. The Dickensian Christmas is one which reaffirms the values of the family and the joyful innocence of childhood. Dickens espouses the qualities of human warmth and kindness, charity for the poor and moral regeneration. But the Dickensian Christmas is not an explicitly religious one: it centres on the family and the hearth rather than the church or the pulpit. Furthermore, the Dickensian Christmas has a historically specific dimension to it, emerging at a moment of rapid population growth, industrialization and urbanization. As John Golby and Bill Purdue point out in their book *The Making of the Modern Christmas*, the Dickensian Christmas represents an attempt to come to terms with social change:

Dickens brought together the mutually supportive preoccupation of nostalgia for a colourful but stable past, where easier and more convivial social relationships were exemplified by Christmas festivities, and anxiety about a rapidly changing present with its many moral and social problems ... *A Christmas Carol* is ... one of the greatest Christmas texts for in it Christmas becomes a bridge between the world as it is and the world as it should be, and here we are at the heart not only of the Victorian Christmas but of the modern Christmas as it has continued to develop. Mr Pickwick's Christmas at Dingley Dell was a Christmas Past, but Scrooge's Christmas pointed to the social problems of the present and anxieties about the future.[8]

Golby and Purdue argue, furthermore, that Dickens's Christmas stories, and the *Carol* in particular, played an important role in what they term the 'refurbishment' of Christmas by the Victorians. Pointing out that in the late-eighteenth and early-nineteenth centuries Christmas was not the popular festival that it had once been, they show how the Victorians rediscovered Christmas as a folk (rather than a religious) festival. It was during the nineteenth century that practices such as carol-singing, exchanging Christmas cards and giving presents to children and other relations became central to the celebration of Christmas, so that by the end of the century Christmas had once again become an important cultural event. 'The late Victorian Christmas,' they suggest, 'had a spiritual significance but it was less a Christian spirituality than one which drew upon the warm but sentimental humanitarianism epitomized by Charles Dickens; it saluted and celebrated the family, childhood and the extended family of the nation.'[9]

For all its historical specificity, however, the Dickensian Christmas also has a timelessness about it. Scrooge's Christmas may have reflected directly the social problems of the 1840s, but the *Carol* has transcended its historical origins to become, after the Nativity, the most definitive of all Christmas stories. It is not merely that the *Carol* has remained a seasonal favourite to be read, often aloud, at Christmas. It is also the fact that the story has been adapted for other cultural forms and practices. H. Philip Bolton has documented the many stage productions, radio performances, films and television adaptations that have been made almost every December since the story was first published.[10] Ever since the first London stage adaptations appeared within a few months of its publication, the *Carol* has become an annual ritual, constantly adapted and readapted to fit the needs of different times and different media. Since the beginning of the twentieth century there have been dozens of film and television adaptations, including straight versions of the story in period costume, updated contemporary reinterpretations, musical treatments, and all variety of novelty versions. In 1996 the cycle of adaptation came full circle when, as part of the series *An Audience with Charles Dickens*, the *Carol* was read on television by Simon Callow, reminding Dickensians that the author himself had given public readings of the book.

This chapter is concerned with movie adaptations of *A Christmas Carol*, focusing on Britain and the USA as the countries in which the cultural currency of the *Carol* has been strongest, though there have also been a number of foreign-language film versions.[11] It will show how the various films of the *Carol* have reinterpreted the story to reflect social and political concerns that were contemporary to the time of their production. And it will also consider the critical and popular reception of the films to place them within the context of the film cultures of Britain and America.[12]

The first known adaptation of the *Carol* was as early as 1901. *Scrooge; or, Marley's Ghost* was a short 'trick' film of the sort which proliferated around the turn of the century. It was produced by British film pioneer R.W. Paul's company Animatograph Works, using the facilities of his studio at New Southgate which was equipped with a glass roof and sliding doors for trick photographic effects. This was the period of what early film historians have since labelled the 'cinema of attractions' when motion pictures were in their infancy and their appeal was based on the novelty of the moving image rather than on narrative. The film itself is hardly an adaptation in the proper sense, focusing as it does on one sequence – the appearance of the ghost of Scrooge's dead partner Jacob Marley – which allows for the sort of optical effects that were an important constituent of the cinema of attractions.

The cinema of attractions remained the dominant mode of film practice until around 1904–5, by which time the origins of narrative film-making can clearly be identified. As films became longer, and as editing developed as a sort of 'grammar' of film language, the trick film gradually gave way to the story film using actors for character identification and inter-titles for simple dialogue and exposition. From about 1908 film-makers turned increasingly to classics of stage and literature for story material, resulting in adaptations of Shakespeare, Ibsen, Scott, Verne, Tolstoy and, of course, Dickens. The use of such sources can be seen as a deliberate attempt at cultural legitimation by early film-makers. As American film historian Eileen Bowser suggests, 'producers and exhibitors could demonstrate that the motion-picture show was an appropriate place for children and that they were bringing high culture to the masses'.[13] In Britain, too, Dickensian adaptations were particularly important in the years immediately preceding the First World War, with Thomas Bentley, who billed himself as 'the great Dickensian character impersonator and scholar', directing versions of *Oliver Twist* (1912), *Barnaby Rudge* (1913),

David Copperfield (1913), *The Chimes* (1914), *The Old Curiosity Shop* (1914) and *Hard Times* (1915). Most of these were made for producer Cecil Hepworth, himself a keen Dickensian, who pioneered an early form of 'heritage' film-making and who, in the words of film historian Rachael Low, turned to Dickensian subject matter 'to keep pace with the great world producers and at the same time retain his reputation for a characteristically English atmosphere'.[14]

These early film adaptations were inevitably much condensed from the original texts. Frank Dubrez Fawcett has explained how early film-makers were able to condense a Dickens novel into one or two reels:

> Take the title of a Dickens story; work some of the best-known incidents into a beginning, a middle and an end; then dress up the players to look like the pictures in the novels. The lettering on the screen would do the rest, and the audience could fill in any blanks from their own stores of Dickensian knowledge.[15]

Jeffrey Richards points out that this presupposes knowledge of the story by the cinema audience. Bowser, however, suggests that audiences would not necessarily have the sophistication to understand the stories. She argues that, at least in respect of American cinema, the practice of using a narrator in the auditorium was necessary to make the story clear to audiences.[16]

The *Carol* proved especially popular with early film-makers, providing as it did an obvious seasonal offering. The earliest American adaptation appears to have been a one-reeler produced for Christmas 1908 by the Essanay Manufacturing Company.[17] Although the film has not survived, it is evident from descriptions in the contemporary trade press that it consisted of ten scenes which dramatized key moments in the story. This version, apparently, omitted Marley's ghost, with Scrooge being visited instead by a beggar whom he had hit after the beggar had approached him in the street asking for alms, and reduces the number of spirits from three to one.[18] The trade journal *Moving Picture World* recognized the cultural aspirations of the film, but felt the narrative was not entirely clear. 'An effort at some high-class work, but in which the details lack some care', it observed. 'In many scenes the actions are too precipitated, consequently giving exaggerated and confused motions.'[19]

Essanay's version of the *Carol* was followed by two adaptations from the Edison Manufacturing Company, one in 1910, the other in 1914, of which the former, featuring Charles Ogle as Scrooge, has survived.[20] Again the film was structured around a succession of individual scenes rather than being a fully integrated narrative, but it was regarded as being much easier to understand than the Essanay version. According to *The Moving Picture World*: 'It is Dickens' story put into motion pictures and so cleverly reproduced that the characters actually live before one ... whether one has read the original or not there will be no difficulty in understanding the picture.'[21] When it was released in Britain a year later a special preview was arranged for the newly formed Dickens Fellowship. Its reception was equally positive. 'It is a true work of art, and will undoubtedly rank with the very highest productions that the moving picture world has yet seen', declared *The Bioscope*.[22] One significant change which the film made from the original, and in which it anticipated some of the later *Carol* films, was in providing a more prominent role for Scrooge's nephew. In this version the Ghost of Christmas Present shows Scrooge a vision of Fred being rejected by his fiancée because he has no money; the next morning Scrooge makes Fred a partner in the business. In the book, of course, Fred is already happily married and does not want for money.

There were numerous other silent screen adaptations of the story over the next decade and a half before the arrival of talking pictures. In Britain the Zenith Film Company produced a relatively long (3000 feet) film entitled *Scrooge* in 1913, starring Seymour Hicks, who had been playing the role on stage since the turn of the century. This was followed in 1914 by a shorter (1200 feet) version entitled *A Christmas Carol* from the London Film Company, starring Charles Rock. *The Bioscope* observed that the latter film lacked 'those vexed social questions' to be found in Dickens, but judged that this was no bad thing as those very questions 'may be considered by many to hamper the novelist's delightful humour and playful fancy'. It further commented that the film embodied 'the very spirit of the Christmas season as everyone would wish it to be'.[23] This provides an early indication of a trend that was to become more pronounced in British cinema during the interwar period of downplaying social criticism in favour of escapist entertainments promoting consensus values and social harmony. The 1920s saw two short British films called *Scrooge*, one a silent film from 1923 which appears to have been an entry in a series entitled *Gems of Literature*, made by theatre director Edwin Greenwood for the British and Colonial Kinematograph Company (B&C), the other an early Phonofilm sound short from 1928 featuring the music-hall Dickensian impersonator Bransby Williams. There do not appear to have been any American adaptations of the *Carol* during the 1920s, a period when, according to Paul Davis, the story was more popular in Britain than it was in America.[24]

The 1930s saw two very different 'talkie' feature films of the *Carol*, one each from Britain and America. *Scrooge*, the British film of 1935, was produced at Twickenham Studios by Julius Hagen – who had been in charge of B & C when the *Gems of Literature* series had been made – and directed by Henry Edwards, a former leading man of the 1920s who turned his hand to directing in the 1930s before returning to the other side of the camera as a character actor (including a small role as a police official in David Lean's 1948 film of *Oliver Twist*). The film is a solid and workmanlike adaptation of the book which, if limited technically, nevertheless has its own points of interest. It again stars Seymour Hicks as Scrooge, and was based on the stage adaptation by J.C. Buckstone in which Hicks had been appearing now for many years. The recently knighted Hicks, who also collaborated on the script, makes a splendidly crotchety Scrooge, a performance which in the view of one commentator 'has yet to be surpassed'.[25] He is ably supported by Donald Calthrop, an actor usually cast as a seedy villain – his best-known role had been as the blackmailer in Hitchcock's *Blackmail* (1929) – who here provides a sprightly, spindly Bob Cratchit.

The opening titles of the film highlight its literary origins as a leather-bound volume of *A Christmas Carol* is picked from a shelf and the credits are shown by turning the pages, ending on Dickens's preface of December 1843, while the refrain of 'Hark the Herald Angels Sing' establishes the tradition of using Christmas carols within the film score followed in later films. Scrooge is introduced as a hunched figure with his back to the camera, which then pans around the dingy offices to the freezing Cratchit, looking round furtively in the hope of putting more coal on the fire. When Cratchit finally plucks up the courage to tiptoe to the coal scuttle, Scrooge observes him in a mirror on the wall, though elsewhere the film makes only fitful use of such self-reflexive motifs about the act of looking and seeing that are so important to the story. The visual style of the film is dark and claustrophobic, with low-key lighting and wisps of studio fog disguising the limited sets. The special effects are also limited – Marley's Ghost, for example, is an off-screen voice ('Look well, Ebenezer Scrooge, for only you can hear me') – though the appearance of the three spirits is actually very close to the book, with the Ghost of Christmas Past represented by a shimmering light and the Ghost of Christmas Yet To Come appearing as the darkly menacing shadow of a pointed finger, with only the Ghost of Christmas Present (Oscar Asche) appearing as a 'person'. The film omits Old Fezziwig, Scrooge's generous first employer, and does not include the younger Scrooge's courtship of his 'fair young girl', but in most key respects it was regarded by critics as a faithful adaptation of the original story.[26]

In certain other ways, however, the 1935 *Scrooge* is very much a product of the British cinema of its time in its construction of the ideology of consensus.[27] Jeffrey Richards points out that it 'stresses the essential social cohesion of the nation'. This is evident in several key scenes which are not in the book. At one point the film intercuts between scenes of the Lord Mayor of London's banquet – the elegant banqueting hall which features only in this one sequence is by far the largest and most elaborate interior in the film – and scenes of the poor outside the gates. Both groups are singing the national anthem, thus asserting the notion of shared values between rich and poor. In this way the film sidesteps the social critique offered by Dickens and instead presents an image of social harmony in which there are no bitter class divisions. A similar effect is achieved later in the film as it cuts from a lighthouse-keeper to the crew of a trawler in a raging sea and then to the more salubrious surroundings of the home of Scrooge's nephew, the national community united in their celebration of Christmas. The film ends with yet another image of social cohesion as Scrooge joins the Cratchits in church. As Richards observes: 'So the film's clear message is that monarchy and religion provide the vital underpinnings of society and all will be well if selfish individuals discover the joys of good neighbourliness and are absorbed into the community.'[28]

The Hollywood version of the story followed in 1938 in the form of MGM's *A Christmas Carol*. David O. Selznick had already produced lavish and celebrated films of *David Copperfield* (1934) and *A Tale of Two Cities* (1936) for the studio, and though he had left Metro before it embarked upon *A Christmas Carol* – which was produced by Joseph L. Mankiewicz and directed by Edwin L. Marin – the film can be placed squarely within the same tradition of handsome, well-mounted, quality literary adaptations and costume dramas that Selznick had initiated. *A Christmas Carol* exemplifies all the expensive production values and technical artistry of a major Hollywood studio at its peak, including as it did among its production team several of the studio's senior creative personnel, such as composer Franz Waxman and art director Cedric Gibbons. Typically for MGM productions of the 1930s, the visual style is characterized by glossy high-key photography and sumptuous, detailed sets with high ceilings, the complete opposite of the claustrophobic British film. Lionel Barrymore, who had become closely associated with the role of Scrooge through playing him annually on American radio since 1934, and who was by now a much-loved member of MGM's roster of stars, usually playing crotchety grandpas and peevish millionaires, was unfortunately prevented from starring in the film by the onset of the arthritis which forced him in later life to act from his wheelchair, so the role of Scrooge went instead to British character actor Reginald Owen.[29] Released for Christmas 1938, and premiering at the prestigious Radio City Music Hall in New York, the film met with a highly enthusiastic reception. Frank S. Nugent, reviewing it for the *New York Times*, was clearly enraptured. 'It is good Dickens, good cinema and good for the soul', he declared. 'We recommend it to all you fellow-bustlers who, weary of browsing through the shops and fighting past crowded gift counters, have begun to feel, like old Scrooge, that Christmas is humbug. Go see it, you sophisticates!'[30]

While faithful to the spirit of Dickens, the film makes more changes from the original text than the British *Scrooge*. 'Hark the Herald Angels Sing' is again played over the opening credits, but a caption announces that the film is set 'More than a century ago', inexplicably setting the story before Dickens had actually written it. There are some changes to the story – here, for example, Scrooge fires Cratchit (Gene Lockhart) on Christmas Eve after the clerk has accidentally knocked off Scrooge's topper with a snowball while playing with his children in the street – and greater prominence is accorded to Fred (Barry Mackay). The film follows the 1910 Edison version in that Fred is unable to marry his fiancée Bess (Lynne Carver) because he is not wealthy enough. But the differences between the British and American films are not only differences in story incident; they are also apparent at the level of narrative ideology. The British film had promoted social consensus, but this consensus was based on the acceptance of class differences. The American film, however, provides a reinterpretation of the story for a supposedly classless society. This is most evident in the relationship between Fred and Cratchit. Whereas in the British version Cratchit had been properly deferential towards Fred, who after all is the nephew of his employer and thus his social better, in the American version Fred and Cratchit are shown as close friends, playing together by sliding on the snow and conversing with each other as equals.

The film also embodies the ideology of the studio which produced it. Under the benign dictatorship of the paternalistic studio head Louis B. Mayer, MGM had evolved its own highly distinctive view of the world, and particularly of America. The studio's idealized image of small-town America was perfectly exemplified by the Hardy Family series of films, beginning with *A Family Affair* (1937) – which coincidentally starred Lionel Barrymore as Judge Hardy, a role taken by Lewis Stone in subsequent films – and continuing for a further fourteen films until 1946. The series was given a special Academy Award in 1942 'for representing the American Way of Life'. MGM's film of *A Christmas Carol* can be seen to have been adapted to fit the studio's world-view. This is most evident in the early scene where Fred makes an eloquent speech about what Christmas means to him. The scene is in the book, but scriptwriter Hugo Butler changes it in line with the studio's own ideology:

Uncle, there are many things that have made me happy, things that have never fattened my purse by even that much [*holding two fingers close together*]. Christmas is one of these. I've always looked on Christmas as a good time, a kind, charitable, forgiving, pleasant time. It's the only time when people open their hearts freely, the only time when men and women seem to realise that all human beings are really members of the same family, and that being members of the same family they owe each other some measure of warmth and solace. And therefore, uncle, though it's never put a scrap of gold or silver in my pocket, I believe that it has done me good, and will do me good, and I say God bless it![31]

This is the sort of homespun philosophy that could easily have come from Andy Hardy himself, a eulogy which illustrates how the Dickensian view of Christmas has been adapted to meet the requirements of the sort of family values endorsed by MGM. One almost expects Fred to mention mom's apple pie.

Paul Davis makes a highly perceptive comparison of the differences in the British and American interpretations of the *Carol* during the 1930s, the decade of the Great Depression. 'The British,' he argues, 'denied the depression by reaffirming a traditional *Carol*, but in America a revolutionary version of the *Carol* emerged that made Cratchit the protagonist.'[32] MGM's *A Christmas Carol* might also be seen as 'revolutionary' because it does not condemn Scrooge for wanting to make money, but rather for failing to put his money to good use ('He has money. And he makes no use of it', says Fred. 'Therefore he's a far more pathetic and unhappy case than a man who has no money at all.') Far from being an anti-capitalist fable, the film endorses capitalism when Scrooge makes Fred a partner in the business. The *Carol* becomes, in Davis's view, 'one of the guiding texts of the New Deal', suggesting that hard work combined with a social conscience can overcome economic difficulty.

The next major adaptation of the *Carol*, and regarded by many as the definitive film version, was the 1951 British movie *Scrooge* (released under the title *A Christmas Carol* in the USA), produced and directed by Brian Desmond Hurst and starring Alastair Sim in the title role. The post-war years had witnessed a renewed interest in Dickensian adaptations in British cinema, but they were very different from their pre-war forbears, being more lavishly mounted, visually exciting and darker in tone. David Lean led the way with his brilliantly cinematic adaptations of *Great Expectations* (1946) and *Oliver Twist* (1948), followed by Alberto Cavalcanti's *Nicholas Nickleby* (1947) and Hurst's *Scrooge*. Richards characterizes this as 'the period of Gothic Dickens', and argues persuasively that these films represented the cross-fertilization of different cinematic trends in the mid-1940s. In Britain the popular Gainsborough melodramas such as *The Man in Grey* (1943) and *The Wicked Lady* (1946) had created a taste for flamboyant costume films, though they had been despised by the critics who argued in favour of a cinema based on realism, emotional restraint and literary quality. The Dickensian films provided the literary quality that the critics demanded, whilst also fulfilling audiences' taste for period

Mervyn Johns as Bob Cratchit and Alastair Sim in the title role of *Scrooge* (1951).

costume drama. At the same time, these films were also influenced by the visual style of Hollywood *film noir* with its chiaroscuro lighting and expressionist shadows.[33]

Scrooge certainly shows elements of these different cinematic trends. It opens, like the 1935 version, with a leather-bound volume of *A Christmas Carol* being taken down from a shelf and opened, asserting its status as a literary classic. This time, however, the music (composed by Richard Addinsell, best known for his 'Warsaw Concerto' from the 1941 film *Dangerous Moonlight*, coincidentally also directed by Hurst) strikes an ominous tone of discordant, heavy brass, before the now familiar strains of 'Hark the Herald Angels Sing' are heard. The visual style of the film is very different from the glossy MGM version with its high-key lighting and crowds bustling on the streets. Hurst's direction makes the city a grim and inhospitable environment, with wind howling down the streets and pavements empty save for the occasional beggar. Here there are no groups of happy, muffled carol-singers, only three poor children whom Scrooge chases away from outside his offices. Many individual shots resemble the style associated with the cinema of German Expressionism:

as Scrooge tramps home through the near-deserted streets he casts a long, elongated shadow, while the interior of his town house, with parallel shadows cast at an angle across the staircase, provides a suitably spooky and slightly unreal environment for the appearance of the ghosts. With his scarf wrapped around his face, furthermore, Sim recalls the first appearance of Ivor Novello as the mysterious stranger in Hitchcock's strongly expressionist *The Lodger* (1926).

With its expressionist style, *Scrooge* clearly belongs to the period of 'Gothic Dickens' identified by Richards. However, it is not only in its aesthetic form that the film is of interest. In certain respects it bears comparison with the celebrated Ealing comedies of the time, such as *Passport to Pimlico* (1949), *Whisky Galore* (1949), *The Lavender Hill Mob* (1951) and *The Titfield Thunderbolt* (1953), in that like them it can be interpreted as a critique of big business and heartless money-grabbing. Fezziwig (Roddy Hughes) is here characterized in an Ealingesque manner in that he embodies the values of the caring small businessman who recognizes that quality of life is as important as money ('I have to be loyal to the old ways … There's more in life than money'). This is contrasted with Jorkins (Jack Warner), a character not in the book, who equates money with power ('Control the cash-box and you control the world'). Scrooge leaves Fezziwig to work for Jorkins; when Jorkins is revealed as an embezzler, Scrooge and Marley take over the company and become money-hoarding misers.

Charles Barr has interpreted the Ealing comedies as complex allegories of the social and political changes taking place in Britain in the late 1940s and early 1950s.[34] Although not an Ealing film, *Scrooge* can also be seen in this context. It was released in October 1951, the very month that Clement Attlee's Labour government, which had been elected by a landslide in 1945 on a tidal wave of expectation of building the New Jerusalem of social justice and state welfare provision, lost a general election to a Conservative Party still led by its wartime idol Winston Churchill. The Labour government had enacted an ambitious and wide-ranging legislative programme that laid the foundation of the welfare state for the next half century. The basis for many of its reforms had been Sir William Beveridge's *Report on Social Insurance and Allied Services* (1942), which had identified the 'five giants on the road of reconstruction' – disease, ignorance, squalor, idleness and want – and had proposed a comprehensive system of social insurance 'from the cradle to the grave'.[35] Labour's fall from office – ironically the vagaries of the British electoral system meant that it won more overall votes than the Conservatives but fewer parliamentary seats – is generally seen to be the consequence of middle-class opinion becoming disaffected by the drab austerity regime of the late 1940s which was caused by continued rationing.[36]

It is possible to advance a contextual reading of *Scrooge* which situates the narrative at this precise moment of change. Scrooge, it might be argued, represents the Conservative Party who during the war had been lukewarm about social reform and who had been opposed to the increased state intervention that the welfare state would entail ('It is enough for a man to understand his own business without interfering with other people's', he remarks). The Conservatives had paid little heed to the Beveridge Report, whereas the Labour Party virtually adopted it as their 1945 election manifesto. Two scenes from the book which had not featured in either of the 1930s films but which were restored in this version acquire further meaning in the context of late 1940s/early 1950s Britain. In the first, Marley's Ghost (Michael Hordern) shows Scrooge a vision of wandering, restless phantoms, which might be read as a lament about the fall of the reforming Labour government ('They seek to inter-fere for good in human madness, and have lost their powers forever'). Labour's majority had been vastly reduced in the general election of May 1950 before they were ousted from office in 1951. In the second scene, when the Ghost of Christmas Present (Francis De Wolff) opens his robe to reveal two starving children ('This boy is Ignorance, this girl is Want') it is impossible not to associate this with the Beveridge Report. However, Scrooge accepts his social responsibilities, just as the Conservatives, during their years of Opposition in the late 1940s, accepted the welfare legislation enacted by the Labour government and agreed not to dismantle it. The Conservatives were returned to power in 1951 on a pledge to maintain the welfare state and to bring an end to austerity and rationing; thus Scrooge makes provision for the poor and sends the turkey to the Cratchits. It is a fanciful reading, admittedly, but an irresist-ible one given the time at which the film appeared.

Another sign of how films reflect the times in which they are made is the discourse evident in *Scrooge* about austerity and rationing. Although the most obvious example of austerity conditions – Cratchit's desire to put more coal on the fire – is missing on this occasion, there are other incidents in the film which are not in the book and which would appear to be have been included for their contemporary resonances. Scrooge eats a meagre meal in a dingy tavern, and decides not to have the extra bread which he wants upon being told that it would cost a halfpenny more – a scene which would surely remind British audiences that bread rationing had been introduced in 1946. Another scene early in the film has Tiny Tim looking in the window of a toy shop full of mechanical dolls and other toys, expensive items which the Cratchits cannot afford – just the sort of luxury goods that were absent from British shops in the 1940s. There is evidence that some contemporary critics were conscious of such elements in the film. Bosley Crowther, the senior film critic of the *New*

York Times, hinted that he saw in the film a reflection of the continuing austerity and food rationing in Britain. 'The usual conceptions of Christmas in terms of puddings and flowing bowls are not visualized in this picture to any conspicuous degree', he observed. 'Even the gay board of the Cratchits is kept on a modest scale, and cheerfulness rather than foodstuffs is apparent in the home of nephew Fred.'[37]

As might be expected, *Scrooge* was more successful in Britain than it was in America. It was well received by the British trade press, with *The Cinema* remarking that '[o]nce more the old tale comes to us as stimulating and salutary' and praising the 'strength and versatility' of Sim's perform-ance, with 'the artiste admirably blending the dramatic with the comic, notably in the final scenes of remorse and regeneration'.[38] But the Holly-wood trade bible *Variety* considered that the film, released in America by United Artists as *A Christmas Carol*, 'hasn't enough entertainment merit to rate it anything but slim chances … There's certainly no Yuletide cheer to be found in this latest adaptation of Charles Dickens' Christmas classic.'[39]

By this time, the first television adaptations of the *Carol* had been seen in America. The earliest appears to have been a one-hour telecast by the East Coast broadcaster WABD in 1947, with John Carradine, which was seen in Philadelphia, Baltimore and Washington.[40] The first networked version appeared a year later as the seasonal offering for NBC's *Philco Television Playhouse*, one of the weekly anthology series which were the dominant mode of early television drama. Scrooge was played by Dennis King, a British-born singer who had appeared occasionally in Hollywood films during the 1930s, while the live performance of the *Carol* was followed by a filmed sequence of Bing Crosby and the Bob Mitchell Boys Choir singing 'Silent Night'. *Variety* described the production as a 'warm, tender and wholly evocative interpretation of the Dickens classic'.[41] This straight dramatization of the *Carol* was followed a few days later by an ABC production using wooden puppets, which *Variety* considered 'a new and completely captivating way of presenting the traditional Dickens story of Old Scrooge'.[42] This adaptation marks the first instance of a trend towards novelty versions of the *Carol* which has become increas-ingly pronounced in more recent years.

The 1950s witnessed a plethora of television *Carol*s, produced on an almost annual basis.[43] Ralph Richardson made his television debut as Scrooge in a half-hour dramatization for NBC in 1951; Melville Keen, who played the Ghost of Christmas Past in that version, graduated to the leading role the following year for the same network's *Kraft Television Theatre*. In 1954 Fredric March played Scrooge, with Basil Rathbone as Marley's Ghost, in a one-hour musical version for the CBS *Shower of Stars* series. It was quite a prestigious production, produced on film and in colour, with a score by Hollywood composer Bernard Hermann.

Rathbone played Scrooge himself in another musical version two years later, entitled *The Stingiest Man in Town*. And in 1957 James Stewart both directed and starred in a half-hour adaptation for the *General Electric Theatre*, entitled *A Trail to Christmas*, which transposed the story to a Western setting and was introduced by Ronald Reagan.

The tradition of novelty adaptations continued in the 1960s. *Mr Magoo's Christmas Carol*, featuring the myopic, bumbling cartoon character voiced by Jim Backus, was screened on NBC in 1962. This adaptation of the story for an established cartoon character anticipates later films featuring Mickey Mouse and the Muppets. The BBC produced an operatic version of the *Carol* in 1963, with music by young American composer Edwin Coleman. The Canadian Broadcasting Corporation produced its own musical version in 1964, entitled *Mr Scrooge* and featuring Cyril Ritchard – a light entertainer whose best-known film role was as the would-be seducer in Hitchcock's *Blackmail* – along with Alfie Bass as Bob Cratchit and Tessie O'Shea as Mrs Cratchit. Back in Britain, the first Christmas television special by the popular 'Carry On' team – entitled, appropriately, *Carry On Christmas* – was a loose comedy version of the *Carol*. Written by Talbot Rothwell, it featured 'Carry On' film favourites Sid James in the Scrooge role, Charles Hawtrey as a camp Marley, Bernard Bresslaw as a hulking Bob Cratchit and Barbara Windsor as a highly flirtatious Christmas spirit.[44]

It was nearly two decades after the classic Brian Desmond Hurst–Alastair Sim movie that the next big screen feature film appeared.[45] Again entitled *Scrooge*, in keeping with other British adaptations of the *Carol*, the 1970 version was a lavish Technicolor-Panavision musical with songs by Leslie Bricusse. The decision to make a big-budget, colour, musical version of the story at this particular moment was due to the success of *Oliver!*, Carol Reed's musical version of *Oliver Twist* made in 1968, which had won five Oscars including Best Film and Best Director. This *Scrooge* was directed by Ronald Neame, who had co-scripted David Lean's *Great Expectations* and produced his *Oliver Twist* in the 1940s. Unlike the dark, expressionist *Scrooge* of 1951, the *Scrooge* of 1970 is a jolly, all-singing, all-dancing colour spectacular. Unfortunately it is handicapped by a severely miscast star. The ideal star for a musical *Scrooge* would have been Rex Harrison, who had provided such a memorable Professor Higgins in *My Fair Lady* (1964), but he had to withdraw from the film when his doctor ordered him to rest. The role went instead to Albert Finney, who, for all his undoubted ability, never looks like anything other than a young man under a lot of make-up. The film introduces some interesting additions to the story: Scrooge is shown a vision of Hell by Marley's Ghost (Alec Guinness), where he is fitted for his chains, while the ending has Scrooge dressed like Santa Claus dancing down the street and dispensing gifts.

The film's reception was mixed. Brian Davis in the *Monthly Film Bulletin* clearly found it all rather ponderous, comparing it unfavourably with contemporary American musicals, though he was warm in his praise for Finney:

> This musical adaptation of *A Christmas Carol* has a Leslie Bricusse score which is if anything even more unmemorable than the one he wrote for *Goodbye, Mr Chips*. The recitative numbers have reasonably adept lyrics – there is some pleasing triple-rhyming in Scrooge's lament 'I Hate People' – but the more sentimental songs, which include a maudlin dirge sung by a winsome Tiny Tim, are consistently banal. The script, which closely follows the original story, is a little better, but Ronald Neame's direction is generally pedestrian. What *Scrooge* conspicuously lacks is the kind of free-wheeling imagination with which Francis Ford Coppola transformed the unpromising *Finian's Rainbow* into an animated screen musical. If Neame had given more opportunities to his talented choreographer Paddy Stone, the songs might at least have been worth looking at, if not listening to. As it is, the sporadic dance numbers feature a determinedly buoyant crowd cavorting inelegantly round cramped, cut-price sets. The only real plus is a finely judged central performance by Albert Finney. Whether drooling over his savings, wistfully recalling his early years, or jubilantly giving away expensive gifts, Finney succeeds throughout in transcending his mediocre material.[46]

A musical is inevitably judged by the quality of its songs, and on this score *Scrooge* simply did not pass muster, for with the exception of the Oscar-nominated 'Thank You Very Much' they are unmemorable in the extreme, lacking the sparkle and panache of Lionel Bart's score for *Oliver!*

Changes in film culture since the last feature film version of the story meant that greater expectations for success were riding on this *Scrooge* than on previous versions. The late 1950s and 1960s had witnessed the emergence of the 'blockbuster' syndrome in both American and British cinema, with production focusing on fewer but bigger films which it was hoped would reap massive rewards. The producers of *Scrooge* obviously hoped that it would repeat the box-office success of *Oliver!*. Several critics pointed out how the message of the film was so much at odds with the motives for making it. 'It is difficult to be miserly about *Scrooge*,' wrote Christopher Hudson in the *Spectator*, remarking pointedly that it 'will give a lot of pleasure to countless children and a lot of money to that notable pauper Twentieth Century–Fox'.[47] And Vincent Canby in the *New York*

Times made a rather facetious play around the notion that Christmas seemed to come earlier each year. '*Scrooge* opened yesterday at the Radio City Music Hall as the Christmas attraction, approximately five weeks early', he remarked. 'The last *A Christmas Carol* to play the Hall, a version produced by Joseph L. Mankiewicz in 1938, was unveiled three days before Christmas. When the next version opens – I estimate in 2001 – it may be on the Fourth of July.'[48]

The next major adaptation of the *Carol* was as different again from the musical *Scrooge* as the musical was from the 1951 film. Produced for American television in 1984, but released theatrically outside the United States, *A Christmas Carol* was a sumptuous $5 million production filmed on location in the English medieval market town of Shrewsbury. It was directed by Clive Donner, who had been editor on the 1951 *Scrooge*, and starred George C. Scott, with a supporting cast of reliable British character actors including David Warner as Bob Cratchit and Frank Finlay as Jacob Marley. Donner spoke of his desire to return to the spirit of Dickens's original *Carol* rather than the sentimentalized version which had become so familiar:

> Owing to the accretions of sugaryness larded onto it since late Victorian times, it has come to be thought of as the most treacly of all Dickens's stories; but I found that he wrote it in a state of considerable outrage and anger … This is why I wanted George C. Scott to play Scrooge. Because I saw Scrooge as a dangerous man, not as the caricature miser that has become the stereotype. A man to be frightened of if you were poor, and to be very wary of if you were a businessman doing a deal with him.[49]

Donner had previously directed Scott in a made-for-television film of *Oliver Twist*, in which Scott had played Fagin, and which provides a companion piece to their version of the *Carol*.

While the 1951 *Scrooge* belonged to the post-war period of 'Gothic Dickens' and the musical *Scrooge* to the last flowering of big-budget musicals at the end of the 1960s, the cinematic context for 1984's *Carol* was the cycle of quality costume pictures and literary adaptations which critics have labelled 'heritage' cinema. Heritage cinema, exemplified pre-eminently by the films of Merchant–Ivory such as *Heat and Dust* (1982), *A Room With A View* (1985) and *Maurice* (1987), is a style of film-making which involves stories set in the past, foregrounding a highly pictorialist visual style, often using real locations for period authenticity, and usually based on classic literature. *A Christmas Carol* is comparable to heritage cinema in that it is a solidly crafted, handsomely mounted costume picture filmed on location and striving for period authenticity through its *mise-en-scène*, sets, dressings, and so forth. It is also a very close adaptation of the book, though it makes one significant change through the addition of Scrooge's father, here called Silas (Nigel Davenport). The film provides a psychological 'explanation' for Scrooge's miserliness in that he was denied affection by his father, something hinted at in previous films but developed much more fully here. In other respects, however, this is probably the closest of all the film adaptations to both the letter and the spirit of Dickens. The veteran British trade journalist Marjorie Bilbow thought that 'this could become the seminal *A Christmas Carol* because it is presented as the human drama Charles Dickens wrote rather than as an animated Christmas card'.[50]

However, this closeness to the original does not mean that the film cannot still be placed in the social and political context of its own time. Just as various commentators have interpreted the heritage films of the 1980s as critiques of the doctrines of Thatcherism, so too this version of *A Christmas Carol* is open to such readings.[51] Thatcherite Britain was marked by an increasingly pronounced gulf between rich and poor. On the one hand the 1980s saw the emergence of a prosperous home-owning, share-holding lower middle class; on the other hand the decade also witnessed increasing unemployment and social deprivation as traditional manufacturing industries were wound down and millions of workers found themselves on the dole. Scott's Scrooge is an out-and-out Thatcherite, the sort of man who believes that there is no such thing as society, that responsibility rests with the individual and not with the state. His refusal to provide for the poor and needy takes on a new significance at a time when the right-wing Tory government was coming under fierce attack from the left for cutting its real expenditure on welfare and under-investing in the National Health Service. Furthermore, when the Ghost of Christmas Present (Edward Woodward) shows Scrooge a homeless family living outdoors, the film brings to mind the social underclass of people living rough on the streets who had become so much more visible in British cities during the 1980s. Several contemporary critics picked up the Thatcherite context of the film, including Pam Cook in her review for the *Monthly Film Bulletin*:

> Screen adaptations of Dickens's moral tale about the change of heart of a hardened monetarist abound, but the appearance of this latest tasteful version at a time of increasing economic crisis makes its paternalistic message especially seasonal. Scrooge operates his business and his life according to the laws of the market. Christmas represents a waste, an excess of spending and consuming which disrupts the process of accumulating wealth.[52]

Ultimately, however, Cook thought it 'a pity that the more subversive aspects of Dickens's story have been missed' and that Scrooge's acceptance of his social responsibilities 'appears more a matter of self-preservation than genuine social insight'. Suggesting that Scrooge's reformation is based on the principle of individual responsibility rather than genuine concern for the poor, she concludes that the film 'champions a "wet" Tory line on economics, rather than anything more radical'.

In 1988 Hollywood produced a modern reworking of the *Carol* in the form of Paramount Pictures' *Scrooged*, directed by Richard Donner, an American unrelated to his British namesake. There was nothing new in the idea of a contemporary reworking of the *Carol*. In 1955 the WCBS–TV series *Eye on New York* had produced a seasonal special which abandoned its usual documentary format for a dramatic adaptation of the *Carol* relocated to contemporary New York, in which Scrooge became the president of the fictitious Metropolitan Plastics Corporation.[53] *Scrooged* is another Americanized reworking of the story in a modern setting. It was a star vehicle for Bill Murray, an abrasive and loud-mouthed comedy actor whose popularity is completely inexplicable but who nevertheless was at the time one of the highest-paid stars in Hollywood following the success of the smash-hit, special-effects comedy *Ghostbusters* (1984).

Murray is typecast as Frank Xavier Cross, a brash, vulgar, tasteless television executive who produces a television film of 'Charles Dickens' immortal classic *Scrooge*' with an improbably cast Buddy Hackett as Scrooge, mini-skirted ice-dancers the 'Scroogettes' and a female Tiny Tim who back-flips rather than hobbles on the set. Cross fires an underling who dares to disagree with him and is rude and heartless to his secretary Grace. Grace, a black single mother, is the film's equivalent of Bob Cratchit, while her son, who has not spoken since his father was shot dead five years ago, takes the place of Tiny Tim. Frank's ruthlessness is contrasted with his ex-fiancée Claire (Karen Allen) who runs a shelter for the homeless. Marley's Ghost becomes that of Frank's former boss, the Ghost of Christmas Past is a cigar-chomping New York cab driver, and the Ghost of Christmas Present is a shrill-voiced fairy who repeatedly punches him. The Ghost of Christmas Future [*sic*] is an altogether more menacing apparition, appearing as a skeletal, shrouded figure on a bank of television screens and reaching out a claw-like hand in a manner reminiscent of horror movies such as the *Nightmare on Elm Street* series which continually broke down the interface between the real world and fantasy. The film ends with Frank, having been shown the error of his ways, interrupting the television transmission with a speech about goodwill and the importance of traditional values.

As might be expected from the personnel involved in its production – star Murray and writers Mitch Glazer and Michael O'Shaughnessy were all alumni of the irreverent *Saturday Night Live* comedy sketch show –

Scrooged is a very hit-or-miss affair. It borrows from different traditions of comedy, mixing satire and slapstick in a haphazard manner. Whether it is funny depends entirely on one's sense of humour. The opening seems to promise a satire about the dumbing-down of American television as Lee Majors (former star of *The Six Million Dollar Man*) is shown rescuing Santa Claus from terrorists in a promotional trailer for *The Night the Reindeer Died*. But this theme is not maintained; indeed, it might be suggested that *Scrooged* itself belongs to the same crass tradition of popular culture which it sets out to satirize. The film is also confused in its attempt to account for Frank's antisocial behaviour. On the one hand it is hinted that his crassness is due to a lifelong exposure to television, but on the other hand it also follows the 1984 *Carol* in that Frank was denied affection by his own father, who in one scene from Frank's childhood is shown giving him a Christmas present of 4lb of veal.

Critical opinion was mixed. '*Scrooged* works in fits and starts', wrote Vincent Canby in the *New York Times*. 'The mundane demands of the sentimental story keep interrupting what are, essentially, revue sketches, a few of which are hilarious.'[54] But *Variety* was especially disparaging, describing it as 'an appallingly unfunny comedy, and a vivid illustration of the fact that money can't buy you laughs'.[55]

While there have been no straight film adaptations of the *Carol* in recent years, there have been a number of novelty versions in which the basic story of the *Carol* has been recast for other characters. At Christmas 1983, for example, the Walt Disney company released *Mickey's Christmas Carol*, a $3 million half-hour cartoon which played in cinemas as a featured attraction. Based on a record album of the same name released in 1974, *Mickey's Christmas Carol* cast familiar Disney cartoon characters in the Dickensian roles: the character of Scrooge McDuck was resurrected from the short *Scrooge McDuck and Money* (1967), while other roles were taken by Donald Duck (voiced for the last time by Clarence Nash) as Scrooge's nephew, Mickey and Minnie Mouse as the Cratchits, Goofy as Marley's Ghost, Jiminy Cricket as the Ghost of Christmas Past, Willie the Giant from *Fun and Fancy Free* (1946) as the Ghost of Christmas Present and Pegleg Pete as the Ghost of Christmas Yet To Come. The result is an enchanting little film which recalls the production values and draughts-manship of the Disney of old. Its mixture of sentimentality with a moral message is so characteristic of Disney that it is surprising the film was not made at a much earlier date. *Mickey's Christmas Carol* was something of a media event in that it marked the first film appearance of Mickey Mouse since *The Simple Things* in 1953, though Mickey himself has a relatively small role and it is Scrooge McDuck, voiced in a Scots accent by Alan Young, who is the real star of the show. Although most critics discussed it in the context of the Disney *oeuvre*, the film is not without interest as an adaptation of the *Carol*, especially insofar as it relocates the *Carol* once again as a children's story. Hitherto films of the *Carol* had been made for the general cinema audience; *Mickey's Christmas Carol* was the first to be aimed directly at children, and, moreover, to give rise to spin-off merchandising.[56]

Disney also had a hand in *The Muppet Christmas Carol*, which uses the same strategy of casting characters familiar from another idiom in Dickensian roles. The Muppets are a group of puppet characters created by actor-director Jim Henson, appearing first on the educational American children's television programme *Sesame Street* and then starring in their own television show in the 1970s. The popularity of the Muppets was such that they appeared in several feature films alongside 'real' actors: *The Muppet Movie* (1979), *The Great Muppet Caper* (1981) and *The Muppets Take Manhattan* (1984). The two most recent Muppet films have been adaptations of classic literature, *The Muppet Christmas Carol* (1992) and *Muppet Treasure Island* (1996). The human star of *The Muppet Christmas Carol* is Michael Caine, giving a wonderfully hammy performance as Scrooge, though he is inevitably upstaged by the likes of Kermit the Frog as Bob Cratchit, Miss Piggy as Emily Cratchit and Fozzie Bear as Fozziwig [*sic*]. Jacob Marley has a brother, Robert, in order to incorporate the cantankerous old hecklers Waldorf and Statler. The most interesting characterization, however, is the Great Gonzo as Charles Dickens himself, who provides a running commentary which not only explains the story for the children at whom the film is aimed but also offers some clever asides to keep the adults amused. It might seem pretentious to claim *The Muppet Christmas Carol* as a postmodern text, but that is precisely what it is. In the first place, like *Mickey's Christmas Carol*, the concept is inherently inter-textual, drawing on the audience's knowledge of both the Dickens story and the Muppets' universe. *The Muppet Christmas Carol* goes further, however, in that it frequently disrupts the narrative to engage in a discourse about its own status as a cultural artefact. 'This is culture', observes Gonzo/Dickens when his companion Rizzo the Rat wonders whether the ghostly scenes will be too frightening for the children in the audience. The film even throws in the concept of the deconstruction of the author for good measure when Rizzo wonders how Gonzo can say what Scrooge is doing when they cannot see him on screen:

> RIZZO: Okay, that does it. How do you know what Scrooge is doing? We're down here and he's up there.
> GONZO: I keep telling you, storytellers are omniscient. I know everything.
> RIZZO: Hoity-toity, Mister Godlike Smarty Pants!

The film also reminds audiences of the education-with-entertainment purpose of the Muppets by asserting its cultural provenance. As Gonzo concludes: 'If you liked this, you should read the book.'

While *Mickey's Christmas Carol* and *The Muppet Christmas Carol* illustrate that the spirit if not quite the letter of Dickens continues to inform film adaptations of the story, a new variation on the theme has been forthcoming from television. *Blackadder's Christmas Carol* represents not only another example of the vogue for novelty adaptations of the *Carol*; it actually offers a narrative which entirely subverts the theme of the original. The Christmas special, made by the BBC in 1988, featured the 'Blackadder' character played by Rowan Atkinson who starred in four six-part series during the 1980s. These were costume comedies which played very loose indeed with history, not unlike the period 'Carry On' films though with a much more satirical and occasionally nasty edge. The eponymous character had featured as an illegitimate son of 'King Richard IV' during the Wars of the Roses, as a courtier during the reign of Elizabeth I, as the butler to Prince George during the Regency period, and as a captain in the trenches during the First World War, but in all those guises had been a conniving, scheming, devious sort with no morals or scruples whatsoever. *Blackadder's Christmas Carol* tells the story of Ebenezer Blackadder, the 'white sheep' of the family in that he is known as 'the kindest and loveliest man in all England'. This Blackadder is honest, caring and charitable, and is regarded as a soft touch by everyone including his grasping niece Millie, Mrs Scratchit and his servant Baldrick (Tony Robinson). On Christmas Eve he is visited by the Spirit of Christmas (Robbie Coltrane), who has stopped off between hauntings, and who shows Blackadder visions of his wicked ancestors. Realizing that 'bad guys have all the fun', Blackadder asks what the future holds, and discovers that if he is bad then one of his descendants will become a space commander who conquers the universe, whereas if he is good then his descendant will be a dogsbody to Baldrick. Blackadder thus decides to alter his ways, and from that moment on is rude to everyone he meets, including Queen Victoria and Prince Albert who have come to reward him for his charity work. *Blackadder's Christmas Carol* is not only very funny, but also an ingenious conceit which completely subverts the meaning of the *Carol* with its cynical conclusion that greed is good and charity pointless. It was written by Richard Curtis, later to write the smash-hit British comedy *Four Weddings and A Funeral* (1994), and Ben Elton, an 'alternative' comedian and satirist known for his anti-Thatcherite views.

What *Blackadder's Christmas Carol* has in common with so many other film and television adaptations of Dickens's story, however, is that it shows how the *Carol* itself remains a highly prominent point of reference in the cultural construction of Christmas in our society. Movie adaptations of the *Carol* have served a twofold purpose as popular entertainments. On the one hand they have provided a medium through which cultural providers have continued to construct images of the 'traditional' Christmas. From the perspective of the twentieth century, the films look back to the Victorian period which seems to offer a Christmas free from the taints of commercialism and vulgarity; the Dickensian Christmas continues to offer a nostalgic view of the way Christmas 'used to be' – or, more accurately, the way Christmas is popularly supposed to have been. On the other hand films of the *Carol* have reinterpreted its essential message of human dignity, moral responsibility and charity according to the social and political climate of the time and country in which they were made. All the films differ slightly in the extent of their fidelity to the original, and most of them emphasize certain elements of the story according to their own concerns, for example the family life of the Cratchits in the 1938 MGM version or the reappearance of the children Ignorance and Want in the 1951 and 1984 versions. Even the novelty versions of Mickey Mouse and the Muppets have served an educational purpose of their own in bringing the moral of Dickens's story home to children at a time when television, videos and computer games have all but replaced books in many households. Indeed, it would probably be fair to say that looking back to the century in which the cinema has been the pre-eminent popular art form, it is through the medium of film – and latterly also television – that most people have gained their knowledge of Dickens in general and the *Carol* in particular. Ultimately, it is due in large measure to the cinema that the continued popularity of the *Carol* has been even more prodigious than possibly Dickens himself could ever have imagined.

Notes

1. Quoted in Philip Collins (ed.), *Dickens: The Critical Heritage* (London: Routledge and Kegan Paul, 1971), p 146. Thackeray's review of *A Christmas Carol* had appeared in *Fraser's Magazine* in February 1844. Thackeray observed that the book's fame had 'so spread over England ... that ... not even the godlike and ancient Quarterly itself ... could review it down'.

2. Charles Dickens to Frederick Dickens, 30 December 1843, in Madeline House, Graham Storey and Kathleen Tillotson (eds), *The Letters of Charles Dickens. Volume Three 1842–1843* (Oxford: Clarendon Press, 1974), p 617.

3. John Forster, *The Life of Charles Dickens*, ed. J.W.T. Ley (London: Cecil Palmer, 1928), p 316.

4. J.B. Priestley, *Charles Dickens and His World* (New York: The Viking Press, 1969), p 54.

5. Michael Slater, 'Introduction', Charles Dickens, *The Christmas Books. Volume 1: A Christmas Carol/The Chimes* (Harmondsworth: Penguin, 1971), pp xi–xii.

6. The critical literature on Dickens is immense. The orthodox view, however, is that the earlier books, such as *The Pickwick Papers* (serialized 1836–7), *Oliver Twist* (1837–8), *Nicholas Nickleby* (1838–9), *The Old Curiosity Shop* (1840–1), *Barnaby Rudge* (1841) and *Martin Chuzzlewit* (1843–4), are more episodic and picaresque. They are also the works in which Dickens's prose style is at its most excessive and his characterizations at their most grotesque. Most Dickensian scholars agree with the verdict of F.R. and Q.D. Leavis in *Dickens the Novelist* (London: Chatto and Windus, 1970) that *Dombey and Son* (1846–8) is 'the first major novel'. '*Dombey and Son* marks a decisive moment in Dickens's career,' they write; 'he offered it as a providently conceived whole, presenting a major theme, and it was his first essay in the elaborately plotted Victorian novel' (p 2). The later novels, including *David Copperfield* (1849–50), *Bleak House* (1852–3), *Hard Times* (1854), *Little Dorrit* (1855–7), *A Tale of Two Cities* (1859), *Great Expectations* (1860–1) and *Our Mutual Friend* (1864–5), are regarded as being tighter in narrative structure and more restrained in their use of language.

7. Eric Midwinter, *Victorian Social Reform* (Harlow: Longman, 1968), p 8.

8. J.M. Golby and A.W. Purdue, *The Making of the Modern Christmas* (London: B.T. Batsford, 1986), p 45.

9. Ibid., p 80.

10. H. Philip Bolton, *Dickens Dramatized* (Boston: G.K. Hall, 1987), pp 234–67. Bolton reckons that by 1987 there had been 357 different adaptations of the *Carol*.

11. This does not purport to be a definitive history of *all* film adaptations of the *Carol*. In the first place, many of the silent film adaptations no longer survive. The National Film Archive has viewing copies of some of the early films, some of which I have been able to see, but there is little point in writing at length about films which the general reader will not have seen. For the most part, therefore, I will be concentrating on sound feature films, which are quite readily available through television broadcast and home video.

12. At this point I should record my indebtedness to the work of two scholars in particular. In his book *Films and British National Identity: From Dickens to Dad's Army* (Manchester: Manchester University Press, 1997), Jeffrey Richards discusses a wide range of Dickensian adaptations and suggests that they have reflected the social and political climate of the times in which they were made. He argues: 'It is the multi-faceted nature of Dickens which makes him susceptible of wholly different interpretations and ensures that he remains, like Shakespeare, completely relevant to and in tune with the moods, needs and mindsets of the nation. Whatever the circumstances, he is likely to remain "Dickens – our contemporary"' (pp 13–14). A similar argument is advanced by Paul B. Davis in *The Lives and Times of Ebenezer Scrooge* (New Haven: Yale University Press, 1990). In contrast to the contextual history of Richards, Davis owes more to the methodologies of cultural studies because he advances the notion of the *Carol* as a 'culture-text', which has been appropriated for different purposes at various moments. Davis's book (which in a sense is a part of the phenomenon it describes, being produced in a large-format, illustrated version) provides a stimulating and theoretically informed account of the role the *Carol* has occupied in popular culture and how it has become part of the folklore of the modern Christmas. In its approach to a fictional character who has taken on a meaning and significance extending far beyond the original text in which he appeared, *The Lives and Times of Ebenezer Scrooge* can be compared to the pioneering cultural analysis of James Bond by Tony Bennett and Janet Woollacott in their *Bond and Beyond: The Political Career of a Popular Hero* (London: Macmillan, 1987), and to the various approaches to the figure of Batman in Roberta Pearson and William Uricchio (eds), *The Many Lives of the Batman: Critical Approaches to a Superhero and His Media* (London: BFI Publishing, 1991).

13. Eileen Bowser, *History of the American Cinema, Volume 2: The Transformation of Cinema 1907–1915* (New York: Charles Scribner's Sons/Macmillan, 1990), p 43.

14. Rachael Low, *The History of the British Film 1906–1914* (London: George Allen & Unwin, 1949), p 190.

15. F. Dubrez Fawcett, *Dickens the Dramatist* (London: W.H. Allen, 1952), p 193.

16. Richards, *Films and British National Identity*, p 330; Bowser, *The Transformation of Cinema*, pp 42–3.

17. It was common practice at this time for film lengths to be quoted in feet: a reel usually meant a thousand feet of celluloid, which, depending on the running speed (this was not standardized until the advent of sound cinema), was usually between 10 and 15 minutes.

18. *The Moving Picture World* (5 December 1908), pp 458–9.

19. *Ibid.* (12 December 1908), p 476.

20. In the same year Ogle had become the first actor to play Frankenstein's Monster in a one-reel adaptation of *Frankenstein*, also produced by the Edison Manufacturing Company. *Frankenstein* was directed by J. Searle Dawley, who according to the British Film Institute's SIFT database also directed the 1910 *A Christmas Carol*. However, Fred Guida identifies John H. Collins as director of *A Christmas Carol*. Fred Guida, 'Merry Christmas from Charles Dickens … and Thomas Edison', *Films in Review*, 45/11 and 12 (November/December 1994), p 4.

21. *The Moving Picture World* (7 January 1911), p 11.

22. *The Bioscope* (16 November 1911), p 483.

23. *Ibid.* (5 November 1914), p 509.

24. Davis, *The Lives and Times of Ebenezer Scrooge*, pp 13–14.

25. Linda Wood, 'Julius Hagen and Twickenham Film Studios', in Jeffrey Richards (ed.), *The Unknown 1930s: An Alternative History of the British Cinema, 1929–1939* (London: I.B. Tauris, 1998), p 48.

26. For example, *Film Weekly* (24 November 1935) commented: 'The makers of *Scrooge* have achieved the creditable end of transferring "A Christmas Carol" to the screen more or less exactly as Dickens wrote it, with authentic characters, backgrounds and atmosphere – even using a good deal of the author's own involved dialogue.' The *Monthly Film Bulletin* (2/22, November 1935) considered that 'the spirit of the original is perfectly conveyed. The settings and costumes have been carefully chosen and excellently reproduced; the actors, like the director, have got inside the characters they are portraying and the period in which the story is set. … Lovers of Dickens will find this film a very successful version of the original and those who are not will enjoy it as an intelligent and restrained production of a story whose interest and values are not confined to any one period.'

27. On the ideology of consensus in 1930s British cinema, see Tony Aldgate, 'Ideological Consensus in British Feature Films, 1935–1947', in K.R.M. Short (ed.), *Feature Films as History* (London: Croom Helm, 1981), pp 94–112; Marcia Landy, *British Genres: Cinema and Society, 1930–1960* (Princeton: Princeton University Press, 1991); Jeffrey Richards, *The Age of the Dream Palace: Cinema and Society in Britain, 1930–1939* (London: Routledge & Kegan Paul, 1984); and Stephen C. Shafer, *British Popular Films 1929–1939: The Cinema of Reassurance* (London: Routledge, 1997).

28. Richards, *Films and British National Identity*, pp 336–7.

29. When the film was released in Britain, the *Catholic Film News* (1/3, January 1939) actually included Lionel Barrymore on its cast list, even though he is not in the film, an indication of how closely he was associated with the role of Scrooge even outside America. The magazine also expressed its surprise at the certificate awarded to the film by the British Board of Film Censors: 'Rather surprisingly, the film has been accorded an "A" certificate: apparently it is considered that Marley's not very frightening (but excellently acted) ghost would disturb the children's slumbers.'

30. *New York Times* (23 December 1938), p 16.

31. In Dickens's original the passage is thus: "'There are many things from which I might have derived good, by which I have not profited, I dare say," returned the nephew: "Christmas among the rest. But I am sure I have always thought of Christmas time, when it has come round – apart from the veneration due to its sacred name and origin, if anything belonging to it can be apart from that – as a good time: a kind, forgiving, charitable, pleasant time: the only time I know of, in the long calendar of the year, when men and women seem by one consent to open their shut-up hearts freely, and to think of people below them as if they really were fellow-passengers to the grave, and not another race of creatures bound on other journeys. And therefore, uncle, though it has never put a scrap of gold or silver in my pocket, I believe that it *has* done me good, and *will* do me good; and I say, God bless it!"' While Dickens implicitly accepts class differences, the film removes those references ('people below them') and substitutes instead the idea of human beings being 'really part of the same family'.

32. Davis, *The Lives and Times of Ebenezer Scrooge*, p 14.

33. Richards, *Films and British National Identity*, pp 340–1.

34. Charles Barr, *Ealing Studios*, revised edition (London: Studio Vista, 1993), particularly pp 108–18, 131–45 and 159–73.

35. *Social Insurance and Allied Services. Report by Sir William Beveridge*, Cmd 6404 (London: HMSO, 1942), 'Introduction and Summary', pp 5–19.

36. See, for example, Peter Clarke, *Hope and Glory: Britain 1900–1990* (Harmondsworth: Penguin, 1966), pp 239–40; Arthur Marwick, *British Society Since 1945*, third edn (Harmondsworth: Penguin, 1996), pp 11–12; and Kenneth O. Morgan, *The People's Peace: British History 1945–1990* (London: Oxford University Press, 1990), pp 104–11.

37. *New York Times* (29 November 1951), p 41.

38. *The Cinema* (17 October 1951), p 13.

39. *Variety* (14 November 1951).

40. *Ibid.* (31 December 1947).

41. *Ibid.* (22 December 1948).

42. *Ibid.* (29 December 1948).

43. The various television productions of the *Carol* are listed by Alvin H. Marill, 'The Television Scene', *Films in Review*, 35/9 (November 1984), pp 629–31.

44. This, and other Christmas specials, are listed in Robert Ross, *The Carry On Companion* (London: B.T. Batsford, 1996), pp 138–47.

45. In the interim there had been a short British film of *A Christmas Carol* produced in 1960 by Anglo-Amalgamated, starring James Hayter as Scrooge. *The Daily Cinema* (21 November 1960) said: 'Charles Dickens' story is no newcomer to the cinema screen in full feature length versions but here the producer has obviously appreciated a showman's need to put a bit of the Christmas spirit into programmes at that time of year.'

46. *Monthly Film Bulletin*, 38/444 (January 1971), pp 13–14.

47. 'Cashing in on Christmas', *Spectator* (5 December 1970), p 736.

48. *New York Times* (20 November 1970), p 29.

49. 'Donner takes up "Christmas" task', *Screen International* (15 December 1984), p 16ff.

50. *Screen International* (8 December 1984), p 2.

51. See, for example, Leonard Quart, 'The Religion of the Market: An American Perspective on the British Film Industry', and Andrew Higson, 'Re-presenting the National Past: Nostalgia and Pastiche in the Heritage Film', both in Lester Friedman (ed.), *British Cinema and Thatcherism: Fires Were Started* (London: UCL Press, 1993), pp 15–34 and pp 108–29.

52. *Monthly Film Bulletin*, 51/611 (December 1984), p 377.

53. *Variety* (28 December 1955).

54. *New York Times* (23 November 1988), p C-16.

55. *Variety* (23 November 1988).

56. Oddly enough, many critics saw it as a film that would appeal to adults who had grown up with Disney. 'For anyone over thirty-five, this little jewel of a film is truly the Ghost of Christmas Past', said Gilbert Adair in the *Monthly Film Bulletin*, 51/600 (January 1984), p 27.

2

A Hollywood Carol's Wonderful Life

Jonathan Munby

It's a Wonderful Life has assumed the status of *the* Christmas movie. The story of how it came to win this honour is itself something of a miracle. Released at Christmastime in 1946, the movie had an inauspicious start, losing at the box-office and dividing critical opinion. *It's a Wonderful Life* was directed by one of Hollywood's most celebrated directors of the pre-war era, Frank Capra (one of the few directors whose name was familiar to audiences). Renowned for purveying upbeat visions of the common folk's triumph against the sinister agents of power throughout the 1930s, Capra had mined a rich vein of public resentment against a discredited establishment fostered in the aftermath of the Wall Street Crash. *It's a Wonderful Life* certainly perpetuated a recognizable Capra (and Depression-associated) formula into the post-war era, telling a tale of a small man's virtuous struggle against the machinations of a miserly, greedy and powerful banker. The relative failure of *It's a Wonderful Life* with audiences at the end of 1946, however, seemed to spell the end of faith in what had come to be known as 'Capra-corn'. Yet the movie's incredible resurrection as a Yuletide television evergreen invites a different account of *It's a Wonderful Life*'s fate.

Of interest here is how a story that is in many ways an American reworking of Dickens's *A Christmas Carol* did not resonate with its original audience, yet has since become an essential part of the American Christmas viewing ritual. Sold to television when the film's releasing company (RKO) went under in the mid-1950s, *It's a Wonderful Life* drifted into relative oblivion until 1974 when no one remembered to renew its copyright.[1] This moment of apparent death, however, provided the conditions for the movie's successful rebirth. With no copyright claims, *It's a Wonderful Life* became part of the public domain, and television companies saw obvious profit in screening this 'free' film as part of their Christmas programming. Even though *It's a Wonderful Life* was set on Christmas Eve, the film had not been conceived as a Christmastime film. As I shall detail later, Capra saw the film as making a more general social commentary about the state of America, and the original release date had been 30 January 1947. The movie's recuperation as appropriate fare for holiday consumption (especially since the early 1980s) has everything to do with the historical distance between today's audience and that of Christmas 1946.

The argument I wish to advance here is that the 1946 film (that text and the interpretations available to audiences of the day) is very different to the film we consume today. In 1946, the film's more fantastic elements would have been understood as just that. An analysis of the contemporaneous contexts of reception will reveal that *It's a Wonderful Life* could not have been consumed as a holiday movie that seamlessly affirmed the regenerative features of what Paul Davies describes as the *Carol* as 'culture-text'.[2] That the movie's central protagonist George Bailey (played

Life and death at Christmas: Clarence (Henry Travers) and George Bailey (James Stewart) in *It's a Wonderful Life* (1946).

by James Stewart) needed an angel to save him sent an ambiguous message to audiences about the capacity of good to triumph over evil in the new post-war world. In its day *It's a Wonderful Life* would have encouraged a more cynical and desperate disposition in its audience: that Christmas was not good enough as a salve to the social and psychic wounds of the time; that Epiphany was a fanciful, even impossible, gesture or contrivance in the face of the secular despair.

It is only when the historical realities of the very period that is the focus of the movie itself (1919–46, a period that includes the Depression and the Second World War) themselves enter the category of myth (a process to which the movie itself has contributed) that *It's a Wonderful Life*'s more bitter elements relinquish their power over the movie's meaning. As I shall substantiate, *It's a Wonderful Life* was self-reflective about the American cinema's mythmaking power. While this latter attribute was partly a product of the pitting of fantasy (the firmament of angels) against realism (the earthly, small town of Bedford Falls) in the movie itself, it was also a product of Capra's own intent to use *It's a Wonderful Life* to review the 'Pollyanna' mythology that had made him Depression America's most successful feature film director. Lost to us today is the movie's pessimistic discourse on the contingency of Hollywood's mythmaking powers. Detailing the contingency of *It's a Wonderful Life*'s meaning in 1946, and the changing relation of the movie to the myth of Christmas since that date, is the focus of the rest of this chapter.

An Independent Life (the Ghost of Christmas Present): 1946

It's a Wonderful Life started out as 'The Greatest Gift', a story oriented around the premise 'I wish I had never been born'. A morally upright protagonist contemplates the taking of his own life because of that life's insignificance. It takes an intervention of God to highlight that every life, no matter how small, counts and that the merits of a 'good' life have to be measured by appropriately small criteria. Working against the grand narrative that attributed agency and power to those of grand influence, the story must have had obvious appeal in a period that had nurtured and extolled the virtues of every American citizen in licking first the Depression and then Axis enemies in the wartime 1940s. As a narrative centred on suicide, however, major studios were insecure about its viability with both audiences and censors.

In spite of various reworkings by established screenwriters, the property was deemed untenable by its owners, RKO.[3] On 1 September 1945, Charles Koerner, head of RKO Radio Pictures, sold 'The Greatest Gift' to Frank Capra and his new independent production company, Liberty Films, for $10,000.[4] Capra was attracted to 'The Greatest Gift' for a variety of reasons. Not least of these was the simplicity (and familiarity) of the original idea which had started out as a tale adorning a Christmas card (written by Philip Van Doren Stern), and which seemed to fit the proscriptions of Capra-corn so perfectly. As Capra himself put it:

> a few typewritten pages bound in Christmas covers. It was the story I had been looking for all my life! Small town. A man. A good man, ambitious. But so busy helping others, life seems to pass him by. Despondent. He wishes he'd never been born. He gets his wish. Through the eyes of a guardian angel he sees the world as it would have been had he not been born. Wow![5]

Unlike the major studios, Capra did not shy away from the 'suicide' premise underpinning the story. Keen to strike a blow for the new cause of independent production, he deliberately wanted to avoid the compromises that characterized Hollywood's 'assembly-line system':

> I had to make a success of Liberty Films. We were the bell-wether of the post-war independents. Hollywood films were being funneled through the tastes of half a dozen studio heads, and film-makers began to get their ideas not from life but from each other's pictures. We were creating within walls of mirrors.[6]

What Capra anticipated about the relationship of Hollywood to the post-war world is briefly outlined in an article he wrote for *The New York Times* in May 1946, entitled 'Breaking Hollywood's "Pattern of Sameness"'. He believed that audiences would notice a new 'individuality' in Hollywood products, and that 'the pattern of sameness' would no longer be present.[7] Independent film producers would foster a more creative and less uniform movie-making culture that was free of the application of 'mass production methods to the creative element'.[8] More specifically, Capra argued this new independent direction would turn away from the 'Hollywood version of how life should be lived' toward 'how it was actually being lived'. Capra believed that the post-war audience had become jaded on the wartime 'machine-like treatment' of life on screen. The war had made the 'sameness' of Hollywood 'glaringly evident', and there was an urgency to remedy this on the part of many film-makers.[9]

Economically, the move to independent production at the end of the war was sponsored by tax relief and the impending divestment of the major studios' assets (the major studios were facing an anti-trust suit that viewed their control of production, distribution and exhibition as monop-olistic). Artistically and politically, the move to independent production was fed by an appetite for more candid treatments of American life. And it is no surprise that many of those associated with the independent movement were devotees of social realism (especially those who left

Warner Brothers). Equally, it is no coincidence that one of the most marked offspring of the independent climate was the dark, topical crime thriller we now call *film noir*.[10] Capra's first independent production displays very similar tendencies aesthetically and thematically. Indeed, *It's a Wonderful Life* can certainly be interpreted as a *film noir* (a subject to which I shall return later). At the same time, *It's a Wonderful Life* extends a trajectory set in motion by his previous film output. And it is against this intertext that *It's a Wonderful Life* must also be evaluated. Not only is the movie significant for the way it mediated the concerns of 1946, but its very failure with audiences begs questions of how and why Capra's vision had lost its cultural currency.

In March 1946, in an interview with the *Los Angeles Times* drama editor, Edwin Schallert, Capra commented on the problem facing 'entertainment' in the context of adjustment to peace:

> People are numb after the catastrophic events of the past 10 or 15 years. I would not attempt to reach them mentally through a picture, only emotionally. Anything of a mental sort, anything apart from the purely human will have to be incidental. Improving the individual and bringing a more hopeful outlook on life to him is the only way that you can improve the nation, and ultimately the world. It is the individual that must be built up in his beliefs, his hopes and his aspirations and then as a matter of course you will find the new world we all talk about developing in a larger way. I think that we must entertain in pictures and then convey our message, whatever it may be, but achieve this quite incidentally.[11]

As such, *It's a Wonderful Life* would take risks only in the name of a cinematic freedom still framed by the obligation to entertain. The resulting movie would be marked by this contradictory desire to acknowledge the 'catastrophic' past on one hand, while providing edifying amusement on the other.

The final version of the screenplay initiated the action in the present of the small town of Bedford Falls on Christmas Eve 1946. George Bailey (James Stewart) is about to jump from a bridge when God decides to send down a 'second class' angel, called Clarence (played by Henry Travers) who is trying to earn his wings by saving a soul. Before his descent, Clarence (and the audience) are provided with the story of George Bailey's life through flashback to 1919. This story narrates the contradictory frustrations of a virtuous small-town citizen wishing to escape the isolation of Bedford Falls on the one hand, and save the town from the corrupting influence of an amoral banker, Potter (played by Lionel Barrymore), on the other. George Bailey's desires to travel the world, to go to college, to exercise his skills as an architect by building bridges and skyscrapers, to fight in the war (to join the grand narrative, as it were), are all frustrated. He forgoes travel when his father dies and he is forced to take over the family's ailing Building and Loan company; he forgoes college when his brother, who should have replaced George in heading the Building and Loan, gets a more attractive high-flying job in the big city; and he cannot fight in the war because he is 4F (a military term meaning unfit for certain types of service) owing to deafness in one ear, an ailment picked up while saving the life of his brother in a freezing pond.

This lamentable tale of sacrifice is not without its redeeming qualities. In running a benign financial institution dedicated to building rather than destroying the community, George fights a good fight against the malevolent Potter who sees no profit in goodwill. George's architectural skills are put to communitarian use as he designs affordable housing for his company's investors. He finds solace in a dedicated wife, Mary (played by Donna Reed), and loving children. In the end, however, his best efforts are compromised by ill-fortune and the machinations of Potter. On Christmas Eve 1946, the Building and Loan faces bankruptcy with $8000 missing. The money has been mislaid by his affable but forgetful uncle (played by

Uncle Billy (Thomas Mitchell), George Bailey (James Stewart) and Mary (Donna Reed) prove that *It's a Wonderful Life* (1946).

Thomas Mitchell), and found by Potter, who pockets it and takes the opportunity to drive the Buildings and Loan to the wall. George knows he will go to jail falsely accused of embezzlement. Reflecting on the failure of his ambitions (his own 'catastrophic' past, as it were) and the need to leave his family with some form of financial security, George decides to commit suicide and let Mary collect on his life insurance policy. Intending to end it all by jumping from the town bridge, he storms out of a home adorned with Christmas decorations and children practising carols.

Having returned to the 'present' of the film's opening, we see Clarence the angel intervene and prevent George from taking his own life. Unconvinced, however, as to the value of Clarence's action, George needs persuasion that his life has amounted to something. Clarence then grants George's wish that he 'had never been born'. Together the two wander into a transformed Bedford Falls, now called 'Pottersville'. George attempts to find key people in his life all of whom not only no longer recognize him, but have experienced drastically different fates without George's influence: Mary is a drab spinster librarian; his mother runs a down-and-out boarding house; his brother does not exist, having died in 1919 (and therefore never grew up to become a business success and war hero) because George was not there to save his life in the icy pond; and so on. Yuletide in Pottersville is now the stuff of *film noir*: a dark space lit up not by Christmas lights, but the neon signs of gambling joints, bars and brothels.

The story ends with George repenting. His realization that even his small life made a beneficial difference is rewarded by a return to the ostensibly 'real' world of Bedford Falls. Yet this return functions as a way to guarantee the fantasy of Christmas itself. In what amounts to an inversion of the film's play with fantasy and realism, George escapes the reality of a Pottersville future through the *deus ex machina* force of Christmas. With a copy of *Tom Sawyer* in hand (a nostalgic gift from Clarence that links George to Twain's pastoral world), George and family gather around the tree in their living room as the community of Bedford Falls rally to his rescue. To the sound of Christmas cheer, the good small-town citizens bring forth their gifts of cash to cover the mislaid money. Friends from the big city call with greater promises of thousands of dollars to guarantee that George and his way of doing things will survive forever. The redemptive power of Christmas wins out. Or does it?

Contemporaneous fears on the part of major studio executives that the darker connotations of the original story would damage box-office returns were confirmed. Capra's uncompromising, independent treatment of this original material only exacerbated the story's more fatalistic features and hampered the task of effecting a believable 'happy end'. The movie eventually lost around $500,000 at the box-office. This failure with audiences in late 1946 and early 1947 can be explained in part by the circumstances that forced the movie into being released ahead of schedule as a Christmastime feature.

The official release date of *It's a Wonderful Life* was 30 January 1947. Capra was compelled, however, to move the release date up to Christmastime 1946, to fill a gap in RKO's release schedule left by *Sinbad the Sailor* which was behind in production.[12] Although *It's a Wonderful Life* was clearly a form of Christmas movie, Capra had always chosen to downplay this aspect: 'I didn't even think of it as a Christmas story when I first ran across it.'[13] He felt that the movie would have a more general appeal, one that was not dependent on holiday sentiment. In fact, that sentiment in the context of 1946 may well have worked against a positive reception of the movie. In the immediate aftermath of the war, *It's a Wonderful Life* addressed the starker realities of a culture transformed and uncertain about its future. In spite of its setting at Christmastime, the movie's deterministic mood and dark *mise-en-scène* belonged to the stylistic and thematic continuum of *film noir*. Ironically, *It's a Wonderful Life* might have won more widespread appeal at any other time of year other than Christmas. But as Christmas holiday fare at the end of the first post-war year the film failed. Given the movie's uncompromising vision of the fate of the American Everyman from 1919 to 1946, the compensatory deployment of Christmas as a guarantee of a happy ending may have seemed just a little too pat to audiences of the day.

The movie lost money at the box-office and failed to garner a single Oscar. The promotion of the movie revealed uncertainty over *It's a Wonderful Life*'s generic status. Publicity surrounding the film disguised its more sinister character and made little or no mention of its Christmas theme. It was sold (somewhat deceptively) to audiences instead as a Capra-film: a humorous family story replete with homey sentimental romance. Although *It's a Wonderful Life* did receive good reviews in influential papers and magazines such as *Nation*, *Life*, *Newsweek* and *Time*, this was countered by not so wonderful appraisals in *The New York Times* ('a figment of Pollyanna platitudes'), *New Republic* ('fights … to convince that American life is exactly like the *Saturday Evening Post* covers of Norman Rockwell'), and *The New Yorker* ('so mincing as to border on baby talk'). *It's a Wonderful Life*'s unstable status as a 'Christmas' movie, inaccurate publicity promises, mixed reviews, competition from other films, and terrible winter weather, all conspired to keep filmgoers away.[14]

Somewhat ironically, however, disappointing box-office returns at Christmastime 1946 probably testify to the way *It's a Wonderful Life* was alive to the contradictions of American society in the immediate aftermath of the war. The elements that made the movie difficult to consume as holiday entertainment have been central to the scholarly fascination with the movie's textual richness. The contradictions of the first post-war year were played out through an amplification of the formal and thematic dichotomies that we can take as definitive of the Hollywood cinema: the familiar structure of oppositions between individual aspiration and social responsibility; between commitments to self or to family; between East and West (here encoded as values of the big city versus the small town); between good and bad versions of capitalism; and so on. Typically, these antinomies were played out as a set of conflicts in need of resolution.[15] *It's a Wonderful Life*, however, did not shirk in showing that there was an imbalance of power between warring parties. Preventing Bedford Falls from becoming Pottersville is understood as a desperate reaffirmation of one set of ailing values in the face of those much more powerful.

In *It's a Wonderful Life*, Hollywood's narrative play on the desire for a sense of an ending is fatalistically reworked and heightened as a desire for suicide. *It's a Wonderful Life*'s struggle to accommodate the convention of the 'happy ending' (with Epiphany) was consistent with Capra's wish to break 'the pattern of sameness' that he thought characterized most of Hollywood. As such, we have a movie that troubles, and is troubled by, the ordering practice of narrative and narrative resolution. Told in flash-back, told as an attempt in many ways to rescue the old way of telling a story from the desperate revision demanded by the present of 1946, *It's a Wonderful Life* communicates its meanings as much through its war with Hollywood's structuring conventions as anything else. And this is typical of the mannered generic experiments that marked what we now call *film noir*. The film's narrative convolutions, in tandem with its dark *mise-en-scène*, reveal how *It's a Wonderful Life* very much belongs to its historical moment. The movie is aesthetically marked as a late 1940s Hollywood movie.

Various film scholars have highlighted how *It's a Wonderful Life* is fascinating for its dichotomous (discordant) *mise-en-scène* and narrative structure. Both Robin Wood and Robert Ray have highlighted the way the movie counterposes the generic conventions of small-town family comedy against those of the post-war crime thriller.[16] A dark (*noir*-like) shadow haunts the affirmative (small-town) story in what amounts to an interrogation of Hollywood conventions. The world of small-town comedy threatens to give way to the crime thriller as a more viable representation of American life. The system of compensatory moral value which traditionally dictated Hollywood narrative patterns is seen to be under duress. Most notably, Potter's crime in stealing $8000 goes unpunished, thus violating a Production Code dictum that crime must never be seen to pay on the American screen. Even worse, Potter (as an ersatz American Scrooge) is deemed irredeemable. This embodiment of capitalist graft and spiritual impoverishment never sees the error of his ways, and he is not even removed from Bedford Falls. In spite of the happy ending, Potter's shadow will continue to haunt the future; a future from which Christmas (and stories with happy endings) may well constitute only a temporary spiritual respite.

It's a Wonderful Life's self-conscious discourse on the conventional limits of Hollywood's version of American life is thematically extensive. In dwelling so obsessively on the difficulty of finding a satisfactory way to contain George Bailey's desires to leave Bedford Falls, *It's a Wonderful Life* raises questions about Hollywood's compensatory ideological function. The movie ends with an idealized image of the nuclear family spiritually buttressed by Christmas. What is at stake, however, is the very credibility of this end image. For, throughout the movie commitment to family (here doubly encoded as Mary and the kids/the Building and Loan as family firm) is convincingly portrayed as a trap. Ideals of continuity wrestle with a desire for difference. The movie encodes obvious but relevant tensions for a culture readjusting to the prerogatives of peace following a world war. *It's a Wonderful Life* catered for a time in which GIs were returning to a world transformed; a world in which domestic values were being consciously reasserted; and a world that had experienced dramatic shifts in the values associated with male and female enterprise.

While these formal and thematic features make the movie a rich object of study, they also made it generically confusing to audiences in 1946, and damaged *It's a Wonderful Life*'s chances of making it as a Christmas movie. Like so many films of its era, *It's a Wonderful Life* is overt in its ideological complexity. The struggle between Mary's world and George's ambition was germane to the post-war audience. *It's a Wonderful Life* is marked by its contradictory relation to the ideological work involved in trying to resanctify 'home sweet home' in an age where men and women had discovered other roles independent of each other at war abroad and on the home front. The hegemonic work required to put men and women back together after the war was never going to be easy, and *It's a Wonderful Life* raised the issue of domestication not simply as a virtue, but as a problem. A problem because audiences in 1946 could not have seen things any other way. Making explicit that which may have been previously implicit in terms of Hollywood's ideological allegiances was a product of an industry trying to re-examine itself; trying to find the right kind of story to tell; trying to establish the right form of national self-representation after the war. And, as we shall see, it was also the product of Capra's own reflection on the value of all his previous work.

The Ghost of Capra's Past

As the film that most deeply communicates Frank Capra's post-war sentiments about America's future, *It's a Wonderful Life*'s box-office disappointment and mixed critical reception at the time of its release tells us much about a national culture in transition. Capra had been the most celebrated movie mythmaker of the Depression era other than Walt Disney.[17] His success at addressing the very subject of Americanism throughout the 1930s led to his appointment by General Marshall to the US Army's Special Services Branch, to head its Film Section.[18] There he produced the seminal 'Why We Fight' propaganda series, designed to win the battle for American minds as to why this was a war worth fighting. Capra's proven abilities to attract a mass audience to films devoted to a discussion of the rights and wrongs of the American way masked, however, an increasingly desperate trajectory in his vision of American possibility. With war's end, Capra turned away from his role as a purveyor of affirmative jingoistic documentaries and returned to the unresolved problems that had been central to his pre-war and early 1940s Hollywood output.

Capra had not made a commercial feature during the war and he approached the making of *It's a Wonderful Life* with a degree of trepidation. Feeling rusty as a man with a Depression-era reputation for life-affirming comedy confronting a transformed America, Capra was uncertain about whether he could still reach out and touch the post-war audience.[19] The jingoistic and war-affirmative rhetoric of Capra's work for the Special Services hid the darker and more sobering realities to which he had been exposed. Photographs of Nazi atrocities (including images of the gas-ovens at Dachau taken by his production partner George Stevens) formed part of the material Capra assembled in order to make the series.[20] Relentless exposure to the darker side of human behaviour must have tempered Capra's traditionally affirmative vision. Even though his films had become progressively darker in theme and style during the late 1930s, they had always found reasonably convincing optimistic resolution.

In the immediate aftermath of the war, however, Capra was worried about how to give dramatic form to a clearly changed order of things. Fear of failure only exacerbated the director's sense of doubt. As he reflected in 1981 about his kind of film-making:

> Perhaps I had put too much faith in the human race – you know, in the pictures I had made. Maybe they were too much as things should be. I began to think that maybe I really was a Pollyanna.[21]

Taking advantage of the new climate of independent film production, Capra settled on entertaining this new world by pursuing the thematic and visual path of his feature film *oeuvre* to its logical conclusion. Although Capra had gained a reputation for his relative autonomy from the control of studio bosses (best expressed in his winning of the right to have his name above the title), his pre-war films display a degree of compromise and compensatory value that are hallmarks of the studio system.

Various film scholars have covered the significance of Capra's Depression era output – seeing him variously as a populist or Jeffersonian agrarian.[22] Capra was dedicated to creating regenerative social fantasies on screen that addressed the problems confronting America in the heart of the Depression. At stake was Americanism itself as his common folk heroes struggled to keep alive pastoral small-town ideals against all odds. Jefferson Smith, Longfellow Deeds, Long John Willoughby (the eponymous heroes of *Mr Smith Goes to Washington, Mr Deeds Goes to Town,* and *Meet John Doe* respectively) all served as forerunners for George Bailey, the chief protagonist in *Its a Wonderful Life*. Whilst only one of these characters was played by James Stewart, they were all similar in character and epitomized an essential ingredient of Capra-corn: common men of high moral principle at odds with a corrupt establishment. Such a conflict would have had strong resonance with a Depression-era audience. And by 1946, the sight of James Stewart fighting a seemingly losing battle on behalf of small-town civic idealism was a definitive part of what one expected from a Capra–Stewart vehicle.

You Can't Take it With You (1938) is also an important forerunner for *It's a Wonderful Life*. Featuring both James Stewart and Lionel Barrymore in leading roles, this film played out a theme that Capra found irresistible: in his own words, 'the viability of the lamb when confronted by a lion'.[23] The story revolved around a conflict between two 'families', the Kirbys and the Vanderhofs. The Vanderhofs were a happy and kind group of rebels (led by an avuncular patriarch, Grandpa Vanderhof, played by Barrymore), while the Kirbys represented a spiritually impoverished Wall Street banking family. The conflict between the avaricial rich and the generous poor is played out over Kirby Jr (played by James Stewart) who falls for Vanderhof's grand-daughter. Kirby Jr's willingness to turn his back on his Wall Street inheritance in the name of love eventually wins over his otherwise mean-spirited father (played by a Scrooge-like Edward Arnold). Through a form of secular epiphany, the Kirbys of the world find a way to love rather than devour their neighbours and compromise is reached through the redemption of the Kirby world via the marriage of family scions. Significantly, such redemption of the miserly banker would be denied in *It's a Wonderful Life*.

It is important to see how *It's a Wonderful Life* constitutes the logical end-game of the trajectory set in motion by these earlier Capra-corn classics. What was at stake was the increasing doubt about the kind of compromise one could make between the fantasy of the common man's triumph and the reality of the fact that everything was stacked against him. The power of the films in question was that they did not avoid contemporaneous realities. Appropriately (for the Depression era), these movies acknowledged the desperate nature of the odds – but found a way to make compromises with the more malignant forces of business and political power that kept the fantasy of a return to pastoral ideals alive.

The declining fortune of Capra's Everymen, between 1936 and 1941, constitutes an index of growing desperation about the efficacy of such protagonists (and their beliefs). In 1936, Longfellow Deeds at least has a twenty million dollar inheritance to redistribute to the needy (in *Mr Deeds Goes to Town*). Yet by 1939, the terms of reforming the establishment have changed drastically, as small-town idealist Jefferson Smith struggles against massive odds to overcome corruption in the US Senate (in *Mr Smith Goes to Washington*). And by 1941, Long John Willoughby's cause is revealed to be nothing but a charade, as his national goodwill enterprise is exposed as a front masking the machinations of a sinister politician (in *Meet John Doe*). George Bailey's struggle re-invokes these previous scenarios – but takes the growing doubt about achieving positive outcomes to its limit (and arguably makes this scepticism the very subject of the film).

As Capra's first post-war feature film, *It's a Wonderful Life* picked up where his last pre-war feature, *Meet John Doe*, had left off. Capra had had trouble trying to find a happy ending for *Meet John Doe*. Significantly, the problematic ending was oriented around how to stop the main protagonist from committing suicide. Long John Willoughby's threat to jump from a high building is 'staged' as a public event designed to persuade and convert a doubting world as to his essential goodness. For Long John, the threat of suicide can be a means to Epiphany for an earthly world looking on. By comparison, George Bailey's suicidal reflections are private and born of the desperate realization that his goodness seems to have amounted to nothing, and there's nothing he can do about it. In his case suicide is the logical confirmation of the worthlessness of a life in which only the angels are listening. Where *Meet John Doe*'s narrative ends with the problem of suicide, *It's a Wonderful Life* starts.

Unlike previous Everyman foes, Bailey's nemesis Potter escapes defeat, punishment, or conversion. Capra felt that Potter's retribution should be left 'to the audience's imagination'.[24] But the representation of Potter was not left to the imagination. Capra was concerned about Lionel Barrymore's face not being villainous enough. Barrymore had been associated with some quite sympathetic avuncular roles on screen – including one as Grandpa Vanderhof in Capra's *You Can't Take It With You*. Scared of Barrymore generating too much sympathy, Capra asked his make-up department to remodel the shape of Barrymore's head on the basis of the portrait of the male farmer in Grant Wood's famous painting *American*

Gothic.[25] Although Barrymore may have been previously typed as sympathetic on screen, Capra himself stated that no other actor would have done for the role of Potter.[26] And this sentiment must have had everything to do with other associations that Barrymore carried with him: most notably his identity with Scrooge in radio performances of *A Christmas Carol*. Guaranteeing that Potter be synonymous with an American Scrooge (albeit a Scrooge unredeemed) was important given the play between fantasy and realism that is essential to this film.

Christmas is key to understanding both the failure and rehabilitation of *It's a Wonderful Life*. More specifically, the movie's changing reception in the second half of the twentieth century has depended on the changing meaning of what Paul Davies has termed the *Christmas Carol* as 'culture-text'. Davies argues that '[e]ach period recreates the story in response to its cultural needs'.[27] In the United States, the *locus classicus* of the American Carol is the Depression. In what was tantamount to an American Epiphany, the Wall Street Crash of 1929 caused profound reflection on precepts associated with *laissez-faire* capitalism, ushering in a period of political and cultural reform. The movies had played a vital role in addressing the woes and needs of Depression culture, and in this context Capra had found his calling in trying to revive American self-belief. Not surprisingly, perhaps, Dickens's *A Christmas Carol* gained a special purchase on the American imagination during the 1930s. The newspapers reminded Americans every Christmas that their President, Franklin Delano Roosevelt, found solace in reading of the redemption of Scrooge and the triumph of Bob Cratchit as part of his Yuletide ritual. The *Carol* could be read as a Depression fable, and its Americanized version became a staple comfort on the radio every Christmas Eve, with the voice of the stateside Scrooge becoming forever associated with Lionel Barrymore (who played the role on radio from 1934 until the mid-1950s).[28]

It's a Wonderful Life constitutes a retelling of the *Carol* that is deliberately compromised. This version tells its story from the perspective not of Scrooge, but Bob Cratchit. It is George Bailey who needs redemption and the guidance of angelic ghosts. Potter, played by the actor so deeply associated with the role of Scrooge, is revealed to be totally irredeemable. *It's a Wonderful Life* featured Barrymore cast against the grain of his previous roles on screen and radio. Although Potter's role as an ersatz Scrooge is important in securing the story as a version of the *Carol*, this Hollywood version is narrated through Bob Cratchit (George Bailey). Paul Davies argues that the retelling of the *Carol* from Bob Cratchit's point of view is symptomatic of the Americanization of the *Carol* – a way to rescue capitalism rather than undermine it. The Cratchits of this world should be seen to be the bourgeois executors of business oriented around small-town civic virtues.[29] Conservative as this message may seem, it leaves the problem of what to do with Scrooge unresolved. The movie openly acknowledges that Scrooge is not a subject of redemption but an immanently evil presence. Here was a Scrooge who rode around town in a horse and carriage decked in undertaker's livery. Such thematic twisting of the *Carol* underwrote the movie's darker implications and begged questions about the redemptive power of Christmas even as it appropriated Christmas to manufacture a happy ending.

How *It's a Wonderful Life* rose to become the Christmas film *sine qua non* has depended on its removal from this original context of production and reception. In fact, it has depended on a dramatic shift in how audiences understand the movie's engagement with the myth of Christmas. In its day the film conveyed a darker message in tension with the mythic codification of Christmas. The idea that even Christmas might not be good enough constitutes an underlying subtext that helps explain the mixed reception of the movie in its year of release. Critics tended to find the movie's recourse to miracle hopelessly sentimental and platitudinous. The *deus ex machina* device of Christmas saving the day was seen to be pat.[30] What more dispassionate analysts have since taken to be the basis of the movie's richness – that generic conflict between sentimental optimism and candid realism – was interpreted quite differently in 1946. Christmas was a device that exposed rather than naturalized the idea that George Bailey's ideals and his world could survive in the post-war 1940s.

Removed from its original context of reception, however, *It's a Wonderful Life*'s artificial devices can be understood as entirely consonant with the 'feeling' of Christmas. Indeed, the movie has since become almost a guarantor of that experience (Christmas just wouldn't be Christmas without it). Today, the fact that Potter/Scrooge remains unredeemed, that in many ways Christmas only saves George Bailey/Bob Cratchit to fight another day in a world unchanged and unredeemed, is rendered irrelevant by the more powerful sentiments the movie raises regarding faith and miracle.

The Ghost of Christmas Future:
The Triumph of the Hollywood Carol Since 1974

Seemingly dead by the end of 1947, *It's a Wonderful Life* experienced an afterlife on television. Capra documents how he continued to correspond with his fans about anomalies in the plot throughout the 1950s and 1960s, because the movie was being aired on the small screen. In fact, the film's resurrection on the small screen constitutes in itself a reworking of Christmas mythology. In 1974, when no one bothered to renew its copyright and the movie went into public domain, *It's a Wonderful Life* claimed its central place in Christmas television programming partly because there were no financial strings attached. In many ways, then, the question 'What would Christmas be without *It's a Wonderful Life*?' has only had relevance in the last twenty years. As John McDonough illuminated in *The Wall Street Journal* in December 1984: '*It's a Wonderful Life* seems quietly to have replaced Charles Dickens' 'A Christmas Carol' as the Great American Christmas Story'.[31]

By the mid-1980s *It's a Wonderful Life* had become an indispensable part of Christmastime programming in the United States, a status it has maintained ever since. That *It's a Wonderful Life* finally found the success its maker so desperately wanted for it some four decades later has rested on a shift in the reception of what the movie communicates. In 1946, *It's a Wonderful Life*'s conflict between historical time and mythical intervention had made it a relatively 'open' text. The desperate struggle to rescue George Bailey from the realities of his secular historical existence through Christmas miracle produced contradictory meanings consistent with a period of maladjustment to peace. The culture confronting the demands of the new post-war world may have had good reason to be optimistic – but it also had good reason to be deeply anxious given the still live memory of a traumatic past.[32] Ostensibly, *It's a Wonderful Life* resolves the struggle between doubt and optimism in favour of the latter. To an audience in 1946, however, the candid treatment of George Bailey's doubts and the fantastic recourse to miracle would have provided an interpretation at odds with the movie's triumphant conclusion.

Today, *It's a Wonderful Life*'s topical commentary on the historical realities of post-war America does not constitute the basis of its mass appeal. The movie's success has been dependent on the way it now services the reinvention of a mythical past. Key to this process of mythification has been the way in which a period, once remembered as reason to doubt, has been translated into a reason to believe. The period in question covers the 1930s and wartime 1940s. These years are at the very heart of *It's a Wonderful Life* and framed the terms of its original reception. The televising of *It's a Wonderful Life* since the mid-1970s has helped the reification of the Great Depression as the site of the American *Carol*. In a reversal of fortune, where *It's a Wonderful Life*'s reworking of the *Carol* and Christmas once served to bring historical realism into competition with myth, it now erases the distinction. The dark 'ghost' of a traumatic past no longer has the power it once had (as a lived experience shared by the vast majority of the movie audience) to compromise the movie's heart-warming but mythic optimism. Nowadays we don't have to see the end as trite and the intervention of angels as ridiculously sentimental. Finally *It's a Wonderful Life* can convince without radical suspension of disbelief.

The fact that Potter has no moment of Epiphany no longer troubles us because the movie's candid realism is no longer understood as such.

Bedford Falls now belongs to the category of movie myth; a beautifully contrived space of the imagination; a sign whose historical referent has been lost; a sign whose new referent is 'Capraville'. *It's a Wonderful Life* is now *the* Christmas movie, *the* Hollywood Carol, *the* benchmark against which all other Christmas films are judged. As a mythical text, *It's a Wonderful Life* has no referent. The movie is instead constitutive of the very language of Hollywood Christmas films. Ironically, perhaps, it may have become the basis of 'a pattern of sameness', exactly the kind of movie Capra would have criticized at the time of *It's a Wonderful Life*'s original release. One could conjecture that the current Christmas movie is precisely a product of 'creating within walls of mirrors' in a house built by Capra. Not that Frank Capra seems to have minded, for he found a form of vindication in the triumph of the movie on the small screen.

The 1946 *It's a Wonderful Life* experience was of the richly duplicitous text – a fantasy replete with its sobering shadow: Bedford Falls versus Pottersville – two equally compelling versions of social possibility locked in a struggle for authority. Robin Wood reminds us that this movie's structural conflict between the generic worlds of happy small-town comedy and *film noir* has a dark implication: that 'behind every Bedford Falls there lurks a Pottersville'.[33] While this is an accurate observation of what we can recover about the film's richness through analysis, the problem is that this reading needs to be historicized. The generic battle that Wood applauds and which makes the film such a 'masterpiece' is not to be denied. But historical distance has changed the terms of the battle between light and dark, good and bad. I have argued that the movie's problematic reception in 1946 rested on its inability to satisfactorily recuperate things to the side of good and effect a convincing suture of all contradictions. As such, *It's a Wonderful Life*'s perceived equivocation in 1946 could hardly fulfil the generic contract of a Christmas film in providing unequivocal messages.

In sum, the loss of the movie's contingent discourse has been key to its success in the last twenty years. One could conjecture that this was always going to happen. This process seems to have started very early in the film's afterlife. For example, the Lux Radio version of *It's a Wonderful Life*, broadcast on 10 March 1947, severely reduced the Potter role in order to abridge the text to a sixty-minute format. The 'abridgement' of the movie's meanings has been a consequence of historical distance. The ghosts of the historical experience of Depression and war, of Capra's *oeuvre*, of *film noir*, of Barrymore's radio Scrooge, no longer haunt and complicate the reception of *It's a Wonderful Life* as they once did. Without those informing contexts, the film assumes an ahistorical immanent status – and the darker (demystifying or sobering) elements of the film lose their power to interfere with the affirmative story and its fantasy of a happy end. *It's a Wonderful Life* gives way to the *Carol*. Where the film once asked questions about the regenerative capacities of the human spirit by begging questions about Christmas' power of Epiphany, it now only asks the question, 'What would Christmas be without me?' In an almost miraculous twist of fate, as a now reified staple of Yuletide television programming, *Its a Wonderful Life* has experienced a resurrection as an ontological guarantee of Christmas itself.

Notes

1. John McDonough, 'A Christmas Movie's Wonderful Life', *The Wall Street Journal* (19 December 1984), reprinted in Jeanine Basinger, *The It's a Wonderful Life Book* (New York: Knopf, 1986), p 72. See also Joel Finler, *The Hollywood Story* (London: Octopus Books, 1988), pp 175–7.

2. Paul Davies, *The Lives and Times of Ebenezer Scrooge* (New Haven, Conn.: Yale University Press, 1990).

3. RKO had commissioned three full scripts from three top screenwriters, Dalton Trumbo, Clifford Odets and Marc Connelly. See Frank Capra, *The Name Above the Title* (New York: Macmillan, 1971), p 376.

4. In partnership with Samuel Briskind, Frank Capra founded Liberty Films in April 1945. In July of the same year, William Wyler came on board, as did George Stevens in January 1946. Whilst RKO sold the property rights to 'The Greatest Gift' to Liberty, RKO would end up operating as the releasing company for the eventual movie. Liberty also leased RKO's Encino Ranch property for the movie's set construction of Bedford Falls. (Basinger: *The It's a Wonderful Life Book*, p 4).

5. Capra: *The Name Above the Title*, p 376.

6. Ibid., p 378.

7. The article is reprinted in Richard Koszarski (ed.), *Hollywood Directors, 1941–1976* (Oxford University Press: Oxford, 1977) pp 83–9.

8. Capra: *The Name Above the Title*, p 86.

9. Ibid., p 87.

10. See Jonathan Munby, *Public Enemies, Public Heroes: Screening the Gangster from 'Little Caesar' to 'Touch of Evil'* (Chicago: University of Chicago Press, 1999); Brian Neve, *Film and Politics in America: A Social Tradition* (London: Routledge, 1992). *It's a Wonderful Life* was made in the wake not only of world war, but profound infrastructural changes in the studio system. The organizational changes that met producer-director desires to have full control over the films they were making took place in a climate of social readjustment to peacetime prerogatives. One result of this combination of forces was that there was increased freedom to pass bleaker comment on life without having to recuperate or contain such commentary within a pattern of resolution (arguably part of what facilitated the rise of the dark crime thrillers we now call *film noir* – a cycle of movies that offer no happy endings). *It's a Wonderful Life* is a fundamentally open text in this regard – a significant part of its narrative interest built around the tension between the ideology of happy resolution and a more deterministic version of things.

11. Basinger: *The It's a Wonderful Life Book*, p 18.

12. Ibid., pp 52–3.

13. Capra cited by McDonough in 'A Christmas Movie's Wonderful Life', in ibid., p 72.

14. Capra: *The Name Above the Title*, p 382.

15. Robin Wood makes this point well in reviewing the antinomies that constitute the deep structure of most Hollywood production and which are integral to *It's a Wonderful Life*. See Robin Wood, 'Ideology, Genre, Auteur', in B. K. Grant (ed.), *Film Genre Reader* (Austin: University of Texas Press, 1986), pp 59–73.

16. Ray sees the movie as typical of how Hollywood is politically dysfunctional – and although Wood dwells on the richness of the movie's aesthetic self-consciousness, he also reads the movie as enforcing a typically conservative outcome. Robert Ray, *A Certain Tendency of the Hollywood Cinema, 1930–1980* (Princeton: Princeton University Press, 1985); and Wood: 'Ideology, Genre, Auteur'.

17. Robert Sklar, *Movie-Made America: A Cultural History of American Movies* (New York: Random House, 1975), pp 195–214.

18. Capra: *The Name Above the Title*, pp 319–28.

19. Basinger: *The It's a Wonderful Life Book*, p 3.

20. Ibid.; and Capra: *The Name Above the Title*, p 378.

21. Capra interview with *Esquire* magazine in 1981 – as cited in Basinger: *The It's a Wonderful Life Book*, p 3.

22. Jeffrey Richards, 'Frank Capra and the Cinema of Populism', in B. Nichols (ed.), *Movies and Methods* (Berkeley: University of California Press, 1976), pp 65–77; and Sklar, *Movie-Made America*, pp 195–214.

23. Capra: *The Name Above the Title*, p 241.

24. Basinger: *The It's A Wonderful Life Book*, p 31.

25. Ibid., p 41.

26. Capra: *The Name Above the Title*, p 377.

27. Davies: *The Lives and Times of Ebenezer Scrooge*, p 13.

28. Ibid., pp 3–5, 152.

29. Ibid., pp 160–70.

30. See Capra's recitation of the press assault on the movie – *The Name Above the Title*, pp 382–3.

31. McDonough: 'A Christmas Movie's Wonderful Life', in Basinger: *The It's a Wonderful Life Book*, p 72. McDonough details how the mass saturation of the American television market with the movie at Christmastime has secured *It's a Wonderful Life*'s status as a Christmas evergreen and annual Yuletide ritual.

32. For broader discussions of the culture of 1940s and its defining anxieties, see William Graebner's appropriately entitled *Age of Doubt: American Thought and Culture in the 1940s* (Boston: Twayne, 1991); Lary May (ed.), *Recasting America: Culture and Politics in the Age of Cold War* (Chicago: University of Chicago Press, 1989); Lewis Erenberg and Susan Hirsch (eds), *The War in American Culture: Society and Consciousness during World War II* (Chicago: University of Chicago Press, 1996); George Lipsitz, *Rainbow at Midnight: Labor and Culture in the 1940s* (Urbana: University of Illinois Press, 1994).

33. Wood: 'Ideology, Genre, Auteur', p 65.

3

Dreaming of Christmas: Hollywood and the Second World War

H. Mark Glancy

It is now hard to imagine a time in which the Christmas season did not bring with it Christmas films, but it was only during the Second World War that Hollywood fully realized the power of Christmas as both a narrative component and a marketing strategy. The circumstances of the war were a key part of this realization. While the war may have seemed far away to many in the United States, it nonetheless caused a massive upheaval in the lives of most Americans. Sixteen million served in the armed forces, and even those who did not serve overseas were usually sent far from home and to distant military camps and postings. The war effort also required the mobilization of civilians, including married and single women, who were called upon to work in war-related production plants. This not only took many out of the home and into the workplace for the first time, but also required them to move away from their home towns and to production centres in distant cities and states. Some twenty-seven million Americans moved a distance of at least one county during the war years, and most moved from rural to more urban areas.[1] Amidst these upheavals, one of the few sources of comfort and constancy was the cinema, and box-office admissions rose to unprecedented levels in the mid-1940s. Hollywood provided its war-weary audiences with a steady diet of escapism, and this took a wide variety of forms. One of these forms was the Christmas film, which during the war years offered what must have seemed to be impossible but very potent scenarios of family unity, reunited lovers, and a return to the customs and traditions of an idealized past.

The development of the Christmas film formula began somewhat tentatively with *Remember the Night* (1940) and *The Man Who Came to Dinner* (1941) and then reached its stride in *Holiday Inn* (1942), *Meet Me in St. Louis* (1944), *I'll Be Seeing You* (1944) and *Christmas in Connecticut* (1945). Throughout all of these films the influence of Charles Dickens's *A Christmas Carol* is clear and strong.[2] Indeed, the Christmas film can be defined according to Dickens's model. They are not merely films with scenes set during the holiday season, but films in which the narrative hinges upon the impact that Christmas has on the characters. Lessons are learned, as the characters embark on journeys of discovery similar to Scrooge's own dark journey. Their lives are found to be lacking and dominated by selfish ambitions and cold materialism. Christmas then serves as the occasion and the solution for these ills, as humanism overcomes materialism, disunity gives way to unity and nearly miraculous reunions are granted to separated families or lovers.

While Dickens served as an overwhelming influence on these films, they do have qualities that are uniquely American and particularly attuned to the needs of wartime audiences in the United States. Whereas Dickens used London as the setting for *A Christmas Carol* and saw no incongruity between Christmas and the metropolis, in Hollywood's Christmas films the settings are primarily small towns or farms, and large cities are embued with values entirely at odds with the Christmas spirit. The image of the United States as a nation of small farms and tightly knit communities is presented as an ideal, and the spirit (and in some cases the names) of patriotic figures such as Lincoln and Jefferson looms large. The epiphanies that the characters experience, it seems, can only take place far from the modern world and in an environment which represents a homage to the nation's heritage. Christmas films, although influenced by Dickens, were made distinctly American during the war years.

A Woman's Place

The first Christmas films of the 1940s were *Remember the Night* and *The Man Who Came to Dinner*. Both served as star vehicles for two of the most popular female stars of the era, Barbara Stanwyck and Bette Davis, and both follow the narrative conventions employed in their earlier and most popular films. Throughout the 1930s, Stanwyck and Davis were routinely cast as strong-willed women who ultimately must pay a high price for challenging social and sexual norms. In both *Forbidden* (1932) and *Stella Dallas* (1937), for example, Stanwyck plays an ambitious girl from the wrong side of the tracks who uses her feminine wiles to attract a well-to-do and prominent man, yet she is ultimately punished for her transgressive behaviour in endings which reveal her to be impoverished and alone. Bette Davis usually played women of a higher social standing. In *Jezebel* (1938) and *Dark Victory* (1939), for example, she is a headstrong heiress who defies convention and social codes, and ultimately finds redemption only through extreme self-sacrifice or her own death. In a sense, it is misleading to place too much emphasis on the final-reel demise of these heroines. An undeniable aspect of the appeal of such films is that they offered their audience, which was likely to be predominantly female, the chance to identify with a strong and uninhibited female character, and to enjoy her flouting of conventions. It is the transgressive behaviour which fills the films, while the punishment often seems to be an obligatory gesture, a nod to the censors and to respectability from the film-makers. However, it is important to note this narrative pattern because in *Remember the Night* and *The Man Who Came to Dinner* it is altered by the heroines' experience of Christmas. Indeed, Christmas offers an opportunity for a happier and less punitive ending because it can be seen to transform the heroine into a more conventional and socially acceptable woman, and to bring her back into the patriarchal fold.

Remember the Night establishes the transgressive nature of its heroine, Lee Leander (Stanwyck), in the very first scene. While Christmas carols play on the soundtrack, and street-corner Santas collect money for the Salvation Army, Leander defies the Christmas spirit and displays her calculating materialism by stealing an expensive bracelet from a Fifth Avenue boutique and then attempting to pawn it. She is caught and jailed, but her guile and charm inspires the sympathy of the district attorney who prosecutes her, John Sargent (Fred MacMurray). Sargent posts her bail and agrees to drive her home to Indiana, where they can both spend Christmas with their respective families. Their journey together is not unlike Scrooge's journey with the ghosts of Christmas past, present and future. The drive out of New York City and into rural America begins as a comic escapade. Then, the Leander home – yet another house on the wrong side of the tracks for a Stanwyck character – proves to be dark and menacing, and Lee's cold and unforgiving mother rejects her daughter. John then agrees to take Lee with him to his own family home, a farm where his kind and supportive family celebrates a warm and traditional Christmas. Christmas cookies are baked, popcorn is strung for the tree, and there are presents for all, including Lee. In a late-night talk with John's mother, Lee learns that John has earned his success in a manner familiar to anyone who has heard the life story of Abraham Lincoln: he worked hard on the farm and put himself through law school by taking on extra jobs. Lee is overwhelmed by the family's warmth and integrity, and John – having seen her background and her transformation – urges her to jump bail and begin a new life. Her transformation is so complete, however, that she goes back to New York and pleads guilty to the charges. She will face her sentence and, when she has paid for her crimes, she and Sargent will marry.

While Lee Leander will be punished for her crimes, which was a necessary outcome under Hollywood's Production Code, Christmas has nonetheless provided an opportunity for her reform and eventual happiness. If this transformation seems unsatisfactory and unnecessary to the audience it is because the screenwriter Preston Sturges, who wrote the script while he was up and coming at Paramount Studios, gives Lee all the best and funniest lines. She is witty, sharp and skilfully flirtatious, and she talks rings round the dull and dependable attorney. In fact, the film works best in its earliest scenes, and as a screwball comedy, when Lee is in control and fires her wit at him. It then loses its footing as it descends into bleak revelations and homespun sentiment. Sturges apparently was attempting to emulate Frank Capra, not least in the move from the vices of the city to the virtues of rural Americana, yet in this instance at least he lacked Capra's deft touch. In the ending, we are meant to believe that a woman who could put a man in his place has learned her place, and that she is even willing to marry her prosecutor. Despite the cosy Christmas cheer, this is both disappointing and unbelievable. When the stars were reunited several years later for *Double Indemnity* (1944), the always sharp Barbara Stanwyck was once again pitted against dull Fred MacMurray, and the denouement – in which her malevolence ensures the downfall of them both – was far more convincing. In *Remember the Night*, however, the spirit of Christmas and the virtues of the heartland are seen to be powerful enough to enable a happy ending.

The Man Who Came to Dinner is Hollywood's most cynical Christmas film. It did not begin as a Bette Davis film, but as a fast-paced, witty and sophisticated play by George S. Kaufman and Moss Hart. Its origins on the Broadway stage (rather than in Hollywood) are betrayed in that it celebrates the metropolitan and urbane at the expense of the provincial and wholesome. The story centres around Sheridan Whiteside, a famous newspaper critic and radio commentator who injures himself while on a speaking tour of the Midwest. He and his personal secretary, Maggie Cutler, are then forced to spend the holidays in the small town of Mesalia, Ohio, and in the home of the Stanley family. The Stanleys are well-to-do and respectable by the standards of Mesalia, yet they are soon put in their place by Whiteside. His acerbic wit is aimed squarely at all Mesalia holds dear. While he may be self-indulgent and vain, he is nonetheless the source of a constant stream of humorous invective, in which small-town manners and mores are mocked and belittled. Whiteside uncovers the respectable Stanleys' dark secret: the flighty aunt whom they hide within their home is an infamous axe murderess. He convinces the Stanleys' son and daughter to run away and chase their dreams in the wider world. And, at the end, the Stanleys' servants readily agree to leave Mesalia and work for Whiteside in New York City.

In contrast to *Remember the Night*, the small town here is not a haven in which souls are saved, it is a narrow-minded backwater from which the intelligent and unconventional must escape. Similarly, the family is not a source of comfort and security, as one might expect within a Christmas story, but instead is seen to stifle aspirations and individuality. Much of this cynicism survived the transformation from stage to screen, including a few hard-hearted jokes that are directed at Christmas itself. Sheridan Whiteside (Monty Woolley) is particularly renowned for his broadcast on Christmas Eve, a fireside chat in which he tells the orginal Christmas story and an angelic boys' choir sings 'Silent Night'. Yet in an early scene Maggie Cutler (Bette Davis) describes his script as 'so gooey I haven't been able to get it off my fingers since I typed it'. The broadcast is introduced as being sponsored by 'Cream of Mush', and Whiteside's opening line – 'On this eve of eves, my heart is overflowing with peace and kindness' – is delivered amidst the chaos and mayhem that his own malice has produced in the Stanley home. Hollywood seldom allowed Christmas to be taken so lightly, but an inescapable part of the play's appeal is its mockery of all that Christmas represents.

There is only one exception to the triumphing of wit over naivety and cynicism over virtue, and that is Maggie's decision to abandon her career and marry the editor of the Mesalia newspaper, Bert Jefferson (Richard Travis). This plot development is a part of the original play, but the screenwriters apparently felt compelled to expand and emphasize it in the film as a means of enhancing Bette Davis's role. Maggie remains a well-bred, intelligent and articulate career woman, but she soon finds peace and serenity in Mesalia's Christmas festivities, and she is overwhelmed when Jefferson gives her a romantic Christmas present. These scenes 'open out' the play (they take place beyond the Stanleys' living room, which served as the stage set), and they increase Davis's time on screen. Equally, they introduce some balance to the pillorying of the small town, and they add a conventional and romantic dimension to the story. But this yet again entails cutting the independent heroine down to size. Having enjoyed a career that took her around the world and into the company of celebrities, artists and politicians, Maggie is seduced by Mesalia and Mr Jefferson. His name, of course, conveys integrity and virtue, but Richard Travis plays the part as though the editor is an eager and enthusiastic farm boy. We are meant to believe that Maggie will be happy with him, and that the experience of Christmas in Mesalia convinced her of this. This may not be entirely convincing, but it is nonetheless remarkable that, as in *Remember the Night*, the Christmas setting has enabled the heroine to survive and smile in the ending. Stanwyck and Davis suffered far worse in the final reels of many of their other films.

Neither *Remember the Night* nor *The Man Who Came to Dinner* was conceived or marketed as a Christmas film. Sturges's initial story idea centred on the romance between a district attorney and a thief, and working out the means of their coming together came, he admitted, after many different scenarios 'almost caused me to commit hara-kiri several times'.[3] The screen rights for *The Man Who Came to Dinner* were bought by Warner Brothers at the instigation of Bette Davis. She admired the play, but her presence in the film meant that it had to be adapted in a manner that would suit her own status and screen persona.[4] Furthermore, neither film was seen as appropriate fare for the holiday season. Both films had their premieres in the month of January and then went into general release over subsequent winter months, long after the seasonal celebrations had ended.[5] Christmas did not become the season for Christmas films until a better formula had been honed. This involved setting aside cynicism, contempt for the heartland, and the taming of wayward heroines, and emphasizing the more sentimental qualities that lurked within these films: nostalgia for home, family, togetherness and the virtues of the American past.

Christmas in the Context of War

It was Irving Berlin's *Holiday Inn* that established the commercial viability of the Christmas film. Berlin, a champion of Tin Pan Alley and the author of numerous stage and screen musicals, set out in 1940 to create a musical comedy that would serve as both a morale booster and as pleasant escapism from the rigours of war. He began working in the autumn of that year, after the Nazi Blitzkrieg through Europe had convinced him that the United States would soon become involved in what was still a European war. The celebration of holidays provided the format for the film. Berlin's experience of the First World War had taught him that war involves patriotism, hard work, separation from family, loneliness and heartache.[6] The holidays celebrating Independence Day and the birthdays of Abraham Lincoln and George Washington would serve the patriotic spirit, while New Year's Day, Valentine's Day, Easter, Thanksgiving and Christmas would offer opportunities for romance, separation and reunion. The initial idea, then, was to celebrate a full year's succession of holidays. While this intention was not abandoned, it was Christmas that took centre-stage in the film.

For Berlin, writing a song for Christmas proved to be the most difficult aspect of *Holiday Inn*. Attempts at summoning the Christmas spirit while he worked in the heat and sunshine of southern California proved fruitless. Finally, he had the idea of writing a song about the very difficulties he was experiencing, and the result was 'White Christmas'. The song originally began with lyrics that contrasted Californian images of palm trees and orange groves with the images of the desired snowy Christmas. This first stanza was dropped, however, so that all that remains is the sense of longing for the ideal. Berlin immediately recognized the power of 'White Christmas'. When he played it the next morning for his transcriber, he introduced it by declaring 'it is not only the best song I ever wrote, it's the best song anybody ever wrote'.[7] The song's sense of bittersweet longing became central to the story of *Holiday Inn*, and its dream of an idyllic and old-fashioned Christmas became the cornerstone of many Christmas films that followed in its wake.

Berlin completed all the songs and a story outline for *Holiday Inn* by the spring of 1941, and sold the package to the producer and director Mark Sandrich at Paramount. Berlin and Sandrich had previously collaborated on the classic musicals that starred Fred Astaire and Ginger Rogers, and Sandrich was now looking for parts that would suit Bing Crosby, Paramount's leading star. The main character of *Holiday Inn*, a lazy singer who seeks a quiet life far from the hustle and bustle of the modern world, fitted well with Crosby's easygoing and gentle manner.[8] Fred Astaire was the natural choice for the other leading role, that of a fast-footed dancer. Astaire, who had found little success since his partnership with Ginger Rogers had been suspended a few years earlier, welcomed the opportunity to take part.[9] With the teaming of Bing Crosby and Fred Astaire, the screen's top singer and its top dancer, Paramount had a certain box-office hit on its hands, but also one heavy with star salaries. Hence, the female roles were given to aspiring actresses, Virginia Dale and Marjorie Reynolds, who made a slighter dent in the payroll costs.[10]

The story of *Holiday Inn* is a light and frothy one. Singer Jim Hardy (Crosby) and dancer Ted Hanover (Astaire) vie for the affections of their fellow peformers, Lila Dixon (Dale) and Linda Mason (Reynolds). Jim gives way all too easily to the more energetic Ted because he wants a quiet life. He drops out of showbusiness because it requires constant travelling, working at odd hours and even working on holidays. He settles on a rural Connecticut farm which he turns into the Holiday Inn, a nightclub that will only open on holidays and therefore enable him to loaf every other day of the year. Most of the holiday songs that are performed at the inn are given a comic delivery. 'Abraham', the song for Lincoln's birthday, is performed by Jim and Linda in blackface so that Ted will not be able to recognize Linda. On Valentine's Day, 'Be Careful It's My

Heart' is meant to be Jim's heartfelt love song for Linda, but as he sings it Linda is swept away by Ted's dancing. For George Washington's birthday, Jim has written 'I Can't Tell A Lie' as a dance number for Ted and Linda, but he gives the song a wildly varying beat so that it will scuttle his sure-footed rival. 'Easter Parade' is performed not 'on the avenue, Fifth Avenue', as the lyrics indicate, but amidst the blossoms of a New England country lane. And at Thanksgiving, 'I've Got Plenty to be Thankful For' is sung by Jim after his fellow performers have gone to Hollywood, where a film based on the Holiday Inn concept is being made. He sings the song in lonely isolation, and while sitting in front of a huge turkey dinner that he does not want.

While many holidays are treated lightly, Independence Day and Christmas are taken very seriously. Independence Day is celebrated with two songs. First, 'Song of Freedom' is sung by Jim to celebrate both well-established freedoms (the Bill of Rights) and newly prized freedoms (two of President Roosevelt's Four Freedoms are acknowledged in the lines 'freedom from want/freedom from fear'). And, as he sings, a screen appears behind him and images of war mobilization unravel in a swiftly edited montage. For the first and only time within the film, the war is referred to directly, but only in visual terms. Ted then appears on stage for a show-stopping tap-dance routine in which he throws firecrackers down around his feet. 'Let's Say It With Firecrackers' is a violent response to the threats alluded to, however indirectly, in 'Song of Freedom'. It provides a cathartic release from the momentary glimpse of war and, as a blasting and triumphant finale to this sequence, it signifies victory and effectively banishes all thoughts of war from the film.

'White Christmas', meanwhile, is the only song in the film to be heard twice. It is first heard when Jim sings it to Linda on a snowy Christmas Eve, while they sit between a Christmas tree laden with decorations and a roaring log fire. It is rendered as a love song, and the poignant delivery and setting make this the film's most sincere and memorable moment. Then, a year later and on the following Christmas Eve, Jim has learned his own Christmas lesson, that he must overcome his malaise and pursue Linda. He travels to Hollywood and gets on to the film set of the Holiday Inn at the very moment that Linda is singing 'White Christmas'. The original scene – a snowy night, the inn, the Christmas tree and the roaring fire – has been perfectly recreated in the studio. As Linda performs the song, Jim begins to duet with her, and they are reunited. Christmas is thus used as both a time of crisis, when feelings of loneliness and despair come to the fore, and as a time of magical deliverance, when the most unlikely resolutions can be conjured and dreams can come true.

With its indulgence of fatigue, its sense of dislocation and its idealization of Christmas and home, *Holiday Inn* touched gently upon timely themes and carefully avoided pointed references. By the time the film was released in August 1942, the war had led many Americans into the military, a round-the-clock and every-day-of-the-year job, and others into the factories, where the forty-eight-hour working week included night shifts and weekends. Jim's fatigue at working round the clock and every day of the year, of course, is related purely to his showbusiness career. Yet his decision to work only in the holidays plays upon wartime weariness in two ways: it renders a world in which every day seems to be a holiday and, conversely, it allows the audience the daydream of working only in the holidays and having every other day of the year free from work. And, while families were separated and uprooted from their communities, *Holiday Inn* offered a vision of home designed expressly for the homesick. The characters travel throughout the film's duration – from New York City to Connecticut to Hollywood and back to Connecticut – yet the rural Holiday Inn itself is a warm haven of homey comforts, and its antiquated New England charm offers a constant and national sense of home to a nation in the midst of transition and dislocation. Particularly in the Christmas scenes, when snow falls gently outside, a log fire glows in the hearth, and Jim sings of his dreams for a Christmas 'just like the ones I used to know', the film summons nostalgia for an old-fashioned and idealized holiday in which 'children listen', Christmas cards are written, and all the days are 'merry and bright'.

The film also soothes the war-weary by avoiding the war itself almost completely. By 1942, Hollywood's trade papers were already warning film-makers that the public had tired not only of combat films, but also of films which explained the meaning of the war.[11] Part of the appeal of *Holiday Inn*, then, must have been its well-attuned escapism. It is a 'why we fight' film that never mentions the fight. It suppresses awareness of the present and at the same time creates a fantasy in which the problems of the present are alleviated and overcome: there is no war and no work, families and couples are reunited, and the city is abandoned in favour of a return to the countryside and the cottage. The Independence Day performances are also careful to skirt round contemporary concerns, and to celebrate national pride without pondering its meaning or its place within an international context. This suited a country with a strong sense of patriotism but a deeply ingrained suspicion of ideology and politics.[12] In this light, Berlin's presentation of the film within the film, which recreates the Holiday Inn on a studio set, can be taken as a prescription for wartime screen entertainment. While real homes may have seemed barren for the duration of the war, and couples may have been parted, Hollywood could provide its audience with the warmth and emotional satisfaction of imagined homes and longed-for reunions.

It was the Christmas setting and the power of the song 'White Christmas', however, which gave *Holiday Inn* its particular poignancy and resonance. When the film was released in August 1942 it was immediately recognized as an assured box-office success, but its potential for the holiday season seems to have gone unnoticed, and 'White Christmas' was seldom singled out for praise by critics.[13] In fact, 'Be Careful It's My Heart' was the first of the film's songs to reach the Hit Parade. Then, as the Christmas season got under way – the first Christmas since war mobilization had hit its stride – both the song and the film were seen (and heard) in a new light. By this time, the film had gone beyond its initial release in the premiere cinemas of major cities, and it was playing in neighbourhood cinemas throughout the country. Reports came from far and wide that *Holiday Inn* had become a seasonal favourite, and cinema patrons were returning for repeated viewings.[14] The 'White Christmas' phenomenon also began to unfold in the Christmas season. It started when Armed Forces Services Radio played the song to its audience of troops stationed around the world. Whether they were in North Africa or the South Pacific, the troops were far from home and 'White Christmas' quickly became an anthem of the homesick.[15] News of its popularity hastened the song's climb to the top of the Hit Parade in the United States, where it remained for nine weeks. By the last week of December 1942, its success warranted a story in *Newsweek* (entitled 'Snowed Under'), which reported that sales of both the sheet music and the recording had passed one million copies.[16]

Yet this was only the beginning. Irving Berlin won an Academy Award for the song. It went back to the top of the Hit Parade during the Christmas seasons of 1943 and 1944. Bing Crosby's version eventually sold twenty-five million copies, and four hundred other versions sold a further one hundred and twenty million copies. By the 1980s, 'White Christmas' had become the best-selling recorded song of all time.[17] *Holiday Inn* became so identified with Christmas and this one song that when Paramount decided to re-make the film they named the new film *White Christmas* (1954). Ironically, *White Christmas* summons nostalgia not for peacetime, but for the wartime spirit. This, too, apparently struck a chord, as *White Christmas* became the top-earning film of 1954.[18] Both films remain seasonal favourites, and are frequently televised during December. In fact, it was during a television screening of *Holiday Inn* in 1951 that an entrepreneur named Kemmons Wilson conceived of the chain of motels that would be known as Holiday Inns.[19] That the thousands of identical and rather soulless substitutes for home should be named after this film is, in a sense, fitting. *Holiday Inn* and 'White Christmas' were designed to evoke the spirit of home in wartime audiences who were denied the real thing.

Christmas in the Past

MGM's *Meet Me In St. Louis* goes much further in distancing its audiences from the war. In this case it is a period setting, at the turn of the century, which enables escapism and the denial of the modern world. The story centres on a happy family and their perfect home. Their house is a grand Victorian mansion, and it is evident that no expense was spared in creating the elaborate sets and period costumes. The use of rich Technicolor enhances a sense of opulence and carefree excess. The songs are nostalgic ('The Boy Next Door', 'You and I') and energetically carefree ('The Trolley Song'). And, because *Meet Me In St. Louis* was released during the holiday season (in November 1944), there is also a Christmas song that captures both the ideal of Christmas and the more disappointing reality of Christmas. 'Have Yourself A Merry Little Christmas' expresses longing for past Christmases and hope for future Christmases, but has only melancholy for the present Christmas.

Meet Me In St. Louis was tailored for a predominantly female audience, and an audience that was undergoing the rigours and trials of the home front. Women not only worked during the war, and worked at jobs previously reserved for men, but also maintained their homes and families despite the difficulties posed by rationing and shortages. Hence, the film offers a sense of empowerment to its female characters while at the same time offering a fantasy of peacetime and carelessness. Throughout much of *Meet Me In St. Louis* the Smith family has only minor troubles and concerns. Sisters Esther (Judy Garland) and Rose (Lucille Bremer) have dreams and schemes about their boyfriends. Their younger sister 'Tootie' (Margaret O'Brien) encounters the rituals of childhood with a bizarre and somewhat macabre imagination. The mother (Mary Astor) looks after her children. The housekeeper (Marjorie Main) observes everything and offers wisecracks and wisdom. The male characters, meanwhile, are notable mainly for their absence. Only Grandpa (Harry Davenport) is a constant presence, yet he is a dotty and kind figure rather than an authoritative one. The son, Lon (Henry Daniels), goes off to Princeton at the beginning of the film and does not return until the end. Mr Smith (Leon Ames) spends most of his time at the office, and even when he is at home his authority is gently undermined. When he tells Mrs Smith with great foreboding that he will be going to New York City on business, she says, 'Is that all? I think we can get along without you for awhile!'. It is the domestic and emotional traumas that are given importance, and the men seem to be external to these. Furthermore, the women have no interest in the world beyond their home and home town. Awareness of the outside world is only manifested within the context of home town pride. The World's Fair is coming to St Louis and the Smiths look forward to their town becoming 'the centre of attraction for the whole universe'.

The world beyond St Louis may be drawn to the city's charms, but the Smiths view the outside world with a sense of alarm. This becomes abundantly clear when, to the dismay of the women of the family, Mr Smith accepts a promotion to a better job in New York City. The women then face the prospect of leaving their beloved home and home town, and of moving into a cramped flat in the anonymous big city. It is telling that this threat is decidedly male and modern, and that Mr Smith seems to be oblivious to the heartache and upheaval his actions bring to the family. It is also telling that the women can only bring him to his senses on Christmas Eve. On that snowy and romantic occasion, Esther receives a much anticipated marriage proposal from the boy next door. She longs to accept the proposal, but acceptance entails remaining in St Louis when her family moves away. Her anxiety is expressed when she sings 'Have Yourself A Merry Little Christmas' as a lullaby to Tootie. The poignancy of the lyrics is centred particularly on separation. They promise that 'some day soon we all will be together if the fates allow', while also intoning that 'until then we'll have to muddle through somehow'. The song sends Tootie into a frenzy of despair. She runs outside and destroys a set of snowmen that represent family members. Seeing this, Mr Smith realizes that home and family come first and the pursuit of money must be put aside to maintain them. This was, of course, the lesson learned by Scrooge himself, but it is the emphasis upon the sanctity of the nuclear family and the rejection of the modern and urban world that made *Meet Me In St. Louis* so poignant for wartime audiences.[20] While the film poses the problem of encroaching modernity, marked by transience, a loss of community and roots, and the pursuit of money and career, it also offers a happy ending. All of these ills are overwhelmed by the affirmation of an innocent and more wholesome past, in which life is centred on the family, the home and the small town.

Christmas and the Returning Soldier

While *Holiday Inn* and *Meet Me In St. Louis* were designed to suit the needs of an audience in the grip of war, hardship and separation, *I'll Be Seeing You* and *Christmas In Connecticut* look forward to the post-war period. Victory and rapid demobilization are taken for granted in these films, and there are no references to contemporary events or war issues. Instead, the emphasis is very much on the home, and the readjustment of both men and women from wartime lives beyond the home to peacetime lives within it. The settings again hark back to an apparently revered concept of the traditional and rural lifestyle, and the rituals of Christmas enhance the atmosphere of tradition and constancy. Yet the experience of Christmas proves to be a liberating one, and one which allows the transformation to be made with relative grace, understanding and good spirits.

I'll Be Seeing You was based on a radio play (*Double Furlough*) that told the story of a holiday romance.[21] The story itself is fairly grim: she is on a furlough from prison, he is a shell-shock victim on a furlough from an army hospital. They fall in love yet cannot be united until she has served her full sentence and he has recovered from his 'neuro-psychiatric' disorder. The producer Dore Schary lightened the film and made it more palatable as a Christmas release through several means. First, Ginger Rogers was chosen to play the lead role, and her air of wholesome conventionality effectively undermines any sense of danger that the character might have presented. Second, the title was changed and the song 'I'll Be Seeing You' was chosen as the film's theme. 'I'll Be Seeing You' is another bittersweet song about a faraway lover, but the refrain – with its emphasis upon the lover's current presence in heart and mind – implies a positive and fulfilling outcome. Third, the film emphasizes Christmas cheer as a means of overcoming the gloom inherent in the story. The first shot of the film shows the couple arriving separately in a train station dominated by a huge and well-decorated Christmas tree, and the lively 'Jingle Bells' is heard playing on the soundtrack. The romance of Mary Marshall (Rogers) and Zack Morgan (Joseph Cotten) then develops as they enjoy Christmas with her family in the small town of Pineville, Texas. The family Christmas – with traditional meals, presents exchanged and carols sung – is a happy, stable and reassuring one. All that Mary and Zack hope for is that one day they can enjoy such a contented family life. And, although Hollywood's Christmas films were secular affairs which rarely mentioned religion or even the original Christmas story, in *I'll Be Seeing You* the rural Texas setting is affirmed as an appropriate environment for a traditional Christmas. As Mary tells Zack, the dry landscape and cool weather are reminiscent of 'the country where they celebrated the first Christmas'.

Despite these reassuring elements, a mood of uncertainty and anxiety over the future lurks within *I'll Be Seeing You*. There is a sense that Mary and Zack represent the couple of the future, the post-war couple who will have to put their wartime experiences behind them and begin life anew. Zack is a war hero who served in the South Pacific and won the Purple Heart, but his heroism has left him with physical and mental scars. He has endured the hell of war (revisited in his flashback), and now cannot readjust to peace. When he first enters the family's house, he says 'I haven't been in a home like this in as long as I can remember', and it is clear that he both feels out of place and yearns to belong. Mary's past and the reason for her imprisonment, meanwhile, remain a secret throughout much of the film. Although the parallel is not explicitly drawn, she is like the original Mary of the bible story in that a cloud of suspicion and doubt hangs over her. The mystery is revealed, and the doubts cast aside, in her own flashback: while working as a secretary, she accidentally killed her boss when he made aggressive and unwanted sexual advances. She was convicted of manslaughter, and although her own version of events makes it clear that her 'crime' was actually committed in self-defence, she also admits that she was ambitious and hoped to marry the boss. In the context of the film, this is made to seem suspect, and the sense of suspicion is compounded by the fact that Zack is the last to learn her secret. Thus, she represents the woman every soldier feared returning to: a woman who had been independent for several years and was now guarding dark secrets about her past. As Mary herself says, 'the dreams I had for the future – a husband, a child, a home – are just impossible now'.

In a wartime Christmas film, however, doubts can be swept aside and dreams can be realized. Mary is not a *femme fatale* from the *film noir* genre, but a redeemable woman who can find happiness once her sentence has been served. As in *Remember the Night* and *The Man Who Came to Dinner*, the experience of Christmas enables a happier ending for the transgressive heroine. However, whereas the earlier films used Christmas to reform the woman alone, in *I'll Be Seeing You* it proves to be therapeutic for both Mary and Zack. The sense of togetherness found in the family Christmas points these troubled individuals toward their own future together. Problems that seem to require the intervention of the state and its officials and experts (his illness, her crimes) are actually solved in the home and during a holiday season which reaffirms the values of home and family. Thus, in *I'll Be Seeing You* the transformative power of Christmas is made greater – it serves both sexes – and it is embued with the spirit of wartime equality.

A similar sense of equality can be found in *Christmas In Connecticut*, but there is no sense of post-war angst. Instead, this bright and flippant comedy both undermines and reaffirms the Christmas film and its settings and situations. The film's title summons an image of New England antiquity which would seem to suggest a celebration of tradition within a patriotic context, and the story is set in motion by a magazine publisher's imagined headline, 'American War Hero Spends Christmas In Perfect Home', which indicates a return to pre-war gender roles. Yet from the outset these ideals are seen to be outdated and impossible; the characters are modern city folk and the couple defy gender stereotypes. The charade that they enact is undeniably enjoyable for the characters and the audience, but the film never allows the audiences to believe that it is anything but a charade, and a very unlikely one at that.

The war hero, Jefferson Jones (Dennis Morgan), is chosen for the publisher's venture because he is 'afraid of marriage and domesticity'. He is then sent to spend the holidays with 'America's most resourceful homemaker', Elizabeth Lane (Barbara Stanwyck). Lane writes lifestyle features and a cooking column feature for the magazine *American House-keeping*. She is a celebrity housewife, and she is famous for her wonderful recipes and her tales of a blissful life in Connecticut with her loving husband and adorable baby. Even her boss, the publishing magnate Alexander Yardley (Sydney Greenstreet) believes her to be 'a fine American wife and mother'. The truth, however, is that Elizabeth Lane actually lives in New York City and has neither a child nor a husband. She is an ambitious and hard-working journalist who gets her recipes from her friend Felix (S.Z. Sakall), and her stories of life on a Connecticut farm from her dull boyfriend, John Sloan (Reginald Gardiner). Lane's real interest is to win a pay rise from Yardley that will cover the cost of her most beloved possession, a fur coat that she has purchased on credit. Hence, she mounts a traditional Christmas at Sloan's farm, and they pose as a married couple with a baby (conveniently borrowed while the baby's mother works in a war production plant) in an attempt to deceive both Alexander Yardley and Jefferson Jones.

One might expect the Christmas experience to transform Elizabeth Lane into the beacon of domesticity that Yardley believes her to be, but this is a comedy that revels both in her sharp city manners and domestic ineptitude. She cannot cook, she does not know how to bath the baby or change a diaper, and in fact she does not even know the sex of her borrowed baby (she refers to the baby as 'it' throughout the film). At the same time, the film reveals Jefferson to be the 'new man' of 1945: he is a dashing war hero and he is practiced at bathing and changing babies. In fact, he not only takes over the tasks that Elizabeth cannot perform, but he does so happily. While the project of the film is to transform these two individuals into a post-war couple, it does not suggest that this requires their own transformation into better or different people. The primary transformation that this Christmas comedy brings about is Yardley's. It is Yardley who sets the charade in motion by bullying those less powerful than himself. This elderly, materialistic and controlling tycoon is the film's Scrooge, and in the ending he has been reduced to apologizing to Lane and singing her praises: 'She can't cook, but what a woman! What a Christmas!'.

Christmas does serve as a means of bringing Elizabeth Lane and Jefferson Jones together. Their romance is the result of sharing seasonal activities: trimming the tree, singing carols, and a long sleigh ride through a snowy landscape. The two independent individuals thus become a couple, but there is no suggestion that their personalities have been transformed. He has not become more masterful, and she has not been made into a dutiful and domestic wife. Furthermore, whereas *Remember The Night* and *The Man Who Came to Dinner* paired their heroines with dull pillars of the community, in *Christmas In Connecticut* the possibility of Elizabeth Lane's marriage to the stolid John Sloane is treated with contemptuous humour. When she tells him she does not love him, he patronisingly replies, 'all that will come in time'. Her reply, 'can you wait *that* long?', indicates that he is no match for the heroine. He is left alone in an ending which rejects traditional and controlling men, and celebrates a couple making a fresh start.

This is a truly remarkable ending for a film made in 1945, and it was feared that the film treats Christmas and marriage too lightly. Warner Brothers released *Christmas In Connecticut* in July rather than during the holiday season. A review in the *New York Times* warned its viewers that, despite the title, the film is not 'a folksy fable that will put the kiddies in the proper spirit for Santa's next visit'.[22] Similarly, the *Motion Picture Herald* complained the film 'is by no means the gently sentimental item of Americana that the title indicates'.[23] The Catholic Legion of Decency gave the film a 'B' rating, indicating that it considered it to be 'objectionable in part'.[24] And in Britain, the title was changed to the more judgemental *Indiscretion*. Yet the film did prove to be a box-office success, and its long and healthy run extended into the Christmas season of 1945.[25] The public was ready, it seems, for a Christmas film that did not take itself too seriously, and one that offered both traditional Christmas festivities and the reassurance that post-war readjustment need not be punitive or stifling.

Conclusion

Wartime Christmas films defined Christmas in uniquely American terms. The setting is always a traditional home within a small town. There is usually snow falling gently outside, while inside a close-knit family has gathered. Images of the United States' humble and wholesome origins are suggested through the settings, the male characters' names and allusions to their past. All of the holiday rituals are observed. There are trees to be decorated, carols to be sung, presents to be exchanged and hearty meals to be eaten. Whether or not the audience had experienced or enjoyed such a traditional Christmas, it would recognize it as a comforting ideal. There is, therefore, all the more drama and pathos to be found when the ideal is threatened. And it is always threatened by some element of incongruity: an independent woman who has rejected the role of wife and mother, a couple or family faced with separation, characters so haunted by the past that they cannot enjoy the present, and selfish materialism at odds with the allusions to an idealized past. The happiness that

Hollywood would like us to believe is inherent in the traditional Christmas is always on the verge of being undermined. In post-war films the crises which occur at Christmastime would often require the intervention of Santa Claus or a heaven-sent angel. In wartime, however, a return to the home and hearth of the past was potent enough to enable happy endings.

The heartaches and anxieties of wartime, of course, were largely unsolvable and insurmountable, but Christmas was seen to have a transformative power. This, too, was an established concept that many in the audience would have brought with them to the cinema, but it derived a particular power in wartime. Audiences enduring long separations from their families, a loss of community and uncertainty for the future were eager to see these threats banished, and found the resolutions all the more convincing and fulfilling for arriving at Christmastime. A key component of the Christmas film is the climactic and joyous scene that occurs as if by magic on Christmas Eve or Christmas Day. Christmas was used as the *deus ex machina* that could deliver all that they hoped for: not only a white Christmas, but a Christmas of intact families and established homes, of reunion and renewal, the return to the past, and, most remarkably, an almost complete disavowal of the war and of the world beyond small-town America. For a country that went to war so reluctantly, the best Christmas scenario would seem to be one in which the problems of the war are solved and the war itself seems to have disappeared amidst the snowflakes. That the Christmas film has endured over subsequent decades with only minor variations and additional implausibilities, suggests that neither the expectations that are built into Christmas stories, nor the anxieties that such stories reflect, were rendered obsolete with the return of peacetime.

Notes

1. William L. O'Neill, *A Democracy At War: America's Fight At Home and Abroad in World War Two* (Cambridge: CUP, 1995), p 249.

2. *A Christmas Carol* had been filmed by MGM as recently as 1938, but it was a low budget film without a major star, and it made little impact at the box-office.

3. Sandy Sturges (ed.), *Preston Sturges on Preston Sturges* (New York: Simon & Schuster, 1990), p 288.

4. Clive Hirschhorn, *The Warner Bros. Story* (London: Octopus, 1979), p 230.

5. A review in Variety declared that the story of *Remember The Night* 'is of a familiar pattern' but praised the 'sparkling comedy dialog'. Christmas was not mentioned in the review. *Variety* (5 January 1940), p 14. The Christmas setting also went without mention in a review of *The Man Who Came To Dinner*, in Variety (7 January 1942), p 7.

6. Laurence Bergreen, *As Thousands Cheer: The Life of Irving Berlin* (London: Hodder & Staughton, 1990), p 385.

7. Ibid., p 386.

8. Stanley Green and Bert Goldblatt, *Starring Fred Astaire* (New York: Dood, Mead, 1973), p 241.

9. See Fred Astaire, *Steps In Time: An Autobiography* (London: Heinemann, 1960), p 249; and Tim Satchell, *Astaire: The Biography* (London: Hutchinson, 1987), p 163.

10. Green and Goldblatt, *Starring Fred Astaire*, p 233.

11. *Motion Picture Herald* (16 January 1943), p 13.

12. O'Neill, *A Democracy At War*, p 325.

13. *Holiday Inn* was said to represent 'a holiday for every showman's calender' in the *Motion Picture Herald* (15 August 1942), p 19; and 'an undeniable box-office parlay, a winner all the way' by *Variety* (17 June 1942), p 13.

14. A weekly feature in the *Motion Picture Herald* entitled 'What the Picture Did For Me' provided reports from cinema owners and managers on the box-office performance of films currently in release. Reports on *Holiday Inn* were consistently positive throughout October and November, but they were particularly enthusiastic in regard to December showings. For example, a report from Alfred, New York stated that 'the folks told me that this is just what they wanted, as they went out smiling ... It ought to do well anywhere, especially in this season of the year' (2 January 1943), p 47. A report on a December showing in Groveton, Texas stated 'it was liked by all and even better the second time ... We can get by in wartime with these releases. Play it in any spot' (6 February 1943). And when it was shown over the period 24–6 December in South Berwick, Maine, the report stated 'a dandy picture for any holiday and particularly suitable for Christmas ... comments all good' (13 February 1943), p 42. *Variety* estimated that the film's total earnings in North America would reach $3,750,000, making it one of the five top earning films of 1942. *Variety* (6 January 1943), pp 58–9.

15. Max Wilk, *They're Playing Our Song* (London: W.H. Allen, 1974), pp 276–7.

16. *Newsweek* (28 December 1942), p 74.

17. John Mueller, *Astaire Dancing: The Musical Films* (New York: Alfred A. Knopf, 1985), p 201.

18. Susan Sackett, *The Hollywood Reporter Book of Box-Office Hits* (New York: Billboard Books, 1990), pp 110–11.

19. David Halberstam, *The Fifties* (New York: Villard Books, 1993), p 175.

20. *Meet Me In St. Louis* earned an extraordinary domestic gross of $5,016,000, making it MGM's top earning film of the year in the domestic market. The gross is reported in *The Eddie Mannix Ledger*, which is held as a special collection at The Margaret Herrick Library of the Academy of Motion Picture Arts and Sciences, Beverly Hills, California.

21. The production history of *I'll Be Seeing You* is recounted in David Thomson, *Showman: The Life of David O. Selznick* (New York: Alfred A. Knopf, 1992), pp 419–22.

22. *New York Times* (28 July 1945).

23. *Motion Picture Herald* (21 July 1945), p 2553.

24. Ibid. (29 September 1945), p 2663.

25. The 'What the Picture Did for Me' reports on *Christmas In Connecticut* indicate that it was still going strong at the box-office five months after its release. See the *Motion Picture Herald* (17 November 1945), p 44; (24 November 1945), p 52; and (1 December 1945), p 42. Warner Bros records indicate that the film's domestic earnings reached $3,273,000, The *William Schaefer Ledger*, The Doheny Library, University of Southern California, Los Angeles, California.

4

Christmas Under Fire: The Wartime Christmas in Britain

Sarah Street

Daniel Miller has observed that in times of national crisis and social upheaval 'we may find a much stronger desire to objectify a solid sense of the social. The starting-point in the objectification of sociality is commonly some immediate form such as the house or family.'[1] The Second World War provided such a focus, the dominant forms of representation – radio, the press, cinema – contributing to a sense of shared community, of a nation united by adversity. The nation was often represented as a family and the family was a central institution in creating a myth of shared national identity.[2] Whether set on the battlefield or on the home front, the majority of British films dealing with the war showed officers and privates working in cheerful collaboration, social classes 'pulling together' and families waiting anxiously for their menfolk to return, if at all possible, for Christmas.

In many ways the symbolic values and conventions of Christmas are accentuated during wartime. Since the central concepts associated with Christmas – peace, goodwill and the family unit – were threatened by the Second World War, it was common for people to make extra efforts to celebrate Christmas, even when the means to do so were severely limited.[3] Christmas represented a memory of normality – peace, optimism, hope (even if in reality this was far from the case) – and as such continued observation of the festival in wartime encapsulated the desire for a peacetime future when Christmas could be celebrated with all family members present. In such circumstances the ritual acquires an intensity which is often lacking in peacetime, the irony being that the best Christmases can frequently occur in these far from perfect circumstances. With key members away from home the family somehow acquires greater significance, its physical unity becoming an ideal, the embodiment of a fondly remembered past and an eagerly awaited future. Each Christmas provides an opportunity to exceed the last in observing this annual occasion for utopian longing to experience 'the best Christmas ever'. Like the family melodrama, Christmas performs the function of satisfying the desire to repeat past pleasures, recapture past memories with the assurance that they can be replayed again next year. 'The best Christmas ever' therefore becomes something to be striven for but never attained for fear of negating the utopian goal, an essential dynamic for the perpetuation of Christmas.

The utopian elements of Christmas were therefore intensified in wartime, acquiring an extra symbolic function in marking off the years and providing a promise of normality. Part of this process involved observing the rituals as far as possible. During the Second World War people made Christmas a focus and used all their resourcefulness in putting on a show: 'war or no war this *is* Christmas'.[4] Rationing prevented many of the traditional accoutrements from being widely available and magazines were littered with ideas for home-made, cheap presents. In a sense the wartime Christmas was egalitarian, with rationing affecting the rich and the poor alike. On the other hand shortages encouraged the 'black market' and material differences were still visible and interpreted in varying ways: a working-class family who saved up for many weeks so that they could have a conspicuously scrumptious Christmas meal were reported as profligate.[5] Many working-class evacuees found that their own families could not compete with the presents they were given by their middle-class 'foster' homes, creating tension and unhappiness.[6] For less fortunate evacuees Christmas was a painful reminder of separation from their loving families. These very real elements of the wartime Christmas were seldom addressed in filmic representations.

The cinema, however, was a key element of recreation and source of home-front propaganda during the war and the industry attempted to produce and exhibit films as far as possible during the disruptive years when studio facilities were requisitioned, projectionists were called up and many cinema workers (a controversial issue) were encouraged to work on Christmas Day. The exhibitor-biased trade paper *Kinematograph Weekly* featured many articles, including one entitled 'Exhibitors Under Fire', which made suggestions as to how cinema managers could keep going under wartime restrictions, blackouts and shortages.[7] Cinemas opened on

Christmas Day rather grudgingly but managers were clearly aware of the positive home-front propaganda value of their work. On Christmas Eve, 1942 *Kinematograph Weekly* gave a general message to all cinema workers: 'May your work at Christmas be recompensed by the satisfaction derived from knowledge of the pleasure you will give to thousands of war workers, who, but for this industry and your efforts, would spend a gloomy time during this year's austere holiday'.[8]

During the Second World War the films released each December rarely featured Christmas and the majority were made in the USA.[9] There were, however, some key films which contained varying representations of Christmas and will be the focus of this chapter. Celebrating Christmas in a context of wartime austerity was indeed an experience shared by many and it appears that the festival itself was sufficient to form a focus for optimism: the concept of the 'Christmas movie' was therefore not really developed. Although they were not released in the pre-Christmas period, the wartime films I am going to discuss, *Christmas Under Fire* (Harry Watt, released 6 January 1941), *Tunisian Victory* (Frank Capra, Hugh Stewart, released March 1944), *A Diary for Timothy* (Humphrey Jennings, trade shown 23 August 1945), *In Which We Serve* (David Lean, released 4 January 1943), *This Happy Breed* (Noël Coward, David Lean, released 7 August 1944) and a more contemporary film, *Hope and Glory* (John Boorman, 1987), offer key representations of Christmas from a documentary and fictional perspective. Essentially, they provide a fascinating insight into the extent to which in a generic sense the conventions of Christmas were observed and perpetuated on screen, and how Christmas provided a narrative excuse to address wider wartime concerns.

The Documentary Vision:
Christmas Under Fire, Tunisian Victory and *A Diary for Timothy*

Christmas Under Fire is a short documentary which was produced by the GPO Film Unit on the instruction of the Ministry of Information. Intended for the American market as a sequel to *London Can Take It* (Humphrey Jennings, Harry Watt, Ministry of Information, 1940), and released early in 1941 before the American entry into the Second World War, its purpose, according to director Harry Watt, was to make Americans feel 'uncomfortable while they celebrated Christmas'.[10] The commentary was written and spoken by an American, Quentin Reynolds, correspondent of *Collier's Weekly* in London, who introduces the film from behind a desk in a comfortable room decorated with Christmas cards, telling us that it is Christmas Day, 1940.[11] The introduction is directed towards an assumed American audience, as a revelation of how Londoners have coped during the Blitz. A sense of urgency is present when Reynolds informs the audience that he will take the film from London to New York that evening. The purpose of his introduction is to give the film an air of authenticity: Reynolds can vouch for the elements of hardship it contains because he has been in London and has seen wartime conditions first-hand. He invites the audience gently, 'Perhaps you'd like to see it?', the implication being that he thinks every American ought to see the film. Throughout the film he occupies the position of omniscient narrator, a role which has been validated by the audience having seen him in this persuasive way at the beginning of the film.

Christmas Under Fire begins with a classic image: the Christmas tree. This is also the occasion for the introduction of one of the film's major dramatic strategies, the overturning of audience expectations by beginning a shot with one image and then shifting to a connected image but with an entirely different connotation. In this case the shot begins with the camera panning across tall trees, gradually gliding down to reveal a man cutting down much smaller trees. The commentary informs us that this year British people can only have small trees because they are forced to celebrate Christmas underground in places with low ceilings, shelters and basements, hiding from overhead bombing. The 'Christmas underground' theme is introduced and with it the idea that because of wartime circumstances this Christmas will be different. The transition from large to small trees also performs a metaphoric function in that they represent the external threat to the nation's stature but at the same time highlight the British people's determination to observe the Christmas festival all the same.

After this scene the film shifts to focus on children who provide the main emotional core of the film. The sequence is introduced with a shot of a church and it is noticeable that *Christmas Under Fire* places religion at the centre of Christmas. Excited children are collecting holly, presumably to decorate the church, running down hills, and the commentary informs us that the war will not prevent people from giving their children as memorable a Christmas as possible: 'The nation has made a resolve that war or no war the children of England will not be cheated out of the one day they look forward to all the year'. This scene therefore connects with the previous one in the sense that it has a pastoral location, continues the theme of a stoical people determined to celebrate Christmas but adds new, significant elements: religion and children.

As before, the following scene links in with the previous one but adds new themes, in this case the observation that of course Christmas is different this year because many men and women are away from home. A montage of various fighting forces includes marching soldiers, Spitfires taking off, warships, tanks overseas, watch patrols and fire fighters, emphasizing that war is experienced by everyone, at home and abroad.

These images are classic documentary footage, reminding the audience of the wider picture – the fighting overseas – but at the same time of its impact on the home front. This develops into the film's major theme that Christmas 1940 is a 'Christmas of contrasts', leading to a sequence which relies on visual counterpoint within a frame. We therefore see farmers working in a field – what would at first appear to be an entirely pastoral shot – but the camera tilts to reveal huge search lights which detect overhead German bombers. Continuing this technique, holly is coupled with barbed wire and we see tinsel on railings. 'A Christmas of contrasts' is further developed with shots of bombed shops, shattered windows and wrecked premises. The address to American audiences is made rather obvious when a shop is singled-out with a resolute sign above its bombed exterior: '5th Avenue basement showroom, the American dress shop – Carries On!' Other shops have shattered windows but they are nevertheless decorated in a minimal way with pieces of defiant tinsel, and the sign of window-cleaner J. Winkle reads: 'Business as usual. If you've got no windows we'll clean your chimneys'.

From these exterior shots the film further elaborates the theme of shopping for Christmas presents by taking us inside a toy shop. The commentary explains that last year children wanted small forts modelled on the Maginot and Siegfried lines whereas today's children want model aeroplanes and tin hats. The supposedly impregnable French Maginot Line had been breached by the German Army in 1940 and Britain was thereafter dependent on the Air Force for protection against invasion; the Siegfried Line was Germany's line of defence in reply to the Maginot Line. In the toy shop, while models of the forts are gathering dust on top of shelves, the new toy model aeroplanes are demonstrated to adults and Quentin Reynolds's commentary, inflected with a sense of irony, is revealing in that the audience is encouraged to feel sad and ashamed that children want war-connected toys and that these are subject to fashion in having to keep up with the latest wartime developments which bring the threat of invasion nearer to home. We leave this scene to another set of exterior shots of children playing soldiers and girls pretending to be nurses. Again, everything has a war connection, the war is ever-present, even at Christmas.

Traditional Christmas events such as the pantomime become the next focus of *Christmas Under Fire* as we see shots of bombed theatres with adults and children nevertheless rehearsing in smaller theatres, hiding underground from the bombs. We also see children making Christmas cards at school and decorating the tree. These shots are interspersed with reminders of the war context – vigilant members of the Observer Corps, cards being written for absent fathers. The commentary makes a direct comparison with the American Christmas: 'Christmas here this year won't perhaps be the Christmas children in America will be lucky enough to enjoy. England is fighting for her life and even the smallest child understands that'. Careful that the audience does not feel that the British are begging for American assistance in a pathetic manner, the film's commentary then shifts to a more measured attempt to secure American admiration by appealing to Americans as champions of democracy.

The 'Torch of Liberty' sequence follows and is probably the most significant in terms of the film's address to Americans and acknowledgement of a 'special relationship' between Britain and the USA. The imagery of light is used throughout this sequence, which begins with church towers shot in low light. The religious theme is stressed again, the commentary mentioning that bells cannot ring in Britain because 'if they do it would mean that the invader has come'. Images that encapsulate the traditional Christmas – starry skies, moonlight 'giving light to a tired world' are given a different meaning when they are placed in a Blitz context – clear, moonlit nights are dangerous because they mean that bombers are more likely to fly to Britain in good weather conditions. This approach allows the theme of the war to be explored further as, for example, shots of shepherds in silhouette, which remind us of Christmas cards, are opened out to reveal that the shepherds are carrying guns: as well as performing their traditional function the war has turned them into watchmen on the lookout for a squadron of overhead bombers rather than a heavenly host of angels. Again the technique of presenting a scene which will be recognized as traditional Christmas imagery and then disturbing it provides an effective way of reminding the audience of the war as the film's meta-narrative.

The commentary which accompanies this sequence introduces the 'Torch of Liberty' theme in an even more overt manner. Britain is presented as a champion of democracy: 'There is no reason for America to feel sorry for England this Christmas. England doesn't feel sorry for herself. Destiny gave her the torch of liberty to hold and she has not dropped it'. The implication here is that Britain has done what America would have done in the same circumstances. With America's national symbol being the Statue of Liberty it is also implied that the two countries are now in a 'special relationship' and that Britain should not have to beg for American help, it should be naturally and readily forthcoming: the torch will not be dropped if it is carried by two natural allies. The sequence continues to play with imagery of light and dark: a woman and child say goodbye to an air-raid warden as he goes on duty during the blackout, again placing children at the forefront as inextricably involved with the routines of war. The sequence ends with a repetition of a series of images of church towers, shot from below in low light. These are suggestive of the theme of invasion, Britain as a fortress 'fighting for her life'.

The finale of *Christmas Under Fire* begins with a choirboy singing in Cambridge and the scene then shifts to a dramatically different location, the London underground. The camera tracks down an escalator on to the platforms where groups of people huddle together to shelter from the Blitz. Christmas is signalled by people decorating a tree on the platform and we hear the choir singing until the organ music swells at the end, a stirring finale to the film. As a narrative the film has come full circle, taking us back to the 'Christmas underground' theme that was introduced in the first scene of small Christmas trees being cut down and also continuing the religious references which have been signalled on several previous occasions. The decoration of the tree underground connects with the film's overall theme of Christmas taking place regardless of the war but the war nevertheless exercising a determining influence on the way it can be celebrated. Christmas therefore becomes even more of a national festival than in peacetime as it becomes inflected with the imagery of war, tinsel and barbed wire.

Celebrating Christmas in the London underground (*Christmas Under Fire*, 1940).

Tunisian Victory was also an attempt to counter the remaining vestiges of American isolationism, although by the time it was shot in the summer/autumn of 1943 America had already entered the war.[12] The film was a collaboration between the British Army Film and Photographic Unit and the US Service Film Units. Although *Tunisian Victory* is a documentary which glorifies Anglo-American military co-operation in North Africa during 1942–43, its production history was riddled with conflict and rivalry.[13] It serves as a companion piece to *Christmas Under Fire* in terms of its focus on Christmas as experienced by servicemen abroad, as opposed to the home front and the London Blitz.

The Christmas sequence occurs when the Allied forces have advanced towards Tunis but are forced to retreat after German retaliation. A moment of respite in the military campaign therefore provides a narrative occasion for a Christmas sequence which is divided into three sections. The first begins with a montage of church towers (similar to those which featured in *Christmas Under Fire*) in silhouette. The towers are seen again at the end of the first section but this time more brightly lit, conveying a transition from difficult times to the optimism represented by Christmas. In between these images the section contains shots of soldiers attending Christian ceremonies in the desert, accompanied by carols and a voice-over commentary which informs us that the soldiers are thinking of home. Allied collaboration is emphasized by the insertion of Christmas scenes from the Allied countries: America, France, India, South Africa, Canada, New Zealand, Australia and Britain, all featuring children. The final shots of this section return to the soldiers, the commentary reminding us of their comrades who have already died, of the cause of 'liberty, tolerance, dignity and peace' they are fighting for, finishing with the ringing of church bells and the commentary heralding the birth of a 'new day', represented by Christmas.

Section two is much lighter, detailing the elaborate preparations for the soldiers' Christmas dinner in the desert. The soldiers try to reconstruct the traditional components of Christmas in what is presented as an alien landscape. Abundance is the major theme (in stark contrast to the home-front representations) as soldiers read letters, collect parcels and consume large quantities of turkey and Christmas pudding. Comradeship is evoked as happy soldiers laugh and enjoy themselves, even finding enough food to feed their pet animals. In stark contrast, the third section of the Christmas sequence in *Tunisian Victory* represents the desert as a 'foreign' place, with its starving children and 'strange' customs: there are shots of off-duty soldiers looking incredulously at Arabs who perform 'mighty strange' performance acts, of Moorish women dressed in their veils; and the tone of the commentary is that the desert is a barbaric place, the Allies creating a civilizing influence. The customs of Christmas therefore function in this sequence as embodying the opposite of the Arab world: Christianity, happy, healthy children and material abundance. In a missionary spirit America, France, Britain and the Empire are presented as the moral alternative not only to Fascism but also to the prevailing customs and values of North Africa. From this perspective, the Anglo-American ideology articulated in *Christmas Under Fire* is externalized, in terms of geo-politics almost anticipating the post-war settlement.

Humphrey Jennings's *A Diary for Timothy*, produced by the Crown Film Unit towards the end of the war, provides an intriguing contrast to *Christmas Under Fire* and *Tunisian Victory* as a documentary vision of Christmas in wartime. The film covers the first six months (September 1944–February 1945) of the life of an Oxfordshire child, Tim.[14] The time-scale covered by the film accords Christmas a central place in the narrative. As well as Tim, *A Diary for Timothy* features four other people whose fates have been influenced by the war: an engine-driver, a farmer, a Welsh miner and a wounded fighter pilot. The pilot provides the frame around which the Christmas sequences are constructed: just before Christmas is first featured in the film we see the pilot being examined by a doctor and we next see him looking much recovered at a New Year's party. In between, the film deals with many issues similar to those raised in *Christmas Under Fire* but from a far more domestic perspective. As with *Christmas Under Fire* the Christmas theme is introduced in *A Diary for Timothy* with reference to Christmas trees. Women decorate trees in a church and men in uniform are shown putting up a tree outside their barracks. Fear of invasion is no longer ever-present and there is none of the underground imagery which was so dominant in *Christmas Under Fire*. The commentary (written by E.M. Forster and spoken by Michael Redgrave) is addressed to Tim, explaining to him that he will look forward to Christmas as 'the day you'll come to love best in all the year' but that this Christmas not everyone will be home because of the war. Tim's father is away but he is 'present' as we are continually reminded of his absence. For example, we see his mother receive a letter from the postman addressed to Tim and we later find out that this contains Christmas greetings from Tim's father, which we hear not as part of the commentary but as a diegetic insert.

As in *Christmas Under Fire* Christmas shopping is featured in *A Diary for Timothy*. Children are not the focus however: this time women's hats are examined by soldiers who are looking into a shop window. In the context of 1945–46 an allusion such as this to fashion and glamour provides a significant anticipation of the end of austerity. The camera glides over the hats to a group of carol-singers outside the shop. Then there is a dramatic break in sound from the carols to bombs as we see a statue of a military figure on a horse in silhouette, followed by a montage of images of

London in darkness as a German counter-offensive is announced. The impression of a city and a people who are tired of the war is conveyed and the commentary becomes very dark: 'In those days before Christmas the news was bad and the weather was foul. Death and darkness. Death and fog. Death across those few miles of water – for our own people and for others – for enslaved and broken people, the noise of battle getting louder and death came by telegram to many of us on Christmas Eve'. The mood shifts yet again as we hear a train and see the engine-driver as the commentary continues: 'Until – out of the fog dawned loveliness, whiteness, Christmas Day'. This leads to some picturesque Christmas images of snow, trees covered in frost and a montage of families and friends celebrating Christmas, toasting 'absent friends' and in the case of Tim's family, 'and Tim' is added as he acquires almost Christ-like significance lying in his mother's arms as a symbol of hope for the future.

Comparing *Christmas Under Fire*, *Tunisian Victory* and *A Diary for Timothy*, it is striking that the films feature similar imagery and themes but from different perspectives. Whereas *Christmas Under Fire* and *Tunisian Victory* are obviously biased towards America *A Diary for Timothy*, released towards the end of the war, looks towards Russia as a major ally in defeating Germany. Except for a brief reference in the commentary in relation to the counter-offensive, America is not mentioned and the film's focus on Tim's future inflects it with a more utopian quality than is evident in *Christmas Under Fire* whose urgency (despite Quentin Reynolds's insistence on everybody's cheerfulness) is located in the immediate context of the Blitz. Fear of invasion pervades this film whereas in *A Diary for Timothy* the war is clearly coming to an end overseas and the scenes of life on the home front are, on the whole, much more relaxed. The films use natural imagery in an interesting and contrasting way. *Tunisian Victory* deploys the vast expanse of the desert landscape as a means of conveying the vulnerability of the troops as they construct makeshift homes from their tents at Christmas, erecting signposts with the names of their home towns outside. As already noted, *Christmas Under Fire* suggests that the war makes ordinary situations difficult to interpret: a dark windy day is welcomed instead of lamented because it means there will be no bombing. Normal registers are threatened in wartime – in this way the film tells us that the world has been turned upside-down. *A Diary for Timothy* also features dark scenes as we hear the news that the Germans are launching a counter-offensive but in this case they are used in the service of a more conventional interpretation: bad news, bad weather. Christmas Day's snow, whiteness and frost is used in a traditional, Christmas card manner in *A Diary for Timothy*, enabling the day to signal a major turning-point in the narrative, the decisive glimmer of hope which promises an end to the fighting. In this film people do not have to shelter underground at Christmas, they can gather together in their homes and in most filmic fictional representations, as we will now go on to discuss, the home functions as a symbol of unity, stability and safety.

Christmas Fictions: *In Which We Serve, This Happy Breed* and *Hope and Glory*

Fiction films that focused on the home front frequently utilized the family as representative of the larger community which in the context of war functioned as an emblem of national unity.[15] In these films Christmas is a narrative excuse for bringing together families, emphasizing the traditional aspects of Christmas, suspending or stifling any behaviour that involves conflict and presenting Christmas as a universal event, celebrated in a similar fashion by all social classes.

The concerns of the documentary representations – the focus on families/absent members, people's determination to preserve the traditions of Christmas at a time when the nation 'is fighting for her life' and the appearance of Christmas as another episode in a longer trajectory of historical development – also feature in fiction films, particularly those like *This Happy Breed* which have been described by Andrew Higson as 'melodramas of everyday life'.[16] In this film Noël Coward used Christmas as an opportunity to project ideas about consensus, family unity and the rituals surrounding Christmas in an extended sequence (examined below) which nevertheless contains a sense that none of these elements are without contestation. An indication of this technique was evident in Coward's previous film, *In Which We Serve*.

A year before *This Happy Breed* Coward featured Christmas in *In Which We Serve* and in this film its representation and narrative function are crucially linked to ideas about class, family and nation. *In Which We Serve* presents 'the story of a ship', *HMS Torrin*, and its sailors under the command of Captain Kinross (Noël Coward), in a series of flashbacks as the crew, clinging to a life-raft, watch their ship sink after it has been bombed during the Battle of Crete. The ship becomes a central reference point serving as a microcosm of British society, a point of connection between men from disparate backgrounds and social classes. The Christmas sequence further emphasizes this by making the ship the focus of attention, implying that it can be taken to represent Britain, the nation under fire.

The sequence is introduced as the *Torrin* is about to sail just after the outbreak of war has been announced by Chamberlain. The sailors, encouraged by an inspiring speech from Kinross, sing 'Good King Wenceslas' and the shot dissolves into a scene of children singing the same carol in a street. From above a window opens and we see a sailor, Shorty

Blake (John Mills), throw down some money to the children, beginning the first of three parallel action scenes of different sailors celebrating Christmas early in the war with their families. Shorty's working-class family is gathered around the table for Christmas dinner in a scene which involves a discussion between Shorty and Bert, his brother-in-law, about rivalry between destroyers and the Marines.[17] Typical of the depiction of women's function in the war, Shorty's mother (Kathleen Harrison) tries to keep the peace, binding the family/nation together, encouraging the two men to settle their differences. They do, each toasting the other's allegiance – Shorty toasts the Marines and Bert 'destroyers and the *HMS Torrin*'.

The scene then dissolves to another toast, taking place at the same time but around another Christmas table: that of Chief Petty Officer Walter Hardy (Bernard Miles) and his wife Kath (Joyce Carey). Also coded as working-class, in a highly decorated room festooned with paper-chains, streamers and cards, their discussion similarly revolves around the services and the war, and about how lucky they are to be together at Christmas (the ship has had to dock for boiler-cleaning). Walter's speech stresses the seriousness of the war ('the whole of civilization happens to be trembling on the edge of an abyss') and his toast, worded as if he is referring to his wife, is also to *HMS Torrin*: 'She is a creature of many moods and fads and fancies [the camera is on Joyce Carey]. She is, to coin a phrase, very often uncertain and coy, hard to please, but I'm devoted to her with every fibre of my being and I hereby swear to be true to her in word and deed'. The inclusion of speeches at the Christmas dinner table is a convention which features in many fictional representations, usually, as in *In Which We Serve* and *This Happy Breed*, delivered in a tone of unaccustomed sobriety and gravity (amidst giggles from younger family members), providing a contrast with the festivities and functioning almost as a sermon, a permissible interlude signalled as important by the head of the family. The description of the ship as a person – a woman – also features in the next scene.

Another dissolve indicates the transition to the third Christmas dinner celebration, this time on board *HMS Torrin* with Captain Kinross, his family and other naval officers. Their table is more minimally decorated than the previous two (not many paper hats in evidence) and after encouragement from Kinross it is his wife Alix (Celia Johnson) who makes the speech, which she addresses to Maureen, a young woman recently engaged to an officer (Michael Wilding). The speech is in many ways an extraordinary example of self-laceration as Alix details the sacrifices made by the wives of naval officers and of their acceptance in taking second-place to their husbands' ships:

I'm going to deliver, on behalf of all wretched naval wives, a word of warning to Maureen who's been unwise enough to join our ranks ['Hear, hear' from the other women present]. Dear Maureen, we all wish you every possible happiness but I think it's only fair to tell you in advance exactly what you're in for [camera moves to medium close-up of Celia Johnson]. Speaking from bitter experience I can only say that the wife of a sailor is most profoundly to be pitied. To begin with, her home life – what there is of it – has no stability whatever. She can never really settle down. She moves through a succession of other people's houses, flats and furnished rooms. She finds herself having to grapple with domestic problems in Bermuda, Malta or Weymouth. We will not deal with the question of pay, that is altogether too painful. [Laughter]. What we will deal with is the most important disillusion of all, that is ['Stop her somebody – this is outright mutiny' – Kinross], that wherever she goes there is always in her life a permanent and undefeated rival – her husband's ship – whether it be a battleship or a sloop, a submarine or a destroyer, it holds first place in his heart. It comes before wife, home, children, everything. Some of us try to fight this and get badly mauled in the process. Others, like myself, resign themselves to the inevitable. That is what you will have to do, my poor Maureen. That is what we all have to do if we want any peace of mind at all. Ladies and gentlemen, I give you my rival. It's extraordinary that anyone could be so fond and so proud of their most implacable enemy, this ship. God Bless this ship and all who sail in her.

It is remarkable that this speech – unusually from the woman's point of view – acknowledges the importance of the ship but at the same time manages to convey a sense of loss. The speech, given with her husband's permission, is clearly not one that the diegetic audience expected to hear. Celia Johnson gives a perfect example of an understated but moving performance, mostly shot in mid close-up and with other people's reactions only heard in the background, the focus remaining on her. Looking at this scene today, with the memory of her subsequent performance in *Brief Encounter* (1945), the same quality of interiority remains with the viewer – the focus on her large eyes, pale complexion, giving a sense of serious contemplation with a tinge of disappointment and sadness. Unlike the other speeches we are not encouraged to identify with the other characters around the table, instead we are invited to consider the full weight of her words which, together with this particular visual strategy, conveys a sense of loneliness, of a voice and words that are heard but not fully appreciated. The wartime context, of course, makes such a speech permissible, together with Alix's careful additions that she has chosen not to fight the isolated and difficult destiny of the naval officer's wife and that she is fond of the ship. This self-censorship lightens the scene but in a curious way it also makes it more pathetic. As well as describing – literally – the problems encountered by naval wives, the speech also can be extended to refer to the wartime national expectation for women to be self-sacrificing, stoical, resigning themselves 'to the inevitable' and with no expectation of reward. At the end of Alix's speech instead of broadening out to encompass the other people around the table to see their reaction the shot remains on her, her glass, her own toast before dissolving back to the present. As such Celia Johnson's speech and performance have stood for the fate of women during the war but despite her words of plucky stoicism in this subtle visual manner the problems of occupying that role have nevertheless been suggested.

Although not set in the Second World War *This Happy Breed* (adapted by Noël Coward, David Lean, Anthony Havelock-Allan and Ronald Neame from Coward's 1939 play) shares the preoccupation with the family and nation which were noted in *In Which We Serve*. The film chronicles the history of a lower-middle-class family, the Gibbons, and the house into which they move in 1919 and leave at the end of the film in 1939. The Christmas sequence occurs in 1925 and is used as a narrative device to develop characters, establish areas of conflict which resurface later in the film and to communicate the film's dominant ideology of political consensus which, in the context of its release in wartime, connected with populist ideas about the family, community and nation.

Even though the sequence makes no direct reference to war there are striking similarities to the representations previously discussed. The first is the absence (or perceived absence) of family members. The father, Frank (Robert Newton), has been given a radio transmitter and his wife Ethel (Celia Johnson) is annoyed because his fascination with the instrument prevents him from engaging with the Christmas celebrations: 'No use talking to your father – he might just as well not be here'. This presence/absence dynamic which haunted the documentaries in particular is repeated here in a comical but significant way. At the end of the extract, as we shall go on to see, however, Frank is allowed the final say as the arbiter of the conflicts that have arisen in the meantime during the Christmas sequence, emphasizing that the father, the traditional head of the family, did not have to be physically present in wartime for his values to be dominant.

Generational differences are also signalled when the younger people stay behind in the dining room after Christmas dinner has been consumed. This provides the occasion for Sam Ledbetter (Guy Kerney), a friend of the family, to make a speech which in its way is as controversial as Celia

Johnson's in *In Which We Serve*, but for very different reasons. The speech looks forward to the subsequent sequence in the family chronicle which deals with the General Strike of 1926, but on this occasion it is de-politicized because of the Christmas setting. Sam is pro-Communist, his speech delivered in a friendly but gradually more aggressive manner, particularly when Queenie, Frank's daughter who aspires to escape from her lower-middle-class background and whom Sam chastises as a member of the bourgeoisie without a conscience, attempts to belittle his ideas. Sam makes the point that many poor children will not enjoy the type of Christmas they have experienced. The speech is potentially disturbing to the other young people but the general friendliness of the occasion contributes to an easy dissolution of the conflict at the end of the scene. Somewhat ironically, however, as it finishes Edie the maid, peering through the hatch, concludes the proceedings with a classic melodramatic interruption: 'All right if I clear away?'

The character of Queenie dominates the next scene when her would-be fiancé Billy (John Mills) asks her to marry him. She rejects him because she says she wants to better herself and not be trapped by a 'common' background. By the end of the film, however, her aspirations have been frustrated after a disastrous affair with a married man. She eventually marries Billy, humbled by her experiences and supporting the film's general ideological bias towards political consensus. Class collaboration rather than class mobility is thus condoned. This viewpoint is most clearly expressed via the character of Frank. When he discusses Sam's ideas with Ethel (who also questions their validity) he makes a case for British grad-ualism ('a nation of gardeners') as the sure route to progress: 'What works in other countries won't work in this one – we've got our own way of settling things – may be a bit slow and dull but it suits us'. In this case, even though the Christmas speech slot was given to Sam as a platform for radical ideas, it is Frank, gradualism, consensus and Noël Coward who have the last word.

A more recent representation of Christmas during the Second World War provides an interesting contrast to these previous films. The Christmas sequence in *Hope and Glory*, produced in 1987, is in many ways a self-reflexive attempt to assemble filmic memories of the wartime Christmas, utilizing past conventions but at the same time making a conscious effort to free them from the constraints of wartime propaganda and dominant ideologies. The narrative revolves around Billy, a small boy, and his recollections of growing up in the war years, filmed through a nostalgic and colourful lens. The Christmas sequence in this film coincides with Billy's father's leave – he is present for Christmas, the family is complete. The sequence begins however at a bazaar, the '1941 Christmas Show' of second-hand clothes, which Billy looks around with his mother. In stark contrast to the other films, women are the focus and we hear and see an entire aspect of the war which was seldom broached in wartime films: sexuality. The bazaar contains rows and rows of female clothing, dresses and undergarments, and provides an occasion for the women to discuss sex and for Billy to become vicariously engaged with their fascination. The camera, at Billy's height, follows him around as he weaves his way through the racks of female clothing, stealing illicit glances at girls who are trying on clothes. There is an entirely different sensibility to this film with its communication of danger, excitement, freedom and chaos; inhibitions are lowered and Billy's mother seems to be enjoying the war. At the bazaar she confesses to a friend that she likes being on her own and her friend admits to having an extra-marital affair: 'my life started when he [her husband] went on night work'. When Billy and his mother attend a piano concert in the next scene she says that she has not had such a good time since before she got married. These scenes allude to the freedoms made possible by the war, freedoms which it was hard for women like Billy's mother to relinquish once the war was over.

Interestingly, the following Christmas meal scene is observant of traditions which were not present in the previous films: the King's speech on the radio and the family standing up for the National Anthem. Their inclusion is somewhat at odds with the rest of the relaxed scene and seems almost 'tacked-on', as if they were conventions which must be included in a spirit of generic homage to wartime films. As we have seen, however, the wartime films did not include these elements, choosing instead to convey the sentiments of patriotism and national pride in other ways, for example in the speeches made by characters at the Christmas dinner table or via the voice-over commentaries of the documentaries. Another important divergence is the speech made by the grandfather in *Hope and Glory*. Instead of the speech being used as device for communicating gravity, seriousness or ideology, his speech is an embarrassing catalogue of all his female conquests over the years, a speech which he apparently makes each year. The tone is much lighter, there is more laughter and game-playing. In keeping, however, with the classic representation, a rupture in a romance is occasioned at Christmas when Billy's sister's Canadian boyfriend is posted overseas and she fears he will transfer his affections elsewhere. The family gather around to support her and the sequence culminates in an affective display of contrasting emotions: sadness and togetherness are intertwined.

Conclusion

All six films use Christmas to promote particular ideas which are pertinent to the wartime context. *Christmas Under Fire* and *Tunisian Victory* seize the opportunity presented by Christmas to appeal to American sentiments about a shared concern for democracy, invoking a 'special relationship' between Britain and America which is welded together by celebrations like Christmas which transcend national boundaries but, particularly in the case of *Tunisian Victory*, also claim superiority over non-Western societies. Although *Christmas Under Fire* and *Tunisian Victory* demonstrate that at home or abroad a wartime Christmas is, by necessity, a different one, 'a Christmas of contrasts', they also promote universal values such as religion, the sanctity of children's joy at Christmas and the significance of communal celebration. Unlike most of the other films *Christmas Under Fire* does not foreground the homestead – the Blitz forces people outside or underground where Christmas is nevertheless in evidence. *Tunisian Victory* shows how the troops overseas attempt to create a sense of 'home' at Christmas even though they are in unfamiliar surroundings.

Locations are important in the films, London being at the centre of them all.[18] For instance, although Tim is from Oxfordshire, *A Diary for Timothy* features shots of the Thames and a montage of city scenes. The focus on London indicates the film's concern to suggest ideas about metropolitan identity being synonymous with national identity, including shots of easily recognized landmarks and the Thames embankment as symbolic of an island under threat of invasion. Apart from the Christmas sequence, *A Diary for Timothy* makes some attempt to suggest regional diversity with its inclusion of the Welsh miner's story, but otherwise the film's focus on London is typical of most British wartime cinema. While regional differences are not really probed in the films there is, as we have seen, some suggestion of disparities between social classes, even if they are presented rather than explored. Small details of *mise-en-scène*, for example, are indicative of class, particularly Christmas 'trappings'. Certain elements are present in all households – the Christmas tree and cards being the most obvious – while the class differences are suggested by the extent of decoration, working-class households being the most elaborate.

Comparing genres, the documentaries make extensive use of voice-over commentaries which direct viewers to support their conclusions. While the relationship between the voice-over and the visuals can, as with *Christmas Under Fire*, be complex, the device nevertheless works to foreclose or discourage other interpretations. The fiction films engage with similar ideas about national identity, community and the importance of negating difference in wartime but have to communicate these in different ways. The strategy used in *This Happy Breed* is to introduce areas of conflict and instability but end the relevant sequence with a dominant figure, in this case the father, defusing the situation. How successful this is depends on the viewer, as in *In Which We Serve* when the closure of the

Christmas speech scene on *HMS Torrin* involves a shift in time to Kinross clinging to the life-raft rather than staying with the previous location to assess the full impact of Alix's speech. In this instance it is by no means clear that the dissatisfactions she has expressed can be easily extinguished.

It is striking that all of the films maintain a level of emotional engagement in spite of their different genres. The documentaries seemingly create a greater sense of distance from their participants than the fiction films but at the same time they still implicate the audience by encouraging an emotional investment via the evocation of national symbols, the iconography of Christmas and a spirit of universality. The fact that *Hope and Glory* was impelled to include such a dominant sense of past conventions concerning the representation of Christmas is evidence of a shared filmic memory. While a Christmas under wartime fire might well have been one of many contrasts, its celluloid representation proved to be remarkably durable.

Notes

1. Daniel Miller (ed.), *Unwrapping Christmas* (Oxford: Clarendon Press, 1993), p 32.

2. See Marcia Landy, *British Genres: Cinema and Society, 1930–1960* (Princeton: Princeton University Press, 1991), pp 298–9.

3. See J.M. Golby and A.W. Purdue, *The Making of the Modern Christmas* (London: B.T. Batsford, 1986), p 115.

4. Quotation from Mass Observation report, 1941, cited in Golby and Purdue (1986), p 128.

5. Golby and Purdue (1986), p 137, quote a Mass Observation report from 1941 in which a middle-class woman complained about a working-class family's lavish Christmas dinner.

6. Gavin Weightman and Steve Humphries, *Christmas Past* (London: Sidgwick and Jackson, 1987), p 171.

7. *Kinematograph Weekly* (14 January 1943), pp 38–40.

8. Ibid. (24 December 1942), p 28.

9. See film lists published in Ibid.: (7 December 1939), 38 films, 7 = UK origin; (5 December 1940), 35 films, 3 = UK origin; (4 December 1941), 34 films, 1 = UK origin; (3 December 1942), 34 films, 3 = UK origin; (2 December 1943), 24 films, 3 = UK origin; (7 December 1944), 32 films, 2 = UK origin.

10. Harry Watt, from his autobiography, quoted in Golby and Purdue (1986), p 131. See also a quotation from Watt in Ministry of Information files in which he refers to the film being for 'super-sentimentalists of the United States. With them Christmas becomes positively orgiastic in its slush'. This reference (Public Record Office INF 5/75) is quoted by James Chapman in *The British at War: Cinema, State and Propaganda, 1939–1945* (London: I.B. Taurus, 1998), pp 39–40.

11. Reynolds made several film reports for the Ministry of Information, also writing and narrating the commentary on *London Can Take It* (1940) and *London's Reply to Germany's False Claims* (1940).

12. I am grateful to James Chapman for alerting me to this example.

13. For an account of the conflicts during the making of *Tunisian Victory* see Anthony Aldgate, 'Creative tensions: *Desert Victory*, the Army Film Unit and Anglo-American

rivalry, 1943–45' in Philip M. Taylor (ed.), *Britain and the Cinema in the Second World War* (London: Macmillan, 1988), pp 158–61.

14. Although the main body of the film covers Tim's first six months there is a shot at the end of VE-Day celebrations, May 1945.

15. See Landy, *British Genres* (1991); Andrew Higson, 'Five Films' in Geoff Hurd (ed.), *National Fictions: World War Two in British Film and Television* (London: British Film Institute, 1984) p 23; and Sarah Street, *British National Cinema* (London: Routledge, 1997) pp 50–9.

16. Andrew Higson, *Waving the Flag: Constructing a National Cinema in Britain* (Oxford: Oxford University Press, 1995) p 262.

17. A Marine was a 'nautical soldier', a soldier appointed to large ships for military duties but under the jurisdiction of the Admiralty. Destroyers, like the *Torrin*, were smaller ships and carried an entirely naval crew.

18. In the montage of home fronts which the soldiers are remembering in *Tunisian Victory* London and Edinburgh are mentioned in the commentary.

5

Crisis at Christmas: *Turkey Time,* *The Holly and the Ivy, The Cheaters*

Jeffrey Richards

Holidays, the psychologists tell us, rank high among the flashpoints for family crises. As the normal routines are disrupted and everyone is cooped up together, tensions rise to the surface, tempers fray and uncomfortable home truths are spoken. This has a particular poignancy during the Christmas holidays, when the season of peace on earth and goodwill to all men can give rise to the most unseasonal feelings and actions.

Both theatre and cinema have found such occasions a ready-made source of dramatic and comic inspiration. In particular the rituals of the middle- and upper-class Christmas have served as the context and counterpoint of crises and complications. Three undeservedly forgotten films illustrate this both in a British and American context: *Turkey Time* (1933), *The Holly and the Ivy* (1952) and *The Cheaters* (1945).

Turkey Time was one of the later Aldwych farces. From 1922 to 1933 the Aldwych farces were a landmark in the history of twentieth-century British theatre. They starred Tom Walls and Ralph Lynn and featured a regular company of supporting players, notably Robertson Hare, Mary Brough and Ralph's brother Sydney Lynn who acted under the name of Gordon James. The farces were all directed by Tom Walls and the majority of them (nine altogether) were written by Ben Travers. With the arrival of talkies in Britain, Tom Walls began the process of transferring the farces from stage to screen and from 1930 to 1937, first at British and Dominions, then at Gaumont British and finally at Capitol, he made film versions of almost all the Aldwych farces. When the stage plays were used up, Ben Travers created original screenplays for the same team. From 1930 to 1933 the Aldwych team were filming by day and performing on stage at night. But after 1933 Tom Walls abandoned the stage completely to concentrate on films.

Walls was the driving force behind the Aldwych farces, as both Robertson Hare and Ben Travers acknowledged in their autobiographies. Hare wrote:

> He proved immediately that he had a flair for producing, on occasions amounting to genius; and he was definite. He rarely changed his mind once it was made up, but he was seldom wrong. His knowledge of character was uncanny, he seemed to know instinctively how the various characters would act in certain circumstances. This ability and understanding was the result of the wide experience of people he had acquired during an unusually varied career, having been a policeman, a race horse owner, a jockey and an actor. His attention to detail with regard to 'effects' was singularly thorough.[1]

Travers also acknowledged Walls' importance:

> Tom's gift for getting the best out of my farces was an absolute revelation. It didn't show itself in flashes; he had a steady, almost lazy application and foresight in discovering possibilities which had never occurred to me ... quite apart from his talent as a producer, Tom was the actuating force which drove Aldwych farce to flourish as it did. Nor could it have done so had not Tom Walls been exactly the Tom Walls he was. That same self-protective arrogance was an essential and guiding factor in the character of this rather coarse, wrong-shaped-headed, ruthless, dissipated, utterly extravagant, optimistic, entertaining, laughing, irresistible man.[2]

But Ralph Lynn also made a valuable contribution, embellishing the script with surrealistic one-liners and constantly devising extra bits of business. Travers thought him:

> an ideal farce actor to work with ... I have never seen or heard any actor in any field with such an instinctive and unerring gift of timing. I soon learned to exploit another distinctive and inimitable feature of his, the throwaway line ... He also relied to a great degree on instinct and impromptu, taking the form of a sudden whim during any one performance, momentary and often unintentional.[3]

Such moments were often kept in.

Travers thought Lynn had

> a nimbleness of wit as individual as his methods on-stage. He not
> only saw the ridiculous side of things; he searched for it. His first
> instinctive thought was to spot something funny in anything he saw
> or heard or read … But Ralph was painstaking about his work. He
> was never satisfied so long as there was a single line of any of his
> scenes which wasn't right. All through the run of a farce he would
> worry and experiment until he got the thing to his liking. In those
> moments there were none of the waggeries and wisecracks of his
> leisure hours; we were concentrating on the solemn problem of
> creating laughter. Nobody ever appreciated so well as Ralph how
> intensely serious is the job of being funny.[4]

Walls and Lynn usually played variants on the same basic characters.
Walls was the hearty, raffish, usually elderly, reprobate; worldly and
easygoing, with a fondness for drink and pretty girls but with a deep
streak of generosity. Lynn was the toothy, monocled, accident-prone but
indelibly good-natured upper-class 'silly ass' with the black patent-leather
hair, a holy fool with a whimsical line in humour, a childlike innocence
and a romantic devotion to women.

It was the introduction of a third actor into the ménage which comple-
mented the chemistry between them and gave the Aldwych farces their
distinctive edge – that was Robertson Hare. Robertson Hare was innately
funny, both visually and vocally. Diminutive, bald, bespectacled, conventional in outlook, pedantically precise in speech and, when exploding in
frustration, given to saying 'Oh-blow' or 'Oh-lawks' or 'Oh-calamity'; he
became the archetype of lower-middle-class suburban respectability who
was the butt of the schemes and misdeeds of the other two. He rapidly
became a regular feature of the farces, there 'to be fleeced of his fair
repute, of his cash, and of his trousers,' and Travers commented:

> I am convinced that this standard victimisation joke would never
> have found its way into the subsequent farces if the third person
> had been any other actor than Robertson Hare. There is nothing the
> farce-going public loves to laugh at more than the sight of the
> familiar, next-door-neighbour type of earnest little citizen in tribula-
> tion or being 'put-upon'.[5]

In *Turkey Time*, all three actors were in vintage form. Set in the seaside
resort of Duddwater, the play was constructed in three acts. The first and
third acts were set in the dining room of Edwin and Ernestine Stoatt and
the second in the gloomy Bella Vista temperance hotel. *The Times* (27 May
1931) reported that the alliance of Walls, Lynn and Travers had provided
'an entertainment which for the greatest part of the evening seemed to fit

the taste of the audience like a glove.' Travers had wanted Walls to play another of his elderly reprobates. But Walls insisted on playing a younger character, a worldly but good-hearted man-about-town, saying 'That's what the women like me to be.' Walls got his way and the public appeared to be perfectly happy with the change.[6]

The play opened on 26 May 1931 and ran for 263 performances. It was filmed by Gaumont British and released on 23 December 1933. The film was to be reissued in 1942 to provide much-needed comic relief during the war. Walls, Lynn, Mary Brough, Robertson Hare and Norma Varden recreated their stage roles and it turned out to be the last performance of the much-loved Mary Brough who died in 1934.

Just as he had produced the stage versions, so Tom Walls directed the film versions. When Gaumont British poached him from British and Dominions, he had struck a hard bargain. Not only did he obtain improved financial terms for himself and his associates, he insisted on choice and approval of story and cast and the right to direct all the films. Michael Balcon, the production chief at Gaumont, hated this arrange-ment and admits that he 'disliked him fiercely'. Years later they made their peace and Walls made a number of notable appearances as a character actor in Balcon's Ealing Studios productions. But Balcon's conclusion was:

> This comeback confirmed for me something that I had known at the time of our original association, that Tom was basically a first-rate performer but, frankly, he did not understand films in any tech-nical or creative sense and would not accept this fact because of his many successes in the early days of sound films. I knew that first-class films could have emerged if only he had placed himself in the hands of a competent director instead of believing he could do everything himself.[7]

This view of Walls's directorial failings was expressed continually in the 1930s. *The Times* (23 December 1933) reported of *Turkey Time*: 'Mr. Tom Walls, as a director, does not depart from his habit of treating the camera as though it were a Kodak and incapable of producing moving pictures.' The *Observer* (29 October 1933) noted: 'This is a director whose idea in making films is to line his stage players against a wall and shoot them at close range.' In an important article on British film comedy in *Film Weekly,* Hubert Cole lamented the popularity of the Aldwych films:

> Their very popularity makes them a menace – for they are nullifying much of the good work and undermining the foundations which the new well-directed British comedies have laid. Mr Walls, inspired by a succession of theatrical winners at the Aldwych, stubbornly

preserves in his pictures a pronounced stagey atmosphere. He has not tried to any extent to adapt his material to screen requirements. Both his direction and acting are theatrical and, therefore, from a screen point of view amateurish. Of course, Mr. Walls may very well reply that his pictures are box-office successes, and that is all he has to worry about. Which is a very sound point. But he might also consider that, with exactly the same material and expenditure of time and money, he could double the appeal and commercial value of his pictures – if only he would forget his past stage triumphs and get down to studying the technical demands of the screen. At present he is doing nothing to further the interests of the British cinema industry.[8]

Such criticism stung Walls. He told the *Evening News* (18 December 1933): 'Who, except a handful of people, wants art in the cinema? The masses go there for entertainment. I break them up as much as I can. We go outdoors where possible, move from room to room and so on. I don't *want* things to look static. But I won't sacrifice good dialogue.'

Turkey Time is certainly filmed in this way. The intricate construction and cumulative chaos of the stage farce is necessarily diluted by being abbreviated and broken up into shorter scenes as the action of the play is considerably opened out. But there was still room for improvisation. Ralph Lynn explained in an article for *Film Weekly*:

> The 'Aldwych team' … is said to be the despair of the script girls because we alter scenes so much as we go along. Ben Travers brings along an idea and dialogue for a scene, and perhaps his treatment gives one of us an additional idea. If it is good, in it goes. So the scene grows. Ben is marvellous about alterations. He doesn't mind a bit when his things are changed.[9]

The newspaper critics were divided about the film. The *Sunday Express* (24 December 1933), *News Chronicle* (23 December 1933) and *Sunday Referee* (27 December 1933) liked it; *News of the World* (24 December 1933) and *Morning Post* (27 December 1933) ('one of the poorest films which has come out of Shepherd's Bush') did not. *Film Weekly* (5 January 1934) thought it 'poorly directed but gloriously played'.[10]

But the trade press was ecstatic. *Kinematograph Weekly* called it 'entertainment riot with box-office appeal', *The Cinema* called it 'great stuff, constituting a comedy booking for all classes', and *Daily Film Renter* 'fun, fast and furious. Another box-office riot, with stars as ace drawing cards.'[11] For they knew – and this is the crucial fact – that whatever the critics said, the public loved Walls and Lynn.

Walls and Lynn regularly made the lists of top ten British film stars in the first half of the 1930s and John Sedgwick has concluded that Tom Walls was in fact the most popular British star at the British cinema box-office in the period 1932 to 1937.[12] Ralph Lynn ranks seventh during the same period. This statistical research confirms the evidence of contemporary newspaper polls of popularity. Walls and Lynn were among the most popular British stars of the 1930s, although Walls was always ahead of Lynn, perhaps because everyone warmed to the old reprobate whereas the 'silly ass' was not to everyone's taste.

In *Turkey Time*, the Aldwych team turned their attention to Christmas. The titles of the film unfold over a picture of a Christmas pudding and the legend 'Turkey Time is Christmastime. A Christmas pudding contains some varied ingredients. So does many a British household at Christmas. Here are some of the ingredients of our pudding.' Then each of the characters of the play is introduced under the heading of an appropriate ingredient: Robertson Hare and Norma Varden as suet and sultanas, Dorothy Hyson as the sugar, D.A. Clarke-Smith as the salt, Veronica Rose as the spice, Mary Brough as the rum, Ralph Lynn as the milk and Tom Walls as the peel.

The setting of the film, the out-of-season seaside resort rechristened

Veronica Rose, Robertson Hare, Ralph Lynn and Norma Varden in *Turkey Time*.

Eden Bay, is evoked by a succession of scenes of pier amusements amid snowy surroundings, and the action takes place on Christmas Eve and Christmas Day. David Winterton (Ralph Lynn) and Max Wheeler (Tom Walls) are cousins of Edwin and Ernestine Stoatt (Robertson Hare and Norma Varden) and have come to stay with them for Christmas at their home, The Warren. Both David and Max continually send up the hapless Edwin who is also tyrannized by his towering, terrifying wife, the magnificent Norma Varden, whose hauteur is positively chilling.

The problems arise when Max tries to do a seasonal good turn for a pretty pierrot performer and David falls for the same girl. Rose Adair (Dorothy Hyson) is appearing with Hal Potts and his Gadabouts in the end-of-the-pier show. David reprimands two small boys for peering in at the show through a window and not paying for admission. But, entranced by the sight of Rose, he is soon up on the window-sill watching the show and sharing a stick of rock with the two boys. Max, who has spent fifteen years in Montana (Canada in the play) and speaks exclusively in highly unconvincing American slang, comes to Rose's rescue when she receives unwelcome attentions from fellow performer Warwick Westbourne (D.A. Clarke-Smith). Max takes her to a tea room, lends her money to pay her rent and warns her against Westbourne.

This act of seasonal goodwill leads to problems as the maidservant of Rose's puritanical landlady, Mrs Gather, reports seeing Rose at the tea room. Mrs Gather suspects an immoral relationship and marches round to inform Mrs Stoatt about her cousin. Despite the suspicions of the puritanical Mrs Gather and the disapproval of the snobbish Ernestine, Max good humouredly explains his way out of it and convinces Louise, Ernestine's sister and his fiancée, of his good intentions. The play opened with Mrs Gather's arrival at the Stoatts'. But the film begins by showing all the actions reported by Mrs Gather (Mary Brough).

After dinner, the Stoatts join a group of carol-singers and Max determines to sort out Westbourne when he discovers that he has appropriated the money Max lent Rose in order to cover a debt she owed him. There follow several funny scenes, none of them in the play. The Stoatts' attempts to sing 'Good King Wenceslas' with the carol-singers are disrupted when a cyclist and then a motorist drive through their group, a band of children pelt them with snowballs and a street musician launches into 'The First Noel' on a trumpet. Max, meanwhile, in search of Westbourne, knocks an innocent bystander through the plate glass window of a shop and has to pay compensation to the man and the shopkeeper so that they will not prefer charges. An angry policeman who has been summoned accidentally pushes a small boy through another plate glass window and is himself pushed through a third by the boy in retaliation. Max and David encounter a man with a baby in a pram. The baby is very accurately playing with a cup and ball but it defeats the two adults when they try it. This has about it the improvisational feel that Ralph Lynn wrote about in his article.

Rose turns up at The Warren in need of a fresh loan to pay her rent. But David and Max are penniless. So they accompany her to Mrs Gather's where Max romances the landlady while David tries to help Rose to sneak out. This fails and Mrs Gather confiscates her luggage. At this point the hapless Edwin turns up with his collecting box, and David and Max talk him out of the proceeds in order to pay the rent. But Edwin complains to Mrs Gather ('This money was filched from me by subterfuge') and she returns the money to him ('I wish you a rotten Christmas and a mouldy new year'). Ernestine and the carol-singers come in search of Edwin, and Max, David, Rose and Edwin lock themselves in Rose's room. David, Max and Rose escape from the window via a ladder but Edwin is discovered by his wife who sets about him with her fists as he disappears inside his coat.

In the play, the hotel belonged not to Mrs Gather but to Mrs Pike and her decrepit uncle, Luke Meate. These characters, played by Ethel Coleridge and Gordon James on stage, were eliminated from the film version and Mrs Pike's role was conflated with that of Mrs Gather. Interestingly *The Times* had noted of the play that it 'sags noticeably in the second act' and recommended shortening or revising the bargaining with the two landladies. This was done for the film.

Back at The Warren, Florence the maid hides Rose, and David and Max concert a plan to get her away next morning. Ernestine and Edwin come down early on Christmas morning to put out the presents and discover Rose in her underwear hiding behind the curtains. Louise catches Max kissing Florence under the mistletoe. Mrs Gather, still in pursuit of the rent, and Westbourne, still in pursuit of Rose, turn up, both drunk. The result is a massive free-for-all, as they pelt each other with the Christmas presents. At the height of the mayhem, David and Rose and Max and Louise sneak out but are buried up to their necks in a snowfall from the roof.

The Aldwych farces are comedies of subversion, sending up traditional morality, playing games with social conventions, mocking the Puritanism of landladies, the snobbery of suburban wives, the timorous conventionality of suburban husbands. As such they qualify, as do Donald MacGill's seaside postcards, which Orwell saw as 'a sort of saturnalia or a harmless rebellion against virtue', and the music hall, for Orwell's definition of comedy:

> Codes of law and morals, or religious systems, never have much
> room in them for a humorous view of life. Whatever is funny is

subversive, every joke is ultimately a custard pie, and the reason why so large a proportion of jokes centre on obscenity is simply that all societies, as the price of survival, have to insist on a fairly high standard of sexual morality. A dirty joke is not, of course, a serious attack upon morality but it is a sort of mental rebellion, a momentary wish that things were otherwise. So also with all other jokes, which always focus on cowardice, laziness, dishonesty or some other quality which society cannot afford to encourage. Society has always to demand a little more from human beings than it will get in practice. It has to demand faultless discipline and self-sacrifice, it must expect its subjects to work hard, pay their taxes, and be faithful to their wives, it must assume that men think it glorious to die on the battlefield and women want to wear themselves out with child-bearing. The whole of what one may call official literature is based on such assumptions.[13]

The virtue of the comic postcards is that

They stand for the worm's eye view of life, for the music-hall world where marriage is a dirty joke or a comic disaster, where the rent is always behind and the clothes are always up the spout, where the lawyer is always a crook and the Scotsman always a miser, where the newlyweds make fools of themselves on the hideous beds of the seaside lodging houses and the drunken, red-nosed husbands roll home at four in the morning to meet the linen-nightgowned wives who wait for them behind the front door, poker in hand.[14]

Many of the elements are to be found in the Aldwych farces in general and *Turkey Time* in particular, which is set with Orwellian appropriateness in a seaside resort. It is a seasonal take on the traditional Aldwych elements and an object lesson in what can go wrong at Christmas. The action revolves around the subversion of the traditional Christmas activities: the carol-singing sabotaged, Christmas shopping degenerating into window-breaking and the present-giving turning into a violent if comic free-for-all. At the centre of it all is hapless suburban husband Edwin Stoatt, henpecked, hectored and humiliated by his wife and bamboozled, bilked and bemused by Max and David. But in fact the complications arise from David's genuine romantic attachment to Rose and Max's altruistic attempt to do a seasonal good deed. And Christmas exacts its own revenge in the end by burying the couples up to the neck in snow. It confirms that at bottom comedy is a safety valve, the laughter a way of letting off steam before convention and seriousness reassert themselves.

The Holly and the Ivy (1952) is a drama of Christmas complications and resulted from an experiment in the early 1950s by producer Alexander Korda in transferring recent stage successes economically to the stage. The casts would be rehearsed at the studio on the set for several weeks and the film would then be rapidly shot in a quarter of the time it normally took to shoot the average film. Four films were made in this way: *Home at Seven*, *Who Goes There?*, *The Ringer* and *The Holly and the Ivy*.[15]

The Holly and the Ivy by Wynyard Browne is a perfect example of the well-made three-act play which graced the West End in the early 1950s and was eclipsed by the theatrical revolution of the late 50s. It opened in 1950 and ran in London for a year and a half, receiving almost unanimous critical praise. Veteran character actor Herbert Lomas gave the performance of a lifetime as the elderly parson at the centre of the action. Charles Duff in his account of post-war British theatre calls it with some justice 'a very English play, full of charm, humour and understanding. A period piece, true, and dealing in understatement, but it is somehow exciting because of its truth and poetry. A lovely play.'[16]

Its truth may stem in part from the fact that many of the characters are based on members of Browne's own Anglo-Irish family. His father Rev.

Celia Johnson and John Gregson in *The Holly and The Ivy*.

Barry Browne was an Irish-born Church of England vicar in Norfolk, as is Rev. Martin Gregory in the play. The two aunts in the play, Aunt Lydia and Aunt Bridget, are based on Browne's English aunt, the widow of the Dean of Battle, and his Irish aunt who lived in Maida Vale.

A distinguished cast of British actors was assembled to play the leading roles, many of them ornaments of the post-war British stage. Ralph Richardson plays Martin Gregory, Celia Johnson and Margaret Leighton his daughters Jenny and Margaret, Denholm Elliot his son Mick, Hugh Williams their cousin Colonel Richard Wyndham, and John Gregson Jenny's fiancé David Patterson. Two members of the original stage cast were retained to repeat their performances: Margaret Halstan as Aunt Lydia, fey, romantic, genteel, longtime widow of a King's Messenger and resident in a succession of hotels, and Maureen Delany as Aunt Bridget, the cantankerous, opinionated, termagant spinster aunt. It was produced and scripted by Anatole de Grunwald and directed by George More O'Ferrall with unobtrusive discretion.

Although it is opened out here and there, the bulk of the action takes place during Christmas Eve and Christmas Day, 1948, in the vicarage at Wyndenham, Norfolk. This Christmas becomes a time for revelation and soul-baring, as the play explores the secrets and evasions within the family, all of which come tumbling out, as they assemble for their annual Yuletide reunion.

Rev. Martin Gregory, vicar of Wyndenham, is the goodnatured, lovable elderly vicar, recently widowed, but unwilling to retire until he has seen son Mick through Cambridge. He has two daughters, Jenny and Margaret. Jenny, the domesticated one who looks after him, wants to marry Scots engineer David Patterson and go with him to South America where he is taking up a new job constructing aerodromes. But she cannot bring herself to leave her father and forbids anyone in the family to tell him about her engagement to David. Margaret is a sophisticated fashion journalist who lives and works in London and rarely comes home. She explains the reason to Jenny during this visit. She had been in love with an American airman during the war. He had been killed, leaving her pregnant. She had given birth to a son Simon but he had died of meningitis at four. Now she drinks. She refuses to come home because she would have to play a role, pretending to be something she is not, to please her father.

Mick, the callow, self-pitying National Serviceman son, is apprised of both secrets and eventually blurts them out to his father. He has claimed that life for the family of a parson is 'a life of perpetual pretence' as they all try not to offend or hurt or upset father or his religious beliefs. This precipitates a major confrontation between Martin and Margaret as he laments that he has failed them all because none of them could talk to him frankly. In the end they do speak frankly about their feelings and beliefs and finally understand one another; Margaret decides that she will come home, freeing Jenny to go to South America with David.

More than in the play, the traditional elements of Christmas are a feature of the film. The credits unfold against a Christmas fantasia by Malcolm Arnold, which blends 'The Holly and the Ivy' and 'The First Noel'. There is an opening montage of Christmas illuminations and shop window displays. Jenny is first seen dressing the crib in the church and listening to the choir rehearse 'The Holly and the Ivy' and later is decorating the tree in the Vicarage and repairing the decorations ('It's only what we always do'). The Vicar attends the nativity play, a charmingly natural rendition by children, and listens to a singing of 'Silent Night'. At regular intervals throughout the film there are carol-singers at the door of the Vicarage. At the end, the Christmas bells ring out. The film concludes with the whole family assembled in church to hear the Vicar's sermon, which is to be on the folklore origins of the Christmas traditions, and to sing 'Oh, Come all ye faithful'.

Despite this strong presence of Christmas imagery, many of the characters express a dislike of Christmas. Mick and Lydia say they loved it when children but it lost its magic when they grew up. David finds Christmas 'depressing'. Even the Vicar declares: 'I hate Christmas. The brewers and the retail traders have got hold of it. It's all eating and drinking and giving each other knick-knacks. No-one remembers the birth of Christ'. The one dissenting voice is that of Jenny:

> But Christmas morning ... there's something about Christmas morning ... the first moment, when you wake up. Somehow I don't know why – you always know it's Christmas morning. It's as if, during the night, while you were asleep, something has happened ... You even expect the world to look as different as it feels. And you lie there, taking it in, realising – and that seems strangest of all – that it's Christmas everywhere.

Her faith in Christmas is repaid. It works its magic. The truth is spoken, new understandings reached and new beginnings are possible.

The film preserves a whole vanished era of British acting, a well-spoken, upper-middle-class school of restraint. It is fashionable to mock the well-bred gentility and well-modulated voices of the early 1950s. But they preserve exactly a particular strand of British life and a well-defined value system which centred on restraint and self-sacrifice, not making a fuss, not hurting people, and doing the right thing. It is the value system which animated *Brief Encounter* and which makes it, like *The Holly and the Ivy*, such a precious cultural document. Celia Johnson's Jenny Gregory has something of the same poignancy, pain and truthfulness that she brought to her celebrated performance as Laura Jesson in *Brief Encounter* and in scenes she shares with Margaret Leighton, who conveys precisely the brittle glamour and neurotic bravado of Margaret, 'the Frozen Queen who went down to the gardens of the dead' (as Jenny calls her), one can see examples of distinctively British acting at its finest. Celia Johnson beautifully conveys her dawning understanding of Margaret's plight and then her horror at the news of Simon's death. These are the film's finest performances. But Ralph Richardson's Vicar with his self-deprecating humour and eccentric saintliness is an engaging study and Hugh Williams's gently concerned cousin is in its own way a classic study in English decency.

Many of the critics pointed out that *The Holly and the Ivy* was a photographed stageplay. The *Daily Worker* (25 October 1952) for instance noted rather sniffily that it was 'a straight transfer to celluloid of a cosy West End play'. But most of the critics who made this observation did not seem to care too much that this was so. The *Daily Mirror* (24 October 1952) called it 'a good copy of a successful stage play ... very pleasant entertainment' and the *Sunday Times* (26 October 1952) observed 'it never shakes off the restraints of the theatre but the cast is good enough for me not to care. The playing of Celia Johnson, Margaret Leighton and Ralph Richardson is a pleasure to watch for its own sake'. *Tribune* (25 October 1952) thought that it did 'not pretend to be any more than a photographed version of a play' but also thought 'the acting beautifully clear, precise and true'.

The Times (27 October 1952) pointed to a paradox:

> It is, from the point of view of those who rightly think that the cinema should develop as an independent art, regrettable that so often the best British films turn out to be photographed stage plays. Indeed it is paradoxically true that their virtues tend to increase the more they depend upon a faithful transcription of the play and upon actors who belong first and foremost to the theatre. Such a film is *The Holly and the Ivy* and an admirable and satisfying film it is.

The Times identified its virtues as a clever mingling of 'those elements of drawing room comedy and domestic drama which constitute the particular strength of our theatre', the 'intelligent inquiry into the problems of the clergy' and the acting which is done with a 'beautiful ease and understanding'. It singled out Celia Johnson's performance for its 'natural magic'.

The *Evening News* (27 October 1952) similarly noted that it had been made 'without any pretensions to film craft but replete with first-class acting' adding, 'it is because of those long static "takes" that the acting seems so good. The thought is disturbing to the student of film craft. The experiment is dangerous unless you have dialogue as excellent as this.'

But this critic was one of several to highlight its specific Christmas message, saying: 'I like the emphasis on the true value of the Christmas festival'.

The *Star* (24 October 1952) commented:

> A photographed stage play? Perhaps producer Anatole de Grun-
> wald does not succeed in turning it into a film but when the result is
> so enjoyable as this I don't think that matters ... All the acting is
> first-rate. Sir Ralph has never done anything better, and Miss
> Johnson and Miss Leighton are particularly good ... it is a picture
> with a wonderfully warm glow, a lovely job which I found as
> comfortable as a crackling log fire with flames shooting high to give
> a ruddy sparkle to Christmas tree snow. Sentimental? Of course, but
> what's the use of a Christmas story without sentiment.

Other critics ignored the film's origins and simply revelled in the story. The *Sunday Telegraph* (26 October 1952) observed that 'the characterisation is so true to life, the dialogue so natural, and the problem so real that the interest is always held ... a film that has a lesson for old and young and is packed with entertainment'. The critic also thought Celia Johnson 'superb'. The *Daily Herald* (24 October 1952) calling it this 'sweet and strangely human little comedy' added 'I must say I never saw better stage acting on the screen' and thought Celia Johnson had even improved on her famous role in *Brief Encounter*. Campbell Dixon in the *Daily Telegraph* (27 October 1952), heading his review 'modest, sincere and charming', felt himself a better man for having seen the film, with its 'natural and intelligent dialogue', 'accomplished' acting and 'tactful' direction. The *News of the World* (26 October 1952) thought it 'a truly rich and digestible feast of polished production and perfect acting'. The *Sunday Chronicle* (26 October 1952) thought it 'good and often very moving' and 'beautifully directed'.

Richard Winnington struck the only note of dissent in the *News Chronicle* (25 October 1952) when he called it 'a damp family drama' with Richardson giving 'his worst performance ever'. However, it was so ecstatically reviewed when it was released in America that the fact was recorded in an article in the *Daily Telegraph* (6 February 1954), reporting that the New York critics had brought out their superlatives, with the *New York Herald Tribune* hailing a 'tour de force of acting', *World Telegram* saying 'England has sent us another of its minor gems to glow in our movie memories', *Journal Americana* calling it 'beautifully made' and the *New York Post* saying:

> It stands squarely in the centre of the great tradition of British
> pictures. It is when you consider the acting and the character both

as performed and written that it assumes the proper position as one of the major British productions. Such performances have seldom been brought together in one film. The result, for this observer at least, is the most deeply moving picture experience of the year.

Where *Turkey Time* and *The Holly and the Ivy* are – a recognized British tradition – film versions of stage plays, *The Cheaters* (1945) is an unacknowledged and unofficial reworking of a previous film, the much-loved 1930s screwball comedy, *My Man Godfrey*. It is in the celebrated tradition of the mysterious stranger who arrives in the bosom of a household and causes them to face up to the truth about themselves and to reform. In the theatre, *The Passing of the Third Floor Back* and *An Inspector Calls* are classic expositions of the idea. *My Man Godfrey* was a variant of this. In the 1930s of the Depression, a down-and-out is picked up, joins the wealthy Bullock household as butler and gradually converts the family from selfishness, flightiness and spitefulness. Recast for Christmas, scripted by Frances Hyland and directed for Republic Pictures by Joseph Kane, *The Cheaters* retold the story with a moral. The similarity to *My Man Godfrey* was underlined by the casting of Eugene Pallette, who played Mr Bullock in the earlier film, as Mr Pidgeon in *The Cheaters*. In this Christmas context, *The Cheaters* can be linked to that late 1940s cycle of films about angels (*It's a Wonderful Life, The Bishop's Wife*) or Father Christmas (*Miracle on 34th Street*) appearing at Christmas to work seasonal miracles.

Largely ignored by the critics on its release, and if noticed at all disparaged (*The New York Times* (21 July 1945) called it 'a compound of witless platitudes'), it is in fact a delightful Christmas fable, beautifully acted and written, and directed by Joseph Kane, who usually made Westerns, with unexpected delicacy, sensitivity and charm. Business tycoon J.C. Pidgeon (Eugene Pallette) prepares for Christmas, although he is short of money and facing mounting debts. His snobbish daughter Therese (Ruth Terry), anxious to impress the Boston socialite family of her fiancé Captain Stephen Bates (Robert Livingston), insists that her mother, the scatter-brained and extravagant Clara Pidgeon (Billie Burke), take in a charity case for Christmas, as Mrs Bates does. They end up with Anthony Marchand (Joseph Schildkraut), a broken-down former matinée idol with a fondness for the bottle. The Pidgeon family, which also includes spoiled brat daughter Angela (Anne Gillis), cynical, bad-mannered, college boy son Reggie (David Holt) and genial, sponging brother-in-law Willie (Raymond Walburn), learn that millionaire Uncle Henry has died leaving five million dollars to a former child actress he once saw and failing her, the Pidgeons. The family plot to find the woman, Florie Watson (Ona Munson), keep her out of sight until the lawyers give up looking for her and then claim the money for themselves. Marchand, sleeping off a binge in a library chair, overhears the plot and offers to help find her through Equity, angrily rejecting Reggie's suggestion that he will want a cut of the money. They track down Florie, a goodhearted but penniless actress, claim she is a long-lost cousin, and invite her for Christmas. As the newspapers publicize the search for the missing heiress, the Pidgeons decide to flee and spend Christmas in a remote country farmhouse which Pidgeon has been trying to sell. They pack up and leave for the snowbound farm but all the servants quit in disgust. Florie organizes them all to rally round with the cooking.

Marchand, who observes that the one part he has never played is 'God', watches as the country life and the need to fend for themselves transforms Therese, Reggie and Angela into natural, decent, goodhearted kids. Mrs Pidgeon weeps at Florie's goodness. The local church choir visits and sings 'Silent Night' and Marchand, to ram home the message, retells the story of 'A Christmas Carol', expressing in particular the chains forged by greed for Marley's Ghost, before passing out drunk. At this point Florie confesses that she is a fraud, taking their hospitality even though she knew she was not their cousin. Angela is so moved she insists on telling Florie about the bequest. Florie goes to find Marchand and discovers he has gone, leaving a note saying he has become fond of Florie and cannot carry on deceiving her. She finds him in a bar in the nearby town, and tells him she has agreed to split the money 50/50 with the Pidgeons. They have a drink together and find that neither of them can pay. The rather lame ending is the only flaw in an otherwise delightful story, in which Schildkraut gives a performance of sardonic authority as the ham actor with the fake limp and fondness for the bottle, and Billie Burke, Eugene Pallette, Ona Munson and Raymond Walburn, cast to type, turn in reliable and engaging performances.

The film fascinatingly links the action to an affirmation of tradition. The family rediscovers the simple life and decent values in an old American farmhouse, dating from 1771, and Marchand pricks its conscience with the retelling of *A Christmas Carol* with its strong anti-greed message. Dickens and Americana are combined to bring a powerful message about the true meaning of Christmas to a 1945 audience.

All three films evoke the by now traditional Christmas imagery with snow falling and carol-singing featured. All involve deception, pretence and evasion and all see the truth coming out after family rows and revelations. All feature a visitor who acts as the catalyst for these revelations. Interestingly all three also revive the medieval tradition of 'the world turned upside down', the reign of the lord of misrule and temporary inversion of norms, as the old learn from the young (*The Holly and the Ivy*), the rich from the poor (*The Cheaters*) and the responsible from the irresponsible (*Turkey Time*). But Christmas works its magic and its centrality to the cultures of both Britain and America is rousingly affirmed.

Notes

1. Robertson Hare, *Yours Indubitably* (London: Robert Hale, 1956), p 115.
2. Ben Travers, *A-Sitting on a Gate* (London: W.H. Allen, 1978), pp 98–9.
3. Ibid., p 91.
4. Ibid., pp 93, 94.
5. Ibid., p 97.
6. Ibid., p 111.
7. Michael Balcon, *A Lifetime of Films* (London: Hutchinson, 1969), p 92.
8. *Film Weekly* (6 April 1934).
9. Ibid. (7 December 1934).
10. I am indebted to Laurie Ede for providing information about the filmed Aldwych farces.
11. BFI microfiche *Turkey Time*.
12. John Sedgwick, 'Cinema-going Preferences in Britain in the 1930s' in Jeffrey Richards (ed.), *The Unknown 1930s* (London: I.B. Tauris, 1998), p 18.
13. George Orwell, 'The Art of Donald McGill', *Collected Essays, Journalism and Letters 2* (Harmondsworth, Penguin, 1971), pp 193–4.
14. Ibid., pp 193–4.
15. John Miller, *Ralph Richardson* (London: Sidgwick and Jackson, 1955), p 144.
16. Charles Duff, *The Lost Summer: The Heyday of the West End Theatre* (London: Nick Hern Books, 1995), p 77.

$$\boxed{6}$$

Santa Claus: The Movie

Mark Connelly

This chapter will explore the way in which Santa Claus has been represented in film since the Second World War. The movies that require most attention are the two versions of *Miracle on 34th Street* (1947 and 1994) and the Disney film *The Santa Clause* (1994). But in addition to this, reference will be made to the quirky *Ernest Saves Christmas* (1988) and *Santa Claus* – also known as *Santa Claus the Movie* (1985). *Miracle on 34th Street* concerns a little girl who does not believe in Santa Claus and yet comes face-to-face with the real thing in Macy's of 34th Street, New York. The film has been regarded as a Christmas classic since its release in 1947 and its fame even engendered a remake in 1994. A leap is then made into the 1980s with *Santa Claus the Movie*, a film in which the origins of Santa, and his problems in dealing with the cut and thrust of the modern world, are explored. Much the same theme fills *Ernest Saves Christmas* and seems to reflect the criticisms of the 'yuppy culture' of the 80s. *The Santa Clause* represents the 1990s where a sales executive finds that he has unwittingly accepted the job of being Santa.

Of the five films mentioned here, four are pure Hollywood products; *Santa Claus* is the only exception. The main thrust of this chapter will therefore be concerned with the way in which the USA perceives the role and nature of Santa Claus. This seems right and proper for Santa is indeed an American preserve; he has been amalgamated with the English Father Christmas and many other European mythical figures associated with the season. But, as Russell Belk has noted, 'the American Santa is more than an amalgam of these characters and is instead uniquely American'.[1] Belk's work is fascinating, for he explores the nature of Santa as an American hero and so provides the backdrop for this particular investigation. The films about Santa, consequently, can be used to tell us something not only about the way in which America understands Christmas but also about the way in which America understands and presents itself. Though, as we shall see, Belk's identification of America with Santa can be questioned when examined in the light of movie interpretations of the figure. The chapter will also show that what are felt to be the modern problems of family life, most poignantly experienced at Christmas, have, in fact, a long history and have been shown on screen for an equally long time. Christmas, and one of its key heralds, therefore becomes significant to national identity and self-perception. The power of cinema, and the subsequent showing of these films on the small screen, allows their images to reach an audience far wider than that of the United States.

Santa Claus: American

When John Wayne died, one of his greatest co-stars, Maureen O'Hara (also the female lead in the original *Miracle on 34th Street*), suggested that a gold medal be struck in his honour inscribed with the simple epitaph 'John Wayne: American'; much the same can be said of the figure of Santa Claus. Unlike the great cowboy, however, Santa is a truly immortal American. Cinema has done more than any other medium to promote this message and ensure its ascendancy over other interpretations. When *Ernest Saves Christmas* was released in the UK in the winter of 1989 *The Times* noted that: 'Americans have perhaps a prerogative of revising the lore of Santa Claus since it was an American ... who invented Santa Claus as we know him.'[2] The reference is to Thomas Nast who created the first standardized image of Santa Claus in the late nineteenth century but the implication is then that the American cinema industry can re-interpret him to fit the circumstances of modern life. This is a theme to which we will return. In January 1995, when *Sight and Sound* commented on the release of the remake of *Miracle on 34th Street*, its correspondent was also convinced that 'the implication for any thinking British child must be ... that Santa is American'.[3] The vision of Santa as an all-American hero can sometimes pose problems. *Variety* worried that *The Santa Clause* might not be a success outside the USA: 'off shore prospects aren't as bright because of the uniquely American flavouring'.[4]

How exactly do these films create this impression? *The Santa Clause* employs Tim Allen, star of the popular television sit-com *Home Improvements*, to take on the job. In the movie he plays the character Scott Calvin (note the significance of the initials), an executive in a toy company. He lives in a handsome house in a suburb and is therefore typical of the

American middle class. It is an image that would be recognized by any viewer of such movies as John Hughes's *Planes, Trains and Automobiles*; *She's Having a Baby* or *Home Alone*. (Ironically Hughes was producing the new *Miracle*, the biggest rival to Disney's *The Santa Clause* for the American Christmas market in 1994). Scott reinforces this image of Santa as, in fact, a typically American guy, by reading his son that classic of American Christmas/Santa literature, Clement Clark Moore's *A Visit From St Nicholas*, also known as *'Twas the Night Before Christmas*. Clark Moore's poem provides the modern definition of Santa:

> Down the chimney St Nicholas came with a bound.
> He was dressed all in fur, from his head to his foot,
> And his clothes were all tarnished with ashes and soot.
> A bundle of toys he had flung on his back,
> And he looked like a peddler, just opening his pack.
> His eyes – how they twinkled! His dimples how merry!
> His cheeks were like roses, his nose like a cherry!
> His droll little mouth was drawn up like a bow,
> And the beard of his chin was as white as the snow …
> He had a broad face and a little round belly,
> That shook when he laughed, like a bowlful of jelly.
> He was chubby and plump, a right jolly old elf.

Later, when Scott has finished delivering toys, we see the sleigh cross the skyscape of a typical American city and the dawn of Christmas Day is heralded by him shouting the last line of the poem, 'Happy Christmas to all, and to all a good-night'.

Both versions of *Miracle on 34th Street*, however, make a far more ambiguous statement about Santa's American credentials. The irony, which immediately stares us in the face, is that in both versions of *Miracle on 34th Street* British actors play Santa – Edmund Gwenn in 1947, and Richard Attenborough in 1994. Both made very good jobs of it, and neither attempts to put on an American accent. Why were British actors cast in these roles given the identification of Santa Claus with America? Should we take such casting decisions as a gesture towards a shared Anglo-Saxon history and set of traditions? Perhaps it was thought that an authentic portrayal of Santa could only come from actors born in the country which gave America so many of its Christmas customs? If this is the case then the *Miracle* films undermine the argument that Santa is a peculiarly American figure. But both versions of the *Miracle* appropriate these British Santas into American life by making them residents of New York. The New York settings and the trappings of the season are undoubtedly American. The original opens with the Macy's Thanksgiving Day Parade. A huge American eagle is carried, the band is playing 'Stars and Stripes Forever' and immediately behind this comes Santa. The juxta-position makes it obvious that Santa may have originated in England, he may be played by a British actor, but he now lines up with the real live nephews of his Uncle Sam. Interestingly in the remake the villain of the piece, Joss Ackland, plays his role with a very definite English accent and so plays a role more often given to British actors in Hollywood films.[5]

The original version of the *Miracle* therefore implies that Santa does have origins outside the USA and goes on to imply a general northern European ancestry. A little Dutch refugee girl is placed upon Santa's knee. She is still clearly distraught at spending her Christmas in New York, a long way from her family. Santa immediately puts her at ease by talking to her in Dutch. This is another hint that the Santa we, the audi-ence, and the other characters in the film are seeing is the real thing and not just another department store copy. But it also seems to have a subtle historical message, albeit one intelligible only to an American audience. By making the little girl Dutch the film refers to the Saint Nicholas legend so strong in the Netherlands; it also connects the modern city to America's history: New York is thrown back to its days as New Amsterdam – Santa has been in America since its infancy. The reference to the Old World also seems significant in the light of the new American position in the world. In 1947 the USA was the undoubted superpower, the protector of Europe. In the same way the film shows the genuine Santa, living in New York, comforting a little foreign girl by showing a great heart and a great desire to do the right thing by the children of the world.

A variation on the European origin of Santa occurs in the British film, *Santa Claus*, as one might expect. The story begins somewhere in Europe in the Middle Ages, when the woodcutter Claus and his wife Anya are busy loading up his home-made toys in order to deliver them to their nephews. Their reindeer sleigh is brought to a halt by a fierce snowstorm and as the snow drifts over them they fall asleep. When they awake they have been miraculously shifted to the North Pole, one of the many loca-tions associated with Santa according to legend and tradition.[6]

In *Miracle on 34th Street*, as the film develops, it becomes clear that though Santa might have lived at the North Pole (a place first visited by American explorers) it probably says on his passport that he is a citizen of the USA. The final proof of this comes in the courtroom scene to decide whether or not Kris Kringle is the real Santa Claus. Both Gwenn and Attenborough are given the name Kris Kringle for it is one of Santa's pseudonyms, a mispronunciation of the German Lutheran term *Christ-kindlein*, meaning a messenger of Christ, a gift-bearer. Fred Gailey, who is a lawyer, played by John Payne, is defending Kris Kringle's claim to be Santa. His final piece of evidence actually comes from the government of the United States itself. The judge had asked for evidence from a 'competent authority' and this duly comes from the government agency of the Post Office, for it delivers to Kris thousands of letters addressed to Santa. The US Postal Service has therefore recognized Kris as the true Santa. The people of the USA make the decision, only the USA can truly recognize Santa for he is one of their own.

The 1994 remake of *Miracle* forces home this point with an added spiritual twist. Fred Gailey has been renamed Bryan Bedford (Dylan McDermott) in this production, but he too has the difficulty of trying to find a way of proving that Kris is the real Santa. Religion, statehood and money are combined when Bryan pulls out his pockets and sees a dollar bill with its legend 'In God We Trust'.[7] Next day Bryan presents this as evidence in court saying that the note is backed by the authority of the government of the United States, which is in turn reliant upon the consent of the people. The logic then follows that it cannot be proved conclusively that God exists and yet the people and state make a statement of belief on their banknotes. These banknotes are not invalidated by the lack of evidence; in many respects they rely on that sense of faith in order for life to be maintained. Bryan then says that the people of the USA believe Kris to be the real Santa Claus, and he then points to the vast crowds gathered outside the court as evidence of this. Accordingly Kris is the real Santa, that is evidence enough; no more tangible proof is required. So once again it is the people of America, seemingly in conjunction with the Almighty, who declare the existence of the true Santa Claus. The fascinating point in this movie is the way in which these concepts come together. This leads on to the next property of the American Santa, that of his quasi-religious/spiritual nature.

Santa Claus as Modern Christ

Belk has written that 'Santa is a secular version of Christ'. This is an interesting point but it is only partly perceptible in the movies I am examining.[8] The simple fact that two of the films under discussion have the word *Miracle* in the title implies a supernatural idea. In both versions of the *Miracle* Santa is invested with the ability to speak many languages as shown in his effortless command of Dutch in the original and his use of sign-language when he meets a deaf child in the 1994 version. Such an ability may be passed off as a sheer love of philology on Santa's part but it also gives him a certain magical quality. It seems to prove that Kris is the real Santa for he can talk to all children. Such an ability has an air of enchantment and mystery, however, rather than of genuine religion or faith.

But the remake does go on to make more obvious parallels with religious themes than the original. When Kris is taken off to Belle Vue, a home for the mentally unbalanced, the warder tells Bryan that: 'If he thinks he's Santy Claus then God Bless him!', he genuflects as he says this. The collusion of the two images subtly stresses the beatific significance of Santa, the symbol of a set of values morally greater than those that usually govern our lives. At the end of the film Bryan and Dorey (Elizabeth Perkins) are lured into church by Kris, Midnight Mass has just ended and he has arranged a wedding ceremony for them. Once again the viewer is filled with a sense of the spiritual, of the mixing of Christian imagery. At another point Kris announces:

> You don't believe in me ... I'm not just a whimsical figure who wears a charming suit and effects a jolly demeanour. I'm a symbol of the human ability to be able to suppress the selfish and the hateful tendencies that rule the major parts of our lives. If you can't believe, if you can't accept anything on faith, then you're doomed for a life dominated by doubt ... If I can make you believe then there'd be some hope for me. If I can't then I'm finished.

The tenets of Christianity, of love and selflessness, are here given expression by a figure associated with Christian mythology, but it is a figure that has become increasingly secular. The original has Kris state that: 'Christmas isn't just a day it's a frame of mind'. This statement seems to throw us back to the source of many of our modern Christmas stories, Dickens's *A Christmas Carol*. Scrooge tells the Ghost of Christmas Yet To Come: 'I will honour Christmas in my heart, and try to keep it all the year.'[9] If the spirit of Christmas is to mean anything, both agree that it should not just be for Christmas!

Faith is also very important in these films. Santa is shown to be a character that only truly appears to those who believe in him. Belief in him becomes a vital test for all other perceptions and understandings of life. In both versions of the *Miracle* the sub-plot of the slowly blossoming love story between Fred/Bryan and Doris/Dorey shows the importance of having faith. Fred grows exasperated at both Doris's lack of interest in him and her desire to ensure that her daughter, Susan (Natalie Wood), does not grow up with her head full of silly ideas about mythical characters. Reality is everything for Doris, this provides a defence against emotional wounds. Fred has so much faith in Kris that he gives up his job in order to defend him properly. Doris turns on Fred and asks him what sort of work he will get now. As a good American Fred knows that the rights of the guy on the ropes need to be defended. He says his clients will be people like Kris, 'tired of being pushed around'. His patience at an end, Fred says to her: 'Look Doris, one day you're going to find that your way of facing the realistic world just doesn't work and when you do don't overlook those lovely intangibles, you'll discover that they are the only things that are worthwhile'. When Bryan takes Susan (Mara Wilson) to see Santa he asks her whether she believes in him. She clearly has a mind closed off to the leap of imagination and faith at this point in the movie for she replies: 'Believing in myths and fantasies makes you unhappy'. Later when Bryan declares his love for Dorey for the first time she rejects him with brusque swiftness. Hurt, he tells her that 'I put my faith in you'. She replies, 'Well if that's true then you're a fool'. Love and faith, two central tenets of Christianity are consequently rejected. Scrooge does much the same thing. When he asks his nephew why he got married he tells him it was because he fell in love. '"Because you fell in love!" growled Scrooge, as if that were the only thing in the world more ridiculous than a merry Christmas.'[10] In *A Christmas Carol* ghosts effect the quasi-religious epiphany, in these movies it is Santa Claus. But there is a fundamental weakness in the test of faith in both *Miracle*s for both rely upon a material test. Susan says she will believe in Santa if she gets a daddy and a house in the country for Christmas; these tests have to be met and, of course, they are, overcoming this new Doubting Thomas. Magic and faith combine to produce a tangible, physical result, a daddy and a house. This is, perhaps, an admission that no modern audience would be made happy by an abstract ending. For such an audience a really good Christmas is about a spiritual well-being combined with a large slice of material happiness. We want to believe in something other than the rat-race of modern life but only in such a way as not to imperil our own possessions and trappings. The *Miracle*s perform this task brilliantly.

Similarly questions of faith are very important throughout *The Santa Clause*. On Christmas Eve Scott reads *A Visit from St Nicholas* to his son Charlie (Peter Boyle). Charlie is constantly badgering his father with questions as to how Santa could possibly do all these magical things. Scott tells his son: 'Charlie, sometimes believing in things means that you just believe in them'. But this seems to be rather an empty statement for when they find themselves on the roof, having accidentally killed Santa(!), it is Charlie who is first to believe and understand what is going on and Scott is bewildered. The vision and innocence of the child becomes clear, he has more understanding and therefore more power than his dad. After a very busy night delivering presents they return to the North Pole. Scott is totally dazzled and bemused, but he is so tired he gets into Santa's bed. He tells the elf that he cannot believe his eyes, she tells him that all children know that 'Seeing isn't believing. Believing is seeing.' But the most interesting definition of faith in *The Santa Clause* is the one Charlie gives to his mother's new partner, Neil. Neil (Judge Reinhold) is a psychoanalyst; he is worried by Charlie's unshakeable belief in Santa and the complexity of the stories he insists upon telling. He confronts Charlie with a barrage of highly rational questions about Santa, hoping to point out the holes in his logic. Charlie replies to each with a perfect alternative logic, culminating in his own rhetorical question, 'Have you ever seen a million dollars?' Neil says he has not, so Charlie replies with devastating finality, 'Doesn't mean to say it doesn't exist'. The logic is perfect but it is the vehicle of the parable that is important – money. The flip side of the debate over faith and innocence in these movies is the nature of American society as a capitalist, consumerist, acquisitive organism.

Santa Claus is Coming to Town

The Santa Claus movies all make reference to the nature of a capitalist society. A critique of that society is always included but it is also always a highly contained and tightly regulated critique. For, to draw on Belk once again, 'Santa Claus is to American material faith what Jesus Christ is to Christian spiritual faith'.[11] The triumph of consumerist ideals in these films comes about only once they have been questioned, and so these ideals are perpetuated by being presented in a seemingly even-handed and honest way. Consumerist and materialist themes are dragged to confession without true repentance. However, this never matters for the films are undoubtedly feel-good movies and are generally good entertainment.

It is in the original *Miracle* that the questioning of a capitalist society is most subtle, most persuasive and most entertaining. Kris states that 'for the past fifty years or more I've been getting more and more worried about Christmas, it seems to me that we're all too busy trying to beat the other fellow and making things go faster and look sharper, Christmas and I are sort of getting lost in the shuffle.' Thus a clear warning is made, that too much commercialization is a bad thing. It leads to an invidious loss of communal identity as each man seeks to out-do the other. Santa survives by being a manifestation of the communal imagination. Kris makes friends with young Alfred, one of the janitors at Macy's. Alfred is fat and slow-moving, which endears him to the audience, and he also has a good heart and likes to dress up as Santa to hand out presents at his local community centre on Christmas Eve. As an innocent he too rejects the values of the modern world. He tells Kris: 'Even in Brooklyn it's the same, don't care what Christmas stands for, just make a buck, make a buck'. When Kris remarks that Christmas is a state of mind and not just a day he adds 'and that's what's been changing'. The condemnation of the modern world by Kris reinforces the idea that he is the genuine Santa for he seems to be able to make grand historical comparisons with confidence and credibility. For those convinced that Christmas past was a far more innocent and pure affair than the orgy of materialism associated with the late-twentieth-century Christmas such lines should serve as a warning. By 1947 America was the greatest economic power in the world, it was the triumphant victor of the Second World War, capable of supplying its ever-wealthier population with more and more material possessions and comforts. The 1947 *Miracle* is about trying to recapture some of the elements of Christmas past; the Christmas we see in the film does not claim to be anything other than modern.

Similar points about a debased modern Christmas are made in both *Santa Claus* and *Ernest Saves Christmas*. In *Santa Claus* there is a great deal of emphasis laid on the fact that all the toys made at the North Pole workshops should be completed with the loving eye and attention to detail of a craftsman. It is the modern shoddiness of Patch's work (Dudley Moore) which leads to his expulsion from the workshop. Patch then offers his services to a ruthless and grasping toy manufacturer who wants to put Santa out of business by setting up Christmas II on 25 March which will bring him huge profits. Quality is of absolutely no interest and everything is sold for the highest possible mark-up. The movie is actually excruciatingly dull and one can't help but wish the venture well. But the overall moral is clear: modernity and profit-making go hand-in-hand and can be taken too far. *Ernest Saves Christmas* makes a comparable statement but in a far more anarchic way. In this movie the evil toy manufacturers arrange for Santa to be arrested and thrown into jail, giving them a free run to pursue a whole range of sick, tasteless and cheap money-spinning projects. These include making a horror film entitled *Christmas Slay*. Ernest blunders around and more by luck than judgement foils these plans and so saves Christmas from such a dreadful fate.

But these criticisms of an overly commercial Christmas do not seem to cut much North Pole ice with film critics. Many British reviewers gave the remake of *Miracle on 34th Street* short shrift. The *Financial Times* condemned it as 'a tie-in puffumentary for Christmas; an on-location hype spree in snowiest Manhattan, filled with a glutinous glow the Yuletide addicts may find appealing but no one else will.'[12] Alexander Walker, writing in the *Evening Standard*, stated that it was cynical free publicity for the stores of New York.[13] This all seems a bit odd for one of the weaknesses of the remake is that it does not make reference to any of the great stores, the names of which bring a magic and an authenticity to the original. The most perceptive comment came in *The Guardian* where it was noted that it 'is a film which tries to make as much money as possible out of Christmas while abjuring the rest of us to do no such thing'.[14] But even the original did not escape some criticisms from the British press. For a Britain suffering from rationing and shortages, desperately trying to convince itself that there might even be some merit in such an existence, the moralizing of *Miracle on 34th Street* must have seemed a bad and hypocritical joke. Back in 1947 *The Times* complained that 'the film as a whole seems expressly designed, possibly with a view to the encouragement of trade, to foster precisely those emotions which lead, fortunately only once a year, to the maximum expenditure for the minimum return'.[15] The British love of irony here appears to shade into sheer curmudgeonliness, for though the films might have these disquieting elements they surely do not override the entertainment value.

The way in which the distasteful elements of this modern, spending-fest Christmas are assuaged is via the analgesic of a caring consumerism. Nowhere is this more obvious than in the original *Miracle*. Kris acts with genuine concern for the children that sit on his knee in Macy's – well he would, wouldn't he? After all he is the real Santa. Further his concern stretches to the pockets of the parents. Instead of plugging Macy's products he recommends parents to go to other stores where the prices are better. At first this infuriates the store manager but customers tell him that they have been given the best advice possible and that Macy's provides a service to be proud of; they say they will come to Macy's more often now. After some trepidation the store manager and Doris tell Mr Macy what has happened and he decides to adopt Kris's approach as general store policy. The store obtains copies of the catalogues of all the other major New York department stores – we see those of Bloomingdale's, Gimbel's, Hearn's and Stern – and if Macy's does not stock it the assistants are told to advise the customer as to the best alternative. But, of course, this is all very good for business, and Macy's stock soars in every respect. Macy's competitors, eager not to be left out, soon follow suit, with Gimbel's being the most keen to get in on the act. Mr Gimbel and Mr Macy join forces to make generous donations to Kris, who is collecting for an x-ray machine for his old folks' home. Gimbel and Macy appear as kind, paternalist, Roosevelt-like figures. They are making money, lots of money, but are being generous with it. The unspoken point is, however, that they do so only once they realize that such an approach will make them even more money.

This theme is far less pronounced in the remake, the major problem being that Macy's refused permission for its name to be used and so the two main rivals, the fictional Cole's and Shopper's Express, are pale substitutes.[16] Instead the main theme is that of the attempt of the owner of Shopper's Express (Ackland) to drive his rival out of business. But we do see a huge 7-Up hoarding proclaiming that Kris is the real thing and the Goodyear blimp circling New York announcing the same fact. When Santa's toy list arrives at Scott Calvin's house it is delivered via a fleet of Federal Express vans. All the nice firms love Santa. Big business still supports Santa.

The Santa Clause shows the cut-throat world of toy manufacturing. But, once Scott starts to settle into his role as Santa his attitude changes. At a planning meeting for the sales drive for this year's toy, the 'Total Tank', he loses his cool. One of the executives explains that the adverts should show Santa rolling into town in his tank. We see his storyboard illustrations, which contain the totally incongruous sight of Santa in his red and white sitting in a camouflaged tank in a street full of snow and conifer trees. Scott complains vociferously and he says Santa must be in his sleigh with his reindeer. This causes some disquiet among his colleagues who are already amazed at his appearance, for magically and unstoppably Scott is taking on the attributes of Santa; his beard grows back at incredible speed and his weight has ballooned. At their working lunch he eats huge quantities of sweets and cakes and gulps down pints of milk. His complaint against the tank comes in two parts. First the lack of tradition which is coupled with the violence of the toy. He yells sarcastically, 'Santa rolling down the block in a panzer ... "Well kids I hope you've been good this year because Santa just took out the Pearson home ... INCOMING!"'. The second problem is the cheapness and shoddiness of the tank – this is similar to the ideas in *Ernest Saves Christmas* and *Santa Claus*. He tells them that the tank takes hours to build and immediately falls apart, breaking its components which then need replacing at a not insubstantial cost. His colleague replies, 'I thought that was the whole point', Scott tells them that they have responsibilities as manufacturers: 'What we got to do is develop a basic, a simple inexpensive toy that will nurture a child's thinking.'[17] In view of the fact that Disney also produced *Toy Story* (1995), and its tie-in range of expensive flashy toys, this is a rather ironic line. The message Santa delivers to the toy manufacturers of the world is clear: they have to think responsibly and imaginatively when designing new toys. Profit does not mean these qualities have to be dropped.

But, once again, some reviewers have not been able to divorce themselves from the wider realities of these movies. The *New York Times* remarked of *Santa Claus* that it was impossible to take the movie's call for a less cut-throat world seriously for the film gave heavy plugs for Bloomingdale's, McDonald's and Coca-Cola.[18] *Screen International* found *The Santa Clause* to be morally moribund: '*The Santa Clause* may have the pretension of being a modern parable, but a moral message is conspicuous by its absence'.[19]

In order to supplement the idea of a caring, but capitalist and acquisitive society the element of nostalgia is introduced. Nostalgia means a lot to these films, they wallow in it in order to help create the image of a golden age, an age that with a little effort can actually be recaptured and resuscitated, that is part of their feel-good charm. The *New York Times* felt this in 1947 when Bosley Crowther reviewed *Miracle on 34th Street*. He said it was a blast against 'all those blasé skeptics who do not believe in Santa Claus – and likewise for all those natives who have grown cynical about New York'.[20] Kris effectively turns the clock back in the film, he turns it back to an idealized New York, a romantic urban landscape, a collective fantasy of the past. *Ernest Saves Christmas* does much the same, despite its quirky approach to the subject. The fascinating slice of wistfulness is the film's use of Haddon Sundblom's paintings of Santa Claus commissioned by Coca-Cola in the 1930s. The Sundblom adverts are quite beautiful and sum up the essence of the American Christmas – consumption, joy and colour. They are also a throwback to a seemingly (and somewhat ironically) less consumerist era, when things, especially Christmas, were more joyful and more colourful.[21]

However, it is the remake of *Miracle on 34th Street* that seems to stress the nostalgia element most strongly. *Variety* noted that 'the overall effect is enjoyable and cosy like a warm fire on a cold night. It also harks back to a bygone, simpler time'.[22] The nostalgia trip is actually the cover for making a comment about modern society, especially its approach to Christmas. This is effected via the differing presentations of the two stores. Cole's is a proper, old-fashioned department store, and we see that it is a real inter-war art deco palace. Shopper's Express by contrast is a modern, 'stack it high, sell it cheap', tacky place. It is a mix of glass, metal, and cheap, pastiche masonry. It looks as faceless and dull as a mall and totally lacks the character and warmth of the department store. A comment about modern shopping habits and shop design is therefore made – the best fun is had by patronizing the stores that have a rich heritage to uphold. Throughout the movie we are told that Cole's is in trouble, it simply cannot compete with the warehouse type of store. Our sympathies are with Cole's, things may be a bit cheaper over in Shopper's Express but say the whole world was like that, how awful it would be. No, it is far better to have the sumptuousness of the genuine department store shopping experience. Just like Santa the whole thing has a baroque campness which the mall cannot imitate.

The idea that the 1930s and the immediate post-war years were the golden age of true Christmases and true, jolly Christmas shopping is upheld in other ways. When a magazine decides to interview Kris and present him as the true Santa we see that the pages are printed in art deco characters. This also has the effect of ensuring that a form of homage is paid to the original throughout. Clearly not all have felt this, for the *New York Times* stated unequivocally that 'it loses the warmth and nostalgia of the old movie'.[23] We must now move on to try to understand what is meant by that comment. Was the reviewer actually talking about the vision of American society and the American Way that the Santa movies also encapsulate?

Kris Kringle and the American Way

We have already noted that Belk has referred to Santa as being a symbol of consumerism and materialism. The Santa films also imply that this is an integral part of the American vision of the world. Gifts, presents, toys and generosity run wild in these movies, it is a vision every kid will fall in love with. Occasionally it can get too excessive, even for a society noted for its consumption. Kris tells Susan in the 1947 *Miracle* that some kids ask for things they could never use 'like real locomotives or B29's'. In *The Santa Clause* Charlie and his dad clamber on to the roof – using the ladder left by Santa and made by the 'Arose such a clatter ladder company' – and see the sleigh and reindeer. Charlie is fascinated and wants to get on with the job of being Santa, Scott tries to deflect him by telling him that they are getting the Disney Channel and this is just a Christmas gimmick. The sense of a society used to consuming big is obvious by the shot of the street: all the houses are beautifully lit for Christmas and are filled with affluent families. Reviewers could not fail to miss this aspect and perceive it as a typically American scene. Geoff Brown writing in *The Times* noted that 'the environment is the usual American dream; large houses festooned with lights, snow deep and crisp and even, families with money to burn'.[24] This was not a reaction evinced solely from a Puritanical streak in the limeys: *Variety* said of the 1994 *Miracle* that it was a warm and cosy vision, 'the portrait of a middle-class, affluent, non-ethnic America is unaltered [from the original]'.[25]

One of the other great American pastimes is also shown in these films – litigation. Court cases and legal wrangles have major roles to play in both versions of *Miracle on 34th Street* and to a lesser extent in *The Santa Clause*. The *Miracle*s also have the whiff of political intrigue and corruption about them, giving the final resolutions a Capraesque *frisson*. In the original the judge who is going to preside over whether Kris Kringle should be consigned to a mental institution is shunned by his grandchildren. His wife sides with them saying it is appalling that he should even consider locking away Santa Claus. The judge's agent has to agree, telling him it will be chucking away any chance of being re-elected. Further, a judgment against Kris will mean a domino effect, for without Santa there is no Christmas and without Christmas there is no toy industry. In turn this will bring the unions out against him. Chances of re-election, zero. As a result the judge searches for every loophole he can and is only too pleased when Fred enlists the help of the Post Office. The whole thing is handled in a very jovial way and so there is no feeling of genuine corruption. The

Monthly Film Bulletin reviewer said he was reminded strongly of Capra's *Mr Deeds Goes to Town*.²⁶ This scene is also reminiscent of the heavenly tribunal in *A Matter of Life and Death* (1946, also known in the States as *Stairway to Heaven*). David Niven defends his right to return to earth and eventually wins his case. At first it is called a 'victory for the common man', but Roger Livesey reminds them that it is the contrary, rather it is a 'victory for the uncommon man' and the law is designed to protect exactly those. Kris's right to be uncommon is upheld in *Miracle on 34th Street*.

The remake, on the other hand, takes a far darker view. Here corruption and collusion are openly shown. Lemburg, the owner of Shopper's Express, bribes lawyers and says he will fund the re-election campaign of the judge if he gets his way. It is the realization of this that leads Bryan to remark to the judge, 'it's all about money isn't it?' We have already noted how this case was resolved, by the people and their clean money. Legal matters take on a slightly different form in *The Santa Clause* for here it is the custody battle between Scott and his ex-wife, a sort of Santa versus Santa I suppose, though it is the facts Charlie tells the judge of his dad's job as Santa, and that Scott has come to the hearing looking like the great man, which persuade the judge to find in favour of his wife Laura (Wendy Crewson), on the grounds that Scott is not mentally fit.

Mental health is the next great American preoccupation to come under scrutiny in these films. Mr Sawyer is the bogus psychoanalyst in *Miracle on 34th Street*. We see that he is an absolute nobody, bullied by his wife and only happy when bossing other people around. Naturally Sawyer is an implacable enemy of Kris and tells Doris that he must be locked up. We find out that Sawyer has no genuine qualifications and just mutters psychobabble the whole time. Kris points out that he has a 'great respect for psychiatry and great contempt for meddling amateurs who go around practising it'. The outburst is provoked by Sawyer's attempts to persuade poor Alfred he has a mental problem thanks to the fact that he likes to play Santa Claus for the local children. The remake avoids many of these scenes and in so doing seems to miss out on a good chance to get in a few laughs.

The Santa Clause, however, satirizes the role of the psychoanalyst from the start; it almost seems to begin where the original *Miracle* left off. Scott constantly snipes at Neil, new partner of Scott's ex-wife, for being a psychotherapist. Scott is resentful of the fact that Neil fills Charlie's head with his jargon. When Scott has a general moan at Charlie about the situation Charlie sympathizes and tells his dad, 'it makes you want to lash out irrationally'. Later, when they have delivered the toys and Scott is in a state of shock, he tells Charlie that the first thing he will do in the morning is to have a CAT scan. The slow transformation of Scott into

Santa convinces Neil that he is indeed mentally unbalanced, he believes it shows signs of a deeply deluded character in need of serious treatment. It is this conviction which leads to the proceedings to exclude Scott from his son's life. As the audience our sympathies are, of course, with Scott for we know what is happening and how true it all is. Further, at the start of the movie Scott is so busy with his work he does not have much time for his son and his son regards staying with his dad as a miserable chore. But in becoming Santa, Scott becomes much more paternal and his relationship with his son improves enormously. Scott's incredulousness at what is happening to him is accepted with ease and aplomb by Charlie, and he resorts to Neil's phraseology, he tells Scott: 'you're in denial dad'. At the end of the film, when Scott flies over Laura and Neil's house in his sleigh, Neil simply cannot believe it and his rational mind suffers overload and breakdown. Once again Charlie digs out a solution Neil would be proud of, only this time it is turned on him: 'that's OK Neil, you're just denying you're a child'.

The problems highlighted in *The Santa Clause* are those of family life in modern America, but it is not a theme confined to this movie, the *Miracle*s are woven with the same thread. The interesting thing in the movies is the fact that the real father is not with the wife and child. To a certain extent Santa provides the universal father in all the films and inspires his earthly substitute to action. We find out that Doris is divorced only by the most indirect and subtle of signs in the original *Miracle*. One could almost be forgiven for thinking that her husband had died, or perhaps been killed in the war so fuzzily is his absence hinted at. But from the start Fred/Bryan provide excellent substitute fathers. Both films start with the Thanksgiving Day parade and Thanksgiving Day dinner. In the remake the significance of the dinner is heightened by the blessing intoned by Bryan, which gives the whole thing a religious aura with Bryan taking the role of rightful head of the family. Perhaps we should expect this from a film produced and co-written by John Hughes. His *Planes, Trains and Automobiles* (1987) similarly shows Thanksgiving to be a crucial moment for the bonding and understanding of the American family. Throughout both films there runs the problem of Doris's/Dorey's reaction to her divorce. Its effect has been to make her distrustful of instinct, intangibles and taking people on trust, all of which she imparts to her daughter. This makes her commitment to being realistic with children seem altogether unrealistic, for she has not reached this decision rationally but out of emotional shock. Fred and Doris argue about the fact that Fred has taken Susan to see Santa against her wishes. Fred says it is good for Susan to exercise her imagination. Doris turns on him saying 'And by filling them full of fairy tales they grow up considering life a fantasy instead of a reality and they keep waiting for Prince Charming to come along and he turns out to be a …' This is the clearest hint that she has been divorced and that it has hurt her deeply. Fred picks up on this and replies 'We were talking about Susie, not you'. The 1994 version has Susan asking her mother whether she believed in fantasies and myths when she was young and whether it made her unhappy. She replies 'When all the things I believed in turned out not to be true, yes I was unhappy'. Santa comes into their lives to wipe away all such fears, he is both a child and a man of incredible longevity, he is the here and now and the past and future.

The Santa Clause treats the whole thing with a great deal of humour, but this does not seek to cover up the facts of modern American family life. Scott is seen to be very laid back at the start and is very casual about his role as a father, as we have noted. The source of this is perhaps hinted at a little later in the film. When Scott grabs Santa's bag of toys it magically carries him up into the air, Charlie shouts 'Dad you're flying' to which Scott replies 'It's OK, I lived through the sixties.' Scott also shows some of the pitfalls of being a modern American trying to imitate Santa. On coming down a chimney which appears magically – the film tells us this is how Santa gets into houses without a good, old-fashioned chimney breast of their own – a little girl awakes from her slumbers and tells him he must drink the milk she has left out for him. He reluctantly does so and, pulling a face of disgust, turns round to tell her he is lactose intolerant. The next year he goes into the same house and the girl has remembered, leaving out soya milk, he pulls a face again for now he is the proper Santa he cannot stand such an appalling imitation. As with colas the message is: only ever drink the real thing.

It is the relationship with Charlie that is the all-important thing. The movie opens with Scott's late arrival home when he is supposed to have his son over for Christmas Eve. He tries to cook dinner while Charlie watches *Miracle on 34th Street* on the television, only he makes a complete turkey of it. So Christmas Eve must be spent eating out. They drive to a Denny's, Scott cheerfully announces 'It's always open … everyone likes Denny's, it's an American institution'. On going in they find it is full of Japanese businessmen and divorced dads with kids who have also made a mess of dinner, one of whom has a bandaged hand thanks to an injury sustained while trying to prepare food. It is a singularly inauspicious start to Christmas. Even when they climb on to the roof things do not improve immediately. Scott does not have the enthusiasm of Charlie and tells him that attempting to do Santa's job is a silly idea. Charlie mournfully mutters 'how come everything I wanna do is stupid?' But once Scott shows the slightest interest in doing the job their relationship begins to make a turn for the better. The Santa Clause, which is a card saying anyone taking this card and putting on the robes has accepted the job of

Santa until accident or illness prevents him from performing it any longer, has actually turned out to be their saviour.

All three movies do reach a resolution on the question of the family. The *Miracle*s show some subtle differences from each other. In the original Fred and Doris have fallen in love and clearly will get married, whereas in the remake they marry on Christmas Eve. What is more, in this version Susan had asked Kris for a little brother. On Christmas Day Susan asks where her little brother is seeing that Santa has delivered on the wedding front. The camera slowly pans down Dorey's body and the implication is obvious. Bryan says, with knowing humour for the adults in the audience, 'If you asked Kris for it you can guarantee it's already on the way'. A not-so-immaculate conception for Christmas. The other great desire of Susan is to have a house in the country. In both films beautiful up-state houses are seen, though the one in the original is slightly less ostentatious. The other side of the American dream and the nostalgia ticket is seen here, for though life in New York might be fine, especially on romantic, snowy days, the only true life is that of the fresh, clean air, of being in communion with the soil. *The Santa Clause* goes for a variant. The nuclear family is not reconstructed at the end of the movie, instead Scott accepts that Neil is a good man, who cares deeply for Charlie and his ex-wife. He tells Charlie that his new commitments as Santa mean it is best if Charlie stays with his mum and Neil. Reflecting what must be the reality for millions of divorced families he says 'we're a family, you, me, your mum ... and Neil'. This is not the idealized solution of the *Miracle*s but Charlie and his dad are back together again in their own way and Santa has made it possible. Now Scott can become the second dad for millions of kids across the globe.

The reactions of the critics to these aspects seem to fall into four categories. The first on my list is that of praise for attempting to come to terms with modern themes. The *New York Times* enjoyed *The Santa Clause* because it managed to mix fantasy with real life: 'a clever, entertaining children's film with a realistic edge and a minimum of seasonal mush ... this film's nicest touch is its sugar-free resolution of Charlie's problems with his parents'.[27] The clever mixture equally intrigued *Sight and Sound*, which called it 'a polished example of festive film-making'.[28] Even the highly conservative English *Daily Telegraph* enjoyed it, noting that 'too often Hollywood's seasonal offerings are battery-farmed turkeys in gaudy wrappings'.[29] Alexander Walker, writing in the London *Evening Standard*, did not like the film but gave grudging admiration to the way in which it tackled the world today: 'On the one hand, such perennial items as divorce, visiting rights and separating parents – not things that usually figure in seasonable fare – are cleverly inserted into the old myth, so modern kids can still believe in Santa coming down the chimney, but needn't necessarily believe in mummy and daddy always sticking together, some kind of advance, I suppose'.[30]

This brings us to the next, and contrary, reaction: that of not being modern enough. This criticism was used with most justification with reference to the remake of *Miracle on 34th Street*. It is a charming film, and Richard Attenborough is excellent as Kris but one cannot help wondering why they bothered in the first place. The critics of *Variety* and the *New York Times* provide perfect summations. The *New York Times* stated that the film 'is too timid to give the story the sharp, contemporary spin it needs'.[31] *Variety* reported that 'it's a bit disappointing that the film-makers huddle in the past rather than press on optimistically into the future'.[32]

A subtle difference can be detected in our next category, that of finding the films far too sentimental. It is interesting to note that it was British reviewers who felt this most strongly; the spirit of Scrooge simply cannot be knocked out of us. We have already come across the venomous reaction to the 1994 *Miracle* of the *Financial Times* critic. The *Guardian*'s reviewer joined him: 'sometimes, watching this feels like swimming naked through a very large bowl of molasses'.[33] Adam Mars-Jones drew upon a similar image for his review in the *Independent*. He said he had to swig vinegar throughout in order to fight off the sweet, sickly taste in his mouth.[34] *The Santa Clause* did not escape: *The Guardian* bemoaned the fact that 'the film has no more than the feeblest of imaginations … You'll have to put up with a lot of sentimental slurp on the way … and an ending at which even Tiny Tim would cringe'.[35]

Just to prove that the critics want it all ways the *Daily Mail* gives us the greatest proof in our final, and once again contradictory, category, that of the films being too modern for our own good. *The Santa Clause* was the real butt of the excellently named William Oddie's column entitled 'Even Disney is destroying family magic'.[36] The film is criticized for showing a dysfunctional America, obsessed with material goods and showing no signs of doing anything other than trying to sentimentalize these problems. No doubt a good old-fashioned Hollywood Christmas film such as the 1947 *Miracle on 34th Street* would never dream of serving up such things as divorce, being content instead merely to entertain us in a middle-of-the-road way.

But when it came to the box-office it was *The Santa Clause* that found the presents in its stocking. Released in the winter of 1994 in the States against the remake of *Miracle, The Santa Clause* out-punched it to take $100 million by Christmas.[37] But both films did far better than the poor old British *Santa Claus* of 1985, which sustained a $37 million dollar loss.[38] As for the original *Miracle*, thanks to television and its all-round quality it remains a Christmas classic. In 1985 it gained a whole new audience in the States thanks to being 'colorized' – oh dear.[39]

'Happy Christmas to all, and to all a good-night': Conclusion

The Santa movies therefore reflect American society, and so it seems many British prejudices about American society. By the same token it would be unfair to say that the movies are only applicable to the USA. They are sentimental but that does not mean to say that they do not show up the problems of society. The great strength is that everybody knows Santa Claus. He is both American and universal, even if this actually means that we are simply accepting an American figure as one of our own. He represents something larger than life but at the same time is intimately connected with the facts of life as we know them. He is magical and yet he acts like a kindly grandfather, or even a rediscovered dad. He inspires a quasi-religious faith and yet there is nothing in him that is remote or removed. His movie incarnations have shown him to be adaptable and yet capable of sustaining certain values and characteristics. It is this element which allows the Santa movie to remain a favourite. I must admit to liking the films I have covered here – well, apart from *Santa Claus* that is – they entertain me and also make me think, which is surely a perfect combination of Christmas and cinema. They are too sentimental but sentimentality has to be at the heart of these films because the season itself is a tide of sentimentality.

Notes

1. Russell Belk, 'Materialism and the American Christmas', in D. Miller (ed.), *Unwrapping Christmas* (Oxford: Clarendon Press, 1993), p 78.

2. *The Times* (11 November 1989).

3. *Sight and Sound* (January 1995).

4. *Variety* (14 November 1994).

5. Examples include Basil Rathbone (*David Copperfield* 1934 and *The Adventures of Robin Hood* 1938), George Sanders, an emigré who adopted an English persona and played gentlemanly cads and crooks (*Rebecca* 1940, *A Picture of Dorian Gray* 1945) and Alan Rickman (*Die Hard* 1988 and *Robin Hood: Prince of Thieves* 1991).

6. The mad plot of *Ernest Saves Christmas* starts with Santa living at the North Pole. But he soon decides he is too old to continue working and considers retiring from his job. He then takes the well-worn track to Florida believing, like millions of Americans, that he will enjoy his retirement far more in the warmth of the sunshine state.

7. It is interesting to note that Bob Clark's 1984 film, *A Christmas Story*, is actually based on the works of the journalist and broadcaster Jean Shepherd. The title of Shepherd's autobiographical memories of Christmases in Cleveland, Ohio, in the late 1940s is *In God We Trust. All Others Pay Cash*. (New York: Doubleday 1966).

8. Belk, 'Materialism and the American Christmas', in Miller (ed.), p 83.

9. Charles Dickens, *A Christmas Carol* (London, 1843), p 107.

10. Ibid., pp 14–15.

11. Belk, 'Materialism and the American Christmas', in Miller (ed.), p 85.

12. *Financial Times* (1 December 1994).

13. *Evening Standard* (1 December 1994).

14. *The Guardian* (1 December 1994).
15. *The Times* (29 September 1947).
16. For Macy's refusal to give permission see *New York Times* (11 November 1994).
17. A similar plot is played out in the Tom Hanks vehicle *Big* (1988). He has an inventive, child's mind hidden in an adult's body, frustrating the pure profit ideals of his colleagues in the toy industry and forcing them to build better, more challenging toys. In this movie too, genuine New York locations are stressed: the toy shop is actually F.A.O. Schwarz.
18. *New York Times* (27 November 1985).
19. *Screen International* (2 December 1994).
20. *New York Times* (5 June 1947).
21. For Santa and Coca-Cola see Belk, 'Materialism and the American Christmas', in Miller (ed.), pp 75–104.
22. *Variety* (14 November 1994).
23. *New York Times* (18 November 1994).
24. *The Times* (30 November 1995).
25. *Variety* (14 November 1994).
26. *Monthly Film Bulletin* (July 1947).
27. *New York Times* (11 November 1994).
28. *Sight and Sound* (December 1995).
29. *Daily Telegraph* (1 December 1995).
30. *Evening Standard* (30 November 1995).
31. *New York Times* (18 November 1994).
32. *Variety* (14 November 1994).
33. *The Guardian* (1 December 1994).
34. *Independent* (1 December 1994).
35. *The Guardian* (30 November 1995).
36. *Daily Mail* (20 December 1995).
37. See *Screen International* and *Hollywood Reporter* (December 1994) for details.
38. British Film Institute Catalogue.
39. *Hollywood Reporter* (22 November, 5 December 1985).

7

You Better Watch Out: Christmas in the Horror Film

Kim Newman

Then Herod, when he saw that he was mocked of the wise men, was exceeding wroth, and sent forth, and slew all the children that were in Bethlehem, and in all the coasts thereof, from two years old and under, according to the time which he had diligently enquired of the wise men.

Then was fulfilled that which was spoken by Jeremy the prophet, saying,

In Rama was there a voice heard, lamentation, and weeping and great mourning, Rachel weeping for her children, and would not be comforted, because they are not.

The Gospel of St Matthew (2: 16–18)

The story of 'the first Noel' is so steeped in violence that no film version of the Nativity has been able to cope with it. As in *Schindler's List* (1993), the story has to concentrate on the few who escaped rather than the many who were slain, so the flight into Egypt gets far more attention than the wholesale murder of every baby in Judea. The slaughter of the innocents – a title used without resonance by James Glickenhaus for a run-of-the-mill 1993 serial killer movie about a maniac who has got his Testaments scrambled and is building an Ark – remains one of the cinema's great taboos, shockingly violated by the likes only of transgressive Jed Johnson (*Andy Warhol's Bad*, 1977) and Peter Greenaway (*The Baby of Mâcon*, 1993). Yet, this literally inconceivable atrocity is at the heart of Christmas.[1]

Charles Dickens's *A Christmas Carol* (1843), which (taking cues from German festival practices imported to Britain by Prince Albert) more or less established the institution of Christmas as celebrated in Britain and America, is as much concerned with the excluded, the miserable, the emotionally poverty-stricken and the dead as it is with merry-makers, puddings and parties. 'Every fool who prattles of Christmas should be buried with a sprig of holly through his own heart,' sneers Ebenezer Scrooge at the outset. Regardless of the never-quite-convincing happy ending, the regularly filmed tale is responsible for the association of Yuletide with ghosts.[2] Though the term 'Dickensian Christmas' came to be associated with holly and family gatherings and a happy exchange of presents, *A Christmas Carol* also sets its most depressing moments – Scrooge's vision of his unloved, lonely death, picked over by scavengers – at Christmas. Dickens' last (unfinished) novel, *The Mystery of Edwin Drood* (1870), contains a potent antidote to the nostalgic glow of *Carol* as a dere-lict woman passes around a succession of institutions on Christmas Day, forever shut out from any hope of cheer.

The instant success of *A Christmas Carol*, which Dickens followed up with a series of less-remembered Christmas stories (*The Chimes*, 1844, *The Cricket on the Hearth*, 1845), further established the linkage of the season with tales of the supernatural. In the 1890s, M.R. James, provost of Eton, read his ghost stories aloud to the pupils as a Christmas treat; and, in the 1970s, the BBC picked up the tradition by presenting an annual adapta-tion of James in a slot known as *A Ghost Story for Christmas*, which slipped a few quiet chills and a strange sense of *fin-de-siècle* despair into a schedule otherwise concerned with Christmas episodes of soaps and sitcoms and the regular Morecambe and Wise special. James's stories tend not to have Christmas settings, but were produced especially for the season, a very specific and double-edged sort of present. One wonders how many of his pupils hated them, and had nightmares which spoiled their holidays; at least as many, probably, as those who took a nasty delight in faces sucked off the bone and wet tendrils of ghost-plasm snaking out from under the pews.

The holiday is, of course, associated with miracles, but these have tended in the cinema to be dark miracles at least as often as they have been happy. The counter-programming use of a Yuletide setting for a grim story is a basic bit of irony that always seems to play: *Die Hard* (1988) would hardly be as suspenseful if Bruce Willis were trapped in a skyscraper with a gang of ruthless terrorists during a Thanksgiving party, and the Deanna Durbin vehicle *Christmas Holiday* (1944) – in which she discovers that her husband (Gene Kelly) is a murderous psychopath – would be a lot less poignantly creepy if it were set over the Easter weekend.[3] The use of holiday trappings for a horror movie made John Carpenter's *Halloween* (1977) a hit, but the genre got round to its own scary holiday only after it had deployed tinsel and cheer for contrast in Theodore Gershuny's *Silent Night, Bloody Night* (1973) and Bob Clark's *Black Christmas* (1972). Carpenter's film was (perhaps amazingly) the first to make much of pumpkin lanterns, trick or treating, childhood ghost stories and the licensed annual anarchy of All Hallows' Eve, but Clark's precursor manages to get its chills among the supposedly delightful trappings of the other major winter holiday.

Clark, who also made the unsentimental *A Christmas Story* (1983), wins points for intercutting an angelic choir of doorstop carol-singers with the Dario Argento-style stabbing of Margot Kidder. Set in a sorority house stalked by a maniac (it uses the 'prank phone calls that turn out to be coming from the attic' urban legend), *Black Christmas* (aka *Stranger in the House*) also trips a minor echo of young Scrooge's primal sense of exclusion (which at least some of James's initial audience must have shared) by making the heroine (Olivia Hussey) one of those lonely, family-free souls who must stay at school over the long holidays. Even before the killer has her in his sights, she is a victim of the cruelty of Christmas, which sends suicide rates soaring annually as the orgy of family togetherness emphasizes how firmly many people are shut out in the cold snow by the happy spectacle glimpsed through the windows of well-lit houses or on television. Clark, of course, has the subjective camera prowl around the sorority, peeking in at the to-be-killed girls, but there is at least as much envy as voyeurism in the use of this device in this instance.

The twentieth-century, purely cinematic, equivalent of *A Christmas Carol* is Frank Capra's dark-hued masterwork *It's a Wonderful Life* (1948), another work whose hard-won happy ending does not really detract from the long, miserable path taken to get there. One of the most referenced and quoted movies of all time, *It's a Wonderful Life* has come to stand for Christmas and, as such, has featured in many works that set out to attack the institution with a savagery unmediated by Capra's bedrock sense of community and family. The single decent sequence in Jim Wynorski's *976 EVIL II* (1991) has the victim sucked into a TV set during a screening of the Capra movie and then suffering when the wielder of the remote control zaps between it and *Night of the Living Dead* (1968), yielding a bizarre black and white melange of the two pictures as the celebrating folks of Bedford Falls are transformed into George Romero's gut-chomping zombies. The feature-length finale of *Dallas* (1991) also plays variations on *It's a Wonderful Life* as the suicidal J.R. Ewing (Larry Hagman) is shown how the city and the supporting cast would be if he had not been born; the angelic visitor Adam (Joel Grey) was finally shown to be not a heavenly messenger but a demonic trickster and the ambiguous finale suggests that his actual mission has been to cause rather than prevent a suicide. That such a modern myth could sustain twisted counter-readings reveals a great deal about its uncertainty.

A more elaborate, horrific revision of Capra's tone is Joe Dante's *Gremlins* (1984), a gleeful trashing of everything America holds sacred about Christmas, which it conflates with the orgiastic abandon of a Roman Saturnalia. As a horde of self-generating toothy monsters wreak havoc in a small town patterned on Bedford Falls, the plot itself collapses as Dante and the gremlins go out of their way to attack such American Christmas sacred cows as *Phil Spector's Christmas Album* and Walt Disney's *Snow White and the Seven Dwarfs*. There is a tension between the overlapping but at-odds world-views of co-executive producer Steven Spielberg, whose small towns and suburbs are havens of eccentricity and bedrock American virtues, and Dante, who cannot see a Norman Rockwell illustration without adding the fanged monsters chewing at the foundations. The Kingston Falls of *Gremlins* is a Recession-era update of Bedford Falls, with snowbound streets and genially chintzy decorations, and Capra is further evoked by the positioning of a portrait of his favourite plutocrat villain Edward Arnold as the late husband of the witchlike wealthy harridan Mrs Deagle.

Kingston Falls evokes a Capra Christmas only to launch a violent assault on everything connected with the institution. Santa Claus is throttled with fairy lights while a couple of cops refuse to get involved, and even posting a Christmas card proves fatal thanks to a gremlin lurking in the mailbox. And the major orgies of devastation are all located in areas of American life familiar from ad lay-outs: the kitchen, where a housewife uses her blender and microwave to fend off the monsters; the living room, where a decorated Christmas tree seems to come to libidinous life; and the shopping mall, where toys, weapons and tools are interchangeable and the most evil gremlin gets to wield a chainsaw and wear a Santa hat. Dante even goes so far as to condemn the very medium that had popularized *It's a Wonderful Life* (which is excerpted), launched the career of Steven Spielberg and fed the imaginations of the movie brat generation, when Keye Luke upbraids the regular American family who have corrupted the childlike Mogwai with 'you taught him to watch *television*!' That *Gremlins* has a depth beyond mere childish cruelty is displayed by the keynote 'why I hate Christmas' speech delivered by heroine Phoebe Cates[4], who reminisces about her father's ghastly death while trying to climb down a chimney with presents.

Because he is the figure who encapsulates all modern meanings of Christmas, even taking aboard the holiday's pre-Christian pagan aspects as a winter solstice festival, Santa Claus – aka Father Christmas, Saint Nick, Kris Kringle, etc – has come in for a lot of grief in anti-Christmas movies. Santa has been forced to duel with demons in the Mexican *Santa Claus* (1959), been abducted by aliens in *Santa Claus Conquers the Martians* (1964), evicted by Rossano Brazzi in *The Christmas That Almost Wasn't* (1966), got mixed up in a drug bust in *The French Connection* (1971), and was zombified by a master villain from the future and gunned down by Tim Thomerson in *Trancers* (1986). The most excessive anti-Santa movie is the cheapjack British slasher picture *Don't Open 'til Christmas* (1984), in which a knife-wielding maniac (Alan Lake), traumatized because he literally saw Mama kissing Santa Claus, murders a succession of deadbeats and winos dressed up as Father Christmas. Even supposedly pro-Santa films – the ghastly *Santa Claus* (1986), the surprisingly dour *One Magic Christmas* (1985) and the negligible *Ernest Saves Christmas* (1988) – have made a fairly feeble case for this beloved old figure of universal benevolence and charity.

It is no surprise, therefore, that Saint Nick should strike back, creating the most familiar of all Christmas-themed horror sub-genre movies, the psycho Santa slasher film. Many children are disturbed by the whole idea of an all-powerful character who can get into their house at night and knows everything about them, and many versions of the tradition[5] have a nasty moral undertone, with Santa punishing bad children as determinedly as he rewards good ones ('he knows when you've been bad or good, so be good for goodness' sake'). Obviously, the idea of Father Christmas as a homicidal maniac strikes a deep chord, for it has been used over and over again. The perfect touchstone of the genre is the first episode of Freddie Francis's *Tales From the Crypt* (1972), adapted from a horror comic by Johnny Craig ('All Through the House', *The Vault of Horror*, 1954). Joan Collins has just bludgeoned her husband to death under the Christmas tree when an escaped madman dressed as Santa begins to terrorize the neighbourhood. The inevitable ironic twist has Collins cover up her crime and barricade herself indoors, only for her angelic daughter (Chloe Franks) to let Santa into the house to strangle her. With a wonderfully bitchy/distressed central performance and wickedly ironic use of decorations and carols to contrast with the slobbering horror, this mini-movie encapsulates the Christmas slasher. When Robert Zemeckis remade 'All Through the House' in 1989, as the pilot for the *Tales From the Crypt* TV series, he stuck a little closer to the stylized comic look, with Larry Drake as a caricature rotten-teethed madman, but added little to the definitive version.

More psycho Santas turn up in *The Silent Partner* (1978), with Christopher Plummer as an especially fiendish bank robber in Father Christmas drag; the sorority-set slasher *To All a Good Night* (1983), which features several red-suited madmen; and the obscure anthology *Campfire Tales* (1990), in which an axe-wielding 'Satan' Claws punishes a wicked youth. The best of the cycle is Lewis Jackson's *You Better Watch Out* (1980, aka *Christmas Evil* and *Murder in Toyland*), with Brandon Maggart as the most sympathetic of the psycho Santas. A put-upon employee of a rapacious toy company, Maggart lives for Christmas and seems to be the only person in the snowbound city actually to believe in goodwill rather than greed. All year he keeps tabs on the local children to see if they've been naughty or nice and, on Christmas Eve, driven mad by the cynical exploitation he sees all around, he gets into his padded red suit and takes to the streets as a pro-Noel vigilante. Besides giving away toys embezzled from his employers to a group of handicapped kids, Maggart uses a lead soldier to gouge out the eye of a Christmas-hating lout and manages to charm children even while he is killing their rotten father with a sharp ornament. This odd mix of psycho wish-fulfillment, urban sleaze and strange innocence climaxes with a touch of *Miracle on 34th Street* as Maggart's van crashes off an embankment during a police chase and takes to the skies, flying northwards while sleighbells jingle on the soundtrack. Jackson's movie, produced by toy tycoon Ed Pressman, is still underrated, though its admirers include John Waters, who said 'I wish I had kids. I'd make them watch it every year, and if they didn't like it, they'd be punished'.[6]

American parent groups cannot have been paying attention, for they ignored ten years of psycho Santas and waited until Charles E. Sellier's feeble *Silent Night, Deadly Night* (1984) to complain about the ill-effects on children of depicting such a sacred institution as Father Christmas as a homicidal maniac. This entirely conventional and dull picture has a child witness his parents' murder by a mugger dressed as Santa and growing up to be a similarly-disguised maniac (Robert Brian Wilson) who commits Christmas-themed killings such as impaling Linnea Quigley on reindeer antlers. With a few tough lines ('it's not all phony sentiment, a lot of it is genuine greed') to add a touch of banal social comment, this by-the-book holiday horror would have sunk without trace were it not for the artificial controversy raised by the protests. However, because of the fuss, *Silent Night, Deadly Night* was the modest hit *You Better Watch Out* deserved to be, and had become a direct-to-video franchise.

The first sequel, Lee Harry's *Silent Night, Deadly Night Part II* (1987) uses over half an hour of footage from the original but surprisingly throws in a few almost interesting, semi-comic vigilante sequences as the original madman's newly afflicted brother (Eric Freeman) takes up the axe and murders numerous irritating characters, including a loudmouth who has the temerity to chatter in the cinema. The three subsequent sequels leave the psycho theme and even the notional Christmas backdrop to concentrate on more science-fictional or occult plot premises: Monte Hellman's *Silent Night, Deadly Night 3: Better Watch Out* (1989) is about mind control and Frankensteinian mad science, and features Santa Claus only as an incidental victim, while Brian Yuzna's *Silent Night, Deadly Night 4: Initiation* (1990) and *Silent Night, Deadly Night 5: The Toy Maker* (1991) feature an insect cult and animated playthings.[7]

Even less-known than *You Better Watch Out* is Rene Manzor's *36:15 – Code Père Noel* (1989), a derivative but spirited French variation on the formula. A fairy-tale action movie made with a gallic post-Besson/Beneix verve, this has a rich kid hero (Alain Musy) who kits himself up Rambo-style to adventure with his dog in a rambling, castle-like home. He hooks up through his computer with a psychotic (Patrick Florsheim) who has a Santa complex, attracting the madman on Christmas Eve, when he has staked out the fireplace to see whether Father Christmas really does come down the chimney. Florsheim arrives with murder in mind, and the kid uses all his ingenuity to protect his elderly grandfather.[8] Like Lewis Jackson, Manzor has a fairly complex attitude to the holidays, refraining from the utter cynicism of the *Silent Night, Deadly Night* films to offer a genuine commitment to the magic of present-giving (the film is all about unwrapping toys) and observing even the most intense life-or-death struggles through frost-rimmed windows, with the jingle of sleigh-bells and the glitter of tinsel well in evidence.

Though indebted to *Santa Claus Conquers the Martians* and the holiday perennial *How the Grinch Stole Christmas* (1966, from the 1957 book by Dr Seuss), the last word on the scary side of the holiday must be Henry Selick's *The Nightmare Before Christmas*.[9] In another example of Santa-bashing, the rather grumpy Father Christmas is kidnapped again, and replaced by the 'Pumpkin King' Jack Skellington (voiced by Chris Sarandon, sung by composer Danny Elfman), whose regular job is the overseeing of Halloween. With the best of intentions, Jack distorts the spirit of Christmas by leaving scary presents for all the children in the world, though the film – like so many Christmas-themed horrors – takes a real delight in subversion. As kids are terrorized by their presents, Selick and Tim Burton deliver a series of gruesome, Charles Addams-like spot gags[10] that are, of course, far more appealing to an audience than heart-warming scenes of happy children enjoying themselves would have been.

The sweetness is acid-edged, but the point is well taken, as it is in most of the films covered in this study. The celebration of Christmas as decreed by Clement Clarke Moore, Charles Dickens, Norman Rockwell (and the Coca-Cola company) and Walt Disney Enterprises is for many a tyrannical regime, emphasizing the shortfall of their own family lives (or lack thereof). Despite the good cheer around the Cratchit table, this fantasy Christmas is available only to those who have the money (and room) for a full-sized tree and a turkey dinner for the whole family. Much of the appeal of the Christmas-themed horror movie is that this illusion is shredded, and those smug, mostly affluent celebrants are assaulted by primal forces, be they gremlins or Santa psychos, which embody the resentment that must be felt towards them by audiences who, even subliminally, cannot look at an idealized representation of Christmas without sparking associative thoughts of malice, horror and shivers.

Notes

1. Arthur C. Clarke's story 'The Star', dramatized on the revived series *Twilight Zone* in 1985, goes even further. In the future, space exploration reveals that the Star of Beth-lehem was a nova that wiped out an ancient extra-terrestrial civilization.

2. See Chapter 1 for more on *A Christmas Carol.*

3. The least Christmassy holiday thriller is Alfred Hitchcock's *Psycho* (1960), which opens on December the 11th and has a plot that takes place over two weeks or so. Under-standably, the Bates Motel has no Christmas decorations or cards on view, but surely the home of the small-town Sheriff should be dressed for the season? Other holiday-set thrillers, war films and black comedies, mostly with soft-soap endings, include *Home for the Holidays* (1972), *Merry Christmas, Mr Lawrence* (1983), *Bloodbeat* (1985), *Dead-Bang* (1989), *A Midnight Clear* (1992) and *The Ref* (1994).

4. This incident may be derived from a singleton cartoon by Gahan Wilson. See Les Daniels, 'Christmas', in *The BFI Companion to Horror*, ed. Kim Newman (London: BFI/ Cassell, 1996).

5. The folkloric version of the myths of Santa Claus and Father Christmas, who were once less interchangeable than they have become, was set in stone by Clement Clarke Moore's poem 'A Visit From St. Nicholas' (1823), more commonly known as ''Twas the Night Before Christmas'.

6. John Waters, 'Why I Love Christmas', *National Lampoon*, December 1985; reprinted in *Crackpot: The Obsessions of John Waters* (London: Fourth Estate, 1988).

7. Because of the controversy, the first film was banned on video in the United Kingdom. Only the last two sequels have been released here, with the series titles subtracted, as *Bugs* and *The Toy Maker.*

8. It is possible that this strong little film did not get an international showing because it was strip-mined by John Hughes for *Home Alone* (1990), which is essentially the same film but with the genuinely dangerous psycho Santa replaced by a pair of comic bunglers.

9. There is some attempt to list the film under the title *Tim Burton's The Nightmare Before Christmas*, but this involves roping in a possessory credit (Burton was a producer and designed some of the creatures) merely because it is on the same card as the title. The film should no more be indexed under 'T' than *Goldfinger* should be filed under 'I' because the card on screen reads *Ian Fleming's Goldfinger* (rather, Ian Fleming's *Goldfinger*). Burton's purest, grimmest take on Christmas comes in *Batman Returns* (1992) in which the Penguin (Danny DeVito) tosses Gotham City's Ice Princess off a roof and she plunges to her death in a giant cake.

10. The opening of *The Addams Family* (1991) is based on the famous cartoon of the gruesome family on the point of pouring boiling oil on to the heads of a party of merry carol-singers.

8

'Peace on Earth, Goodwill to All Men': The Depiction of Christmas in Modern Hollywood Films

Rowana Agajanian

There are a surprising number of 1980s and 1990s Hollywood films that offer significant representations of Christmas for detailed analysis. But, for the purposes of this study, I have selected eight popular Hollywood films with Christmas narratives: *A Christmas Story* (1983), *Lethal Weapon* (1987), *Die Hard* (1988) and the sequel, *Die Hard 2: Die Harder* (1990), *Home Alone* (1990) and *Home Alone 2: Lost in New York* (1992), *The Long Kiss Goodnight* (1996), and *Jingle All the Way* (1996).

The eight films represent two distinct genres: the children's or family entertainment film and the action-adventure film. Five of the eight, *Lethal Weapon*, *Die Hard*, *Die Hard 2*, *Home Alone* and *Home Alone 2*, made the top ten list of box-office hits of their year in the USA.[1] The remaining three fared less well at the box-office and were marked by the press as 'Christmas turkeys'. Contrary to expectations and despite their narrative setting, not all were released at Christmas. *Lethal Weapon* and *Die Hard* were released in the USA in March and July respectively. Nevertheless, the Christmas vacations along with spring and summer have traditionally been viewed by the film industry as the time to release blockbuster films, particularly family entertainment films. But much has changed in the industry in the last twenty years, both in terms of its structure and in terms of its products. During this period there were numerous upheavals among the Hollywood majors: Twentieth Century Fox, Warner Brothers, MCA/Universal, Paramount Pictures, MGM, United Artists, and Columbia. Many entered into lucrative national and international deals in order to take advantage of the changing marketplace both at home and abroad. With the power to market and distribute world-wide, it is not surprising that the majority of the films in my selection were produced either by or in conjunction with the majors cited above. Twentieth Century Fox Film Corporation was responsible for no less than four of the films chosen: *Die Hard*, *Home Alone*, *Home Alone 2: Lost in New York*, and *Jingle All the Way*. MGM/UA Entertainment was responsible for *A Christmas Story*, and Warner Brothers for *Lethal Weapon*.

Average production costs rose considerably from $6 million in 1979 to $24 million in 1990. *Die Hard 2: Die Harder* cost a record-breaking $70 million to produce in 1990. By 1996, this sum no longer raised eyebrows in Hollywood; even a relatively small family entertainment film such as *Jingle All the Way* cost $75 million to produce.[2] By the 1990s the average movie needed to take two and a half times its production costs (including prints, distribution and promotion) to break even. With the introduction of VHS and Betamax recording systems in 1976, new and highly lucrative markets were established with home video sales and rentals. In addition, the introduction of cable and satellite film channels created a combination that would revolutionize home viewing in the next two decades. In 1979, the average movie could already expect to earn 20 per cent of its receipts from video and television sales, 80 per cent from its theatrical release. By 1988 a staggering 50 per cent of US households owned VCRs. By 1993 the video and television markets had turned the earnings equation almost on its head, now accounting for a massive 65 per cent of a movie's earning with the theatrical release accounting for only 20 per cent, and a further 15 per cent attributed to foreign theatrical exhibition.[3] Thus films no longer relied on their theatrical release for the bulk of their returns, and though seasonal releases were still evident, film producers began to make films with a view to capturing the domestic audience both in the cinema and at home.

In 1967, US cinema attendance figures rose for the first time since 1947. With massive investment in new cinemas, in particular the new multiplex structures in the 1970s and 1980s, there seemed to be a revival in cinema-going. Yet by the early 1990s the figures were once again cause for concern as David J. Fox of the *Los Angeles Times* reported. Fox observed that most Hollywood studios were trying to combat the decline in theatre attendance by making 'transgenerational' movies with stars that would appeal to multiple age groups, such as Arnold Schwarzenegger,

Harrison Ford and Macaulay Culkin; even comic cult heroes such as the Super Mario Brothers and Batman.[4]

Although in the 1980s and 1990s films were still being made in the traditional Hollywood genres, as Joseph Sartelle points out 'they coexisted with an explosion of new categories which made use of older elements by recombining them in various ways'.[5] A prime example of this is *Die Hard*, where the action-adventure epic is combined with the disaster movie, a cop thriller with Western motifs, and an inter-racial buddy film with a touch of marital discord/romance thrown in for good measure. Moreover, film-makers needed to adjust their products to attract, in terms of viewing expectations, an increasingly sophisticated younger audience. By 1991, according to box-office statistics, 56 per cent of the audience were under the age of 30.[6]

Before analysing the films themselves it would be useful to begin with a summary of images and concepts associated with a modern Christmas, many of them stemming from the Victorian era. Today Christmas conjures up images of Christmas trees, decorations and lights, presents, snow and snowmen, Santa Claus and reindeer, food, the nativity, church, carol-singing, cards, pantomimes and parades, and, depending on age and religious beliefs, the items on this list vary in importance. Christmas has also come to signify family gatherings, cosy homes, a focus on the children, humanitarianism toward the under-privileged and vulnerable, and a feeling of nostalgia for good times past. However, the more negative associations with Christmas include resentment toward the increasing commercialism surrounding the festival, and the escalating expenditure on food, drink and particularly presents.

So how has Hollywood cinema portrayed Christmas in the 1980s and 1990s? Do they offer a mixture of the traditional and the modern Christmas? Is the iconography of Christmas trees, presents and so on used as one expects? Is it a utopian world that celebrates the festival or a dystopian one that inverts the ideals of Christmas? Similarly, is it a realistic one or a fantastical Christmas? Do these films contain religious messages or are they purely secular stories? What do they tell us about the culture that produced them? Covering two distinct genres, the films seem to be aimed at specific audiences. The family entertainment film is in effect designed for children, and the action thriller expects to attract a predominantly male audience. Again, this begs the question; do these categories reveal significantly different images of Christmas? Do they simply reflect the desires or fears of their targeted audience?

Finally, screen violence has been the focus of attention from film critics, academics and related experts for some time, the 1980s and 1990s being no exception. Certainly, what struck me initially about these films are the contradictory messages inherent in the majority. The idyllic domestic or work scene is disrupted not simply by the chaos of Christmas shopping, but by robbers, drug gangs, spies, and a range of unsavoury characters. Indeed, all eight films contain weapons and violence; whether slapstick or real, it is incongruous to the Christmas message of 'peace and goodwill to all men' with which we are so familiar. Therefore it would seem appropriate to take a look at this issue in more depth.

The Family Entertainment Film – Fun for All the Family?

A Christmas Story, Home Alone, Home Alone 2 and *Jingle All The Way* were all intended as Christmas theatrical releases. Of course these films would be competing with the ubiquitous Disney offering, which in the last few decades has almost become synonymous with Christmas despite the lack of festive stories.[7] Nevertheless, they do contain stories about good versus evil, good triumphing after much tribulation. More conspicuous by their absence are biblical stories produced for the big screen during this period. Some television companies have ventured to make television features, particularly animations aimed at the child audience. But the story of the nativity has failed to feature in a motion picture for several decades now.[8] Few of the films within our selection make any reference to the biblical event on which these celebrations are based. None of the families in my selection are shown making a visit to church, with the exception of

Nostalgia for good times past, *A Christmas Story* (1983) set in Indiana in the 1940s.

young Kevin McCallister who seeks refuge from his foes by hiding in the nativity display and who later pays a visit to listen to carol practice. On the whole these are secular stories. However some, including the action-thrillers, do contain a degree of religious symbolism.

A Christmas Story, directed by Bob Clark and released in the USA in November 1984, tells the story of eight-year-old Ralphie who dreams of getting a Red Ryder air rifle for Christmas. Set in the 1940s, Ralphie comes from an average middle-class family living in an Indiana suburb. The humour is provided, in the main, by Ralphie's fantasy life and his various manoeuvres to secure the prized rifle. For example, Ralphie conjures up in his imagination a scene where he defends the family and the homestead from marauding bandits. With his Red Ryder rifle and dressed in full cowboy regalia he expertly picks off the villains. Clark employs a mixture of slapstick and silent comedy styles to enhance the humour of this episode. However, his parents' idiosyncrasies also provide cause for mirth, especially when his father wins the prize of an electric lamp in a competition. The lamp is shaped in the sensuous form of a lady's leg, and much to his mother's dismay his father insists on displaying it in full view in the front room window. Fortunately, Ralphie's mother manages to dispatch the offending object in time to erect and decorate the traditional Christmas tree. Decorating the Christmas tree is a generic feature shared by all the family entertainment films discussed here. In *Home Alone*, Kevin is shown selecting and cutting down a small treetop from his garden in order to decorate his house. The tree becomes a symbol round which Kevin fights to protect hearth and home. In *Jingle All the Way*, Howard insists it is his job, as head of the family, to put the Christmas star on the tree and resents anybody, especially his neighbour Ted, usurping his role both physically and metaphorically.

For a more traditional story it is surprising that some of the seasonal icons in *A Christmas Story* are reversed. For example, Santa Claus and the elves prove positively nightmarish with their heavy-handed tactics. Also the Parker's Christmas dinner is ruined as the neighbour's dogs invade the house and devour the cooked turkey. As a result the family have to eat in the only restaurant open on Christmas Day – the Chinese. Nevertheless, the Christmas dinner of duck is a joyous occasion, especially as the Chinese waiters serenade the Parker family with Christmas tunes.

Although the film is made for children, its real appeal is for their parents who immerse themselves in feelings of nostalgia for this period. Young Ralphie provides the visual focus but adult Ralphie, who recounts his childhood via a voice-over narration, provides the real point of view. The film opens with him reminiscing about his old home. But this is not a picture-postcard image of Christmas in Indiana for the background shot is of an industrial site and the Parker family, albeit comfortable, are hardly well off. Yet, the film takes great pains to focus on the closeness of the family unit and the narrative closes with the parents sitting together beside the Christmas tree watching the snow falling outside whilst the children are tucked up in bed clutching their favourite presents. But these are not presents on the Christmas list of the contemporary child audience. Indeed children from the 1980s would not be able to identify with Ralphie's desire for a Red Ryder gun. Far more likely they would be looking for the latest video games. Similarly, the radio that plays such a central role in the Parker's family life would not strike a chord in the contemporary child audience since it has been supplanted not only by the television but also by the computer screen and all its accessories. Still, other aspects such as the schoolroom antics and bullying would have some resonance with young audiences whatever the era. Perhaps it is just as well the adult jokes, such as the fetishist appeal of the electric leg lamp, would not have been picked up by the child audience. With this kind of content and some explicit language, mainly from Ralphie's father, the film was given a 'PG' rating by the Motion Picture Association of America (MPAA).[9] And despite its setting in the 1940s, it is a surprisingly secular story, for one would expect the Parkers to be depicted as paying the customary visit to church. Indeed, there is only the smallest degree of religious sentiment in the film with the brief inclusion of some carol-singing at the Christmas parade.

On both sides of the Atlantic the film received a mixed response. The *Variety* critic found the story unrealistic and unlikely to appeal to kids: '*A Christmas Story* is a version of Christmas as it exists only in the imagination. Though it is told through the eyes of a child, adults should find more to respond to in this nostalgic look at growing up in the 1940s'.[10] But Andrew Sarris of *Village Voice* called it, 'the best Christmas qua Christmas entertainment I've seen in years', and praised the creative performances given by Melinda Dillon and Darren McGavin as the Parker parents and Peter Billingsley as the bespectacled boy who wants a Red Ryder rifle for Christmas.[11] The British press too offered a mixed response. Ian Christie of the *Daily Express* said: '*A Christmas Story* should be avoided if you wish to have fond feelings towards children during the forthcoming festive season'.[12] On the other hand, David Castell of the *Daily Telegraph* felt that the film was 'a trifle unfocused, yet it touches so many nerves and dips into so many memory banks that you are quickly won over by its easy, unforced charm'.[13]

What is most interesting about this film and indicative of things to come is the film's soundtrack which contains a mixture of traditional and popular music. For example, the numbers range from traditional songs such as 'Silent Night' and 'Jingle Bells', to more contemporary popular songs performed by Bing Crosby such as 'Santa Claus is Comin' To

Town' and 'It's Beginning To Look Like Christmas'. From now on it would seem compulsory for films to enforce the season by using familiar Christmas songs and tunes. Some films, such as *Home Alone 2* and *Jingle All the Way,* employ these Christmas numbers in a literal way. For example, when Kevin misses his mother the soundtrack plays 'Please Come Home For Christmas' and when Howard is shown rushing around town on Christmas Eve in search of a specific toy, the soundtrack plays 'Run, Rudolf, Run'. Moreover, the vast majority of these popular tunes are from the 1950s and early 1960s.[14] The regularity with which these songs appear would suggest that the Christmas film of the 1980s and 90s has its own 'musical' iconography. *Die Hard* particularly emphasizes the need for familiarity with musical tradition when McClane fails to recognize that the rap music playing in the limousine is in fact the latest Christmas song ('Christmas in Hollis' performed by Run DMC). Both *Die Hard* films prefer the more traditional sound of Vaughn Monroe's 'Let It Snow! Let It Snow! Let It Snow!' Moreover, in these Christmas films it would seem that many of the traditional values invoked by the music are from America's golden period – the 1950s – rather than the Victorian era.

In contrast to the box-office failure of *A Christmas Story* was the phenomenal success of *Home Alone*. Costing a mere $18.2 million to produce, *Home Alone* grossed $17.1 million in its first three days.[15] Its early success can partly be attributed to timing, clever promotional publicity and 'saturation' screening. *Home Alone* opened on Thanksgiving weekend and was shown on 1,202 screens in its first week.[16] Earning nearly $280 million in domestic gross and a further $200 million abroad, the film not only became the top-grossing film of 1990 but joined the ranks of the 20 top-grossing films of all time.[17]

Home Alone is set in the present and told from the point of view of a child. Marketed to appeal to the child audience its strapline read 'A Family Comedy Without the Family'. Nevertheless, the content and language still required the MPAA to give it a 'PG–13' rating. Fundamentally it is a David and Goliath plot. Eight-year-old Kevin McCallister (Macaulay Culkin) is accidentally left at home as his extended family goes on holiday to France. Having been blamed, somewhat unfairly, for all the arguments and accidents, Kevin had been banished to sleep in the attic. Angry with his family, Kevin, wishes that they would all disappear. The next morning the McCallisters wake up late and in their rush to the airport forget Kevin. Unaware of the parental error, Kevin thinks his wish has been granted. Instead of being distressed at finding himself alone, Kevin makes the most of his new-found freedom, helping himself to all the food, normally restricted, from the refrigerator, playing with his brother's out-of-bounds toys and watching old gangster movies till late. However, as the house comes under threat from two burglars Kevin fights ingeniously to protect his house. Eventually, an old neighbour, Marley, whom he befriends at the local church, comes to his assistance to capture the thieves. Meanwhile his family, realizing their mistake, battle to make their way home despite the busy Christmas holiday bookings and difficult weather conditions. The film ends happily with Kevin and the old man united with their respective families.

Both American and British critics were taken by the 'picture-postcard' images of Christmas with snow-decked streets and houses covered in Christmas lights. As *Variety* reported, the 'Pic's psychology of comfort and abundance – Kevin's house is a roomy showplace stocked with all the good stuff and money never seems to be an obstacle to anyone's actions – may not ring true for much of the audience but it's probably a welcome Christmas fantasy'.[18] But from this cosy picture emerged a heated debate with regard to images of the family, the community, the American Dream, race, and screen violence. Heading the vitriolic attack was *New York Times* editor Mary E. Mitchell who wrote: 'The other night I saw a Christmas movie in which a little boy leaves a church and goes home and shoots two men in the genitals and face.' Mitchell was not taken in by the picturesque setting, insisting instead that 'violence is what the movie is about – violence that would make Rambo blush ... In *Home Alone*, violence is a chuckle. Abandonment is amusing. Cruelty is a boffo part of modern family life.'[19]

Similarly, media historian Marsha Kinder argued the plot was reminiscent of vigilante films that are popular with adult males. She surmised that 'this strange combination turns *Home Alone* into a third-grader's *Die Hard* or a second-grader's *Straw Dogs* – a transgenerational hybrid that enables kiddy spectators to grow into the more mature action-genre and their parents to enjoy a non-saccharine children's film with a cutting edge.[20]

Less concerned about the violence, Fabian Worsham concentrates on the images of the family and society in *Home Alone*. He argues that the film appeals both to parents' hopes and aspirations and their worst fears, particularly the fear of failing as parents, and it appeals to children in the way it offers 'a vision of autonomy and power' lived out in the character of young Kevin'.[21] Worsham argues that the film is a critique of the American way of life particularly in its promotion of affluence and material goods. The image of success as represented by the McCallister's luxury three-storey house is challenged by the chaos and dysfunction apparent in the family relations, especially in the way Kevin is picked on by the other children and blamed by the adults for causing accidents.

Indeed the chaos and the dysfunction are evident in the first few minutes of the film as we view the McCallister's seemingly neat and ordered home from the outside but can hear the bedlam reigning within. The following shots from within confirm our fears as children and adults run in all directions. Kevin quickly wins our sympathy as the children call him a variety of names including a 'jerk', 'disease', 'idiot', and 'incompetent' amongst others.

Worsham stresses that '*Home Alone* is a complex film. It's a family comedy while addressing the failures of family; it's about material success while pointing to its inadequacies; and it's a Christmas story even though its most powerful symbol is the glinting gold tooth of the malicious burglar Harry.'[22] And here is where Worsham provides a most interesting reading of the film. He argues that it is Harry who is the most magical character in the film – a role usually reserved for Santa Claus in Christmas stories. 'Harry is, in fact, an anti-Santa, the evil power that comes on Christmas Eve to take the goodies away. The glint from the gold tooth is a transmogrification of the twinkle in Santa's eye.'[23] Indeed, the cartoon style used to superimpose the glint of Harry's tooth and the speeded-up action used to exaggerate the McCallisters' rush to get to the airport on time are deemed unproblematic, unlike the depiction of the violence.

Interestingly much of the British press came out in favour of the film's cartoon precedents and over-the-top pantomime style. As Shaun Usher of the *Daily Mail* remarked, the film contained 'some of the best slapstick since Laurel and Hardy … Ignore the plot, think Tom and Jerry – for after a gentle start, here's a carnival of harmlessly-heartless mayhem'.[24] Iain Johnstone had a particularly British reading: 'there is a pantomime aspect to the villains that makes this less of a nightmare and more of a fantasy'.[25] But Worsham argues that the problems revealed in the *Home Alone* narrative are very real rather than fantastic. For instance, the technology fails – telephone and alarm systems break down and airports come to a standstill due to bad weather conditions. Moreover, there are gaps in the fabric of American society as outlined by the lack of family or friends nearby, and by the incompetence of the police. Worsham concludes that 'despite the sentimental subplot and "happy" ending, *Home Alone* subverts the American Dream and easy clichés about the meaning of Christmas'. [26] Marsha Kinder has further concerns about *Home Alone* and its sequel, arguing that they contain conflicts, not only of class but also of race, 'between the charmed well-to-do middle-class Anglo-Saxon family and the ethnic criminal have-nots'.[27] The character of Harry is played by actor Joe Pesci who is more usually cast in Italian-American gangster roles, while Daniel Stern, playing against the 'shrewd Jew' stereotype, wishes himself a 'Happy Chanukah', as he steals children's charity money in *Home Alone 2*. The McCallister family are bored and unhappy in Florida, being subjected to rain rather than sunshine. (Kevin specifically complains that he does not want to go to Florida, as there are no Christmas trees, without which Christmas is not the same.) Moreover, the class discourse that was suppressed in the first film re-emerges in the sequel, with the homeless pigeon lady of Central Park. Only it is diverted to personal rather than social conditions, so Kevin ends up giving her his friendship rather than food, money or shelter. Kinder is right to highlight the stereotyping of race and class in the *Home Alone* films. On further scrutiny of all these films one is painfully aware that there is little ethnic diversity nor is there any significant religious pluralism, which is neither realistic nor representative of the vast land and multi-ethnic peoples that make up the United States of America.

Home Alone 2: Lost in New York reunited the original production team and actors for a two-hour sequel. The title is somewhat misleading since Kevin is not 'home alone' on this occasion. Instead, he is separated from his family as a result of accidentally boarding the wrong plane, so rather than accompanying his family to Florida for Christmas he finds himself in New York with his father's credit card and cash. Undaunted by the error, Kevin decides to check into a first-class hotel and enjoy himself. However, his festivities are hampered by the arrival of his old adversaries the 'Wet Bandits' who plan to raid a toy store and steal the money set aside for a children's hospital. With the help of a homeless lady who looks after pigeons in the park Kevin sets out to atone for his selfishness and scupper the thieves. However, he does so with unusual zeal, luring them to his uncle's abandoned home to inflict all sorts of injuries on them.

Joe Levy of *Village Voice* argued that *Home Alone 2* 'made *A Clockwork Orange* seem pretty dated ... Ultraviolence isn't for kids, unless it's Saturday morning – so be glad the bigger the explosions and collisions get, the less human Pesci and Stern look. They get covered in paint and ash, get their hair burned off or shocked into a fright wig, and generally become cartoon characters'.[28] But not everyone agreed with this reading. For example Neil Norman of the *Evening Standard* was deeply alarmed at the moral imbalance of the film: 'It is simply not good enough to claim that all kids view violent acts from a different perspective to that of adults ... While the villains (indeed all the adults) are presented as a bunch of amusingly ineffectual incompetents, the violence is given the teeth-jarring impact of virtual reality'.[29]

Certainly the critics were divided in their assessment of the violence depicted in the *Home Alone* films. And although I do not hold with the humourless reading by Mitchell, I do believe Norman is right to point to problems raised by the virtual reality of the sounds and images presented to the child audience. Indeed, there is a significant difference between the unrealistic violence played out by one-dimensional animated figures, often in the form of animals (e.g. Tom the cat and Jerry the mouse), and the human characters and tangible violence displayed in *Home Alone*. The audience, young and old, can actually identify with the pain of the characters as they get their hands burnt, or tread on nails, or get hit by heavy objects such as an iron. The fact that they seemingly recover from these incidents does not make it less realistic in terms of identification.

Indeed, the majority of the British press were appalled at the unjustified violence and sadism perpetrated by Kevin in the sequel. Several critics pointed to the illogic of the narrative and asked why Kevin could not have simply called the police as this time all the telephones were working. In fact, Kevin, no longer defending the family hearth, is seen to be enticing the villains to his uncle's home to inflict more misery, asking vindictively, 'Have you had enough pain?' Obviously not, as the villains get bashed, crushed, electrocuted, stapled and pecked into submission. More disturbing is how the kind, homeless person is left out in the cold, while the least needy children in New York, the McCallister clan, are spoilt with a mountain of expensive toys in their cosy, luxury hotel penthouse. Despite complaints about length, unoriginal narrative and violence *Home Alone 2* once again did well at the domestic box-office, earning $173.6 million and became the second top-grossing film in the USA in 1992.[30]

Yet it is film critic Jonathan Romney of *New Statesman and Society* who makes the most interesting connection between Christmas and the violence of both the *Home Alone* and *Die Hard* series:

> Both sequels set themselves the same-but-different challenge, and do it as self-consciously as possible so you can see how smart they are; and curiously, all four films take place at Christmas. This is no accident: Christmas is associated with the theme of eternal return and rebirth that informs both pairs. Just as the saviour Bruce can never be killed, so little Kevin remains forever young while his mortal enemies are actually immortal, forever rising to take further falls no matter how lethally they seem to get minced up.[31]

And there is a further religious reading to be made from the narrative. In both *Home Alone* adventures, the only family member Kevin truly misses is his mother, which is fitting since the festival of Christmas celebrates the relationship between mother and son, between Mary and Jesus. But it is Santa rather than God who Kevin asks for help in restoring his family, despite his visits to church. Similarly in the sequel Kevin prays at the foot of the Rockerfeller Christmas tree to see his mother. Neither are religious symbols but rather secular substitutes.

Directed by Brian Levant and produced by *Home Alone's* Chris Columbus, *Jingle All the Way* could not match the success of *Home Alone* and its sequel, despite being a vehicle for top box-office star Arnold Schwarzenegger. Schwarzenegger plays businessman Howard Langton who has been so engrossed in his work he has forgotten to buy his son Jamie the Christmas present he most desires – an action-figure Turbo

Man. In a desperate attempt to acquire this toy Howard searches all over the city to no avail and gets into a lot of trouble with the police, a postman named Myron, not to mention a belligerent reindeer. The weak plot ends up with Howard performing as Turbo Man in a Christmas parade and becoming a real hero in the eyes of his son who had felt neglected up till then. The film preys on the madness of Christmas shopping, and the fears of most parents of disappointing their children. But again this is a film for parents rather than children as it is told from the point of view of Langton not Jamie. Indeed, none of the adult characters appears suitable for a children's film for they include Ted, a seedy neighbour lusting after Langton's wife, Myron, an aggressive postman, and a corrupt Santa played by James Belushi. Fortunately they pose an insidious threat to Langton rather than the child. And with Schwarzenegger as the star the film is somewhat predictable in its ending as he turns into a super hero. Indeed the film's press pack played on his famous tough image, 'He's "terminated" predators around the globe, "erased" the world's toughest "commandos", but now, in *Jingle All the Way*, Arnold Schwarzenegger is facing his greatest challenge ever ...'. Neither the American nor British press were impressed. The *Variety* critic pointed out that the film played on the same parental feelings of guilt employed by *Home Alone*, only this time the point of view was reversed. This resulted in 'an erratic comedy that will frustrate children, the film's main target audience, because the kid doesn't get as much screen time as Dad'.[32] The British press went to town on the film, criticizing the narrative, the characters and in particular the violence, as being totally unsuitable for a children's film rated 'PG'. Philip French of the *Observer* found Schwarzenegger's character somewhat back-to-front if not implausible:

> This is a crude piece of slapstick film-making, and begins with the initial unlikelihood of Arnie as a suburban middle-class husband in the Midwest. This freak of Nietzsche is a Superman who could never pass as Clark Kent. At the end, when he's dressed up as Turbo Man and flying around the sky-scrapers of Minneapolis the movie at last becomes plausible, if not very funny.[33]

Evening Standard critic Alexander Walker was outraged at the violence contained in the film calling it 'the family comedy from hell', and criticizing the British Board of Film Classification for being lenient in granting the film a 'PG' certificate. Walker was not taken in by the narrative, 'posing as the heart-warming story of a dad's heroic endeavours to lay hands on a hard-to-obtain toy for his kid, it's actually a non-stop advertisement for family rage and uninhibited greed'.[34] Walker also pointed to the irony of putting into neutral the customary 'killing-machine' persona of Schwarzenegger while Langton's child is turned into a mini-killing machine with karate lessons. Again, critics like Walker had cause for concern. The film contained acts of violence totally unsuitable for the child audience, for example, Myron spraying mace into the eyes of Langton. Also unsuitable is the way Langton punches the reindeer then tries to make amends by drinking beer with the animal. More worrying is how Langton is mistaken for a paedophile when he tries to retrieve a lottery ball that has fallen into the hands of a child.

Adam Mars-Jones of the *Independent* seemed to suggest that the violence was realistic in terms of the experience of modern-day shopping: *'Jingle All the Way* … deals with one of the new varieties of anger: not road rage but shopping mall rage, toy shop trauma'.[35] Certainly, we tend to regard Christmas as increasingly commercialized. But not only is the trauma of Christmas shopping highly exaggerated, the film sets a poor example of charity, selflessness and goodwill to others. It is not until the very end that these ideals are confirmed by young Jamie who hands over his coveted Turbo-Man action figure to Myron for the postman to give it to his son. Jamie declares that he has no need of the toy since he has the real thing in the shape of his father. Yet it is not Jamie who is lauded but Langton posing as Turbo Man who is lifted on to the shoulders of the crowd.

In both *A Christmas Story* and *Jingle All the Way* the emphasis is on the acquisition of presents. For Ralphie Parker Christmas remained a relatively innocent experience. The department store's Christmas window is like an Aladdin's Cave to Ralphie and his friends. In *Home Alone* presents do not tend to feature but in the sequel the producers try to offer a balance between the modern Christmas, as symbolized by Kevin's high-tech camcorder, and Mr Duncan's toy shop, which is full of more traditional goods. In *Jingle All the Way* the commercialism of the toy industry takes on a more worrying perspective as everyone tries to make a profit from children's dreams. Despite having an image of Captain America plastered across his bedroom wall Jamie seems obsessed with the figure of Turbo Man. Not only does he watch him on television but he also wears Turbo Man pyjamas and eats Turbo Man Cereal. Moreover, the Christmas Parade looks like a veritable shopping list with giant figures representing Paddington Bear, Barbie, Snoopy, Ninja Turtles, Crayons, Boxing Robots not to mention Turbo Man and his pals. However, Christmas presents take a more sinister form in the action-adventure thriller to be discussed later.

The Action-Adventure Film – for Men Only?

As John Belton points out, the 1980s and 1990s saw a new generation of film-makers, screenwriters, and actors come to the fore, a generation that had grown up on sitcoms and made-for television movies rather than classic films of the 1950s. Whereas director John McTiernan trained at the American Film Institute for Advanced Film Studies, Chris Columbus had no formal film training. It is hardly surprising, therefore, that Columbus's work shows little to none of the classical influences of his predecessors. That is not to say these directors ignored the genre they were working within, far from it. Columbus and Hughes, in particular, made literal references to Hollywood Christmas classics by wittily incorporating them in rather subtle ways, such as featuring extracts on television sets in the McCallister home and hotel rooms. In the hotel in France one sees *It's A Wonderful Life* (1946) playing on the television but it is dubbed into French, much to the annoyance of the family. The same thing happens on vacation in Florida where they are subjected to the film again but this time dubbed in Spanish. Clips of *Miracle on 34th Street* (1947) as well as *How the Grinch Stole Christmas* (1957) also flash on the television screen.

Director Richard Donner, however, utilized more classic generic conventions and motifs in *Lethal Weapon*. Indeed he admitted trying to make the action-thriller-adventure 'more like an old-fashioned western'.[36] Released in March and with a MPAA 'R' rating the film was not expected to attract large holiday audiences, but nevertheless became a box-office hit on both sides of the Atlantic.[37] Starring Mel Gibson and Danny Glover, this action-thriller has two cops thrown together to solve a murder which is connected to a drugs gang. One is a mature black officer named Murtaugh. A family man, Murtaugh is looking for a quiet life until his forthcoming retirement. The other, Riggs, a younger white officer, is deemed unstable since the tragic loss of his wife. The two get involved in investigating a ruthless drugs cartel whose members have Vietnam War connections. Whilst investigating the case they manage to overcome their differences and learn to respect and care for one another.

The film wastes no time in suggesting something sinister is afoot, for even before the opening credits roll we see the reflection of Christmas lights appear in the cocaine mirror of the first victim. Being Los Angeles there is no snow to indicate the time of year and so the soundtrack with accompanying images of Christmas trees and lights has to provide the setting. Similarly Murtaugh makes a big play about his wife's awful cooking and forthcoming Christmas dinner as he invites Riggs to join the family. Moreover, the villains appear even more heinous as they attempt to destroy Murtaugh's family celebrations by kidnapping his teenage daughter.

The *Variety* critic felt the film owed a great deal to the *Rambo* series (1982, 1985, 1988) and *48 HRS* (1982), and although entertaining enough to satisfy the fans it also contained some disturbing attitudes about heroes and violence in America.[38] Released in the UK in August 1987, the timing for this violent action-thriller could not have been worse, following the Hungerford massacre, and out of respect for the dead the local Cannon cinema in Newbury refused to show the film. Elsewhere in the UK it attracted substantial audiences. However, the critics were vociferous in their concern about the film's violence as Alexander Walker exemplified:

> Torture, kidnapping, sadistic humiliation, masochistic catharsis: the movie's capacity to see excessive violence as the way out of every crisis and the way back to self-respect and love of country is predictably impressive considering the high-tech talents that made it …The makers of this movie are committed only to cynicism and manipulation. Not that audiences for *Lethal Weapon* will care that much I fear.[39]

Times critic David Robinson reflected that 'the dubious moral of the film is that a good shoot-up like this, topped off by a hand-to-hand struggle with the nastiest nasty (Gary Busey) is sovereign therapy: our hero ends up as normal as the next man'.[40]

Intended as a summer blockbuster, *Die Hard* was released in July and given MPAA 'R' rating for its adult content. Director John McTiernan had already made his name in this action-genre with films like *Predator* (1987). But *Die Hard's* star Bruce Willis was relatively new to the big screen, having made his name with the television series *Moonlighting*. Indeed, Willis, like Gibson, appealed to female audiences as well as male because they promoted a smoother image than the usual tough 'he-man' offered by other stars such as Arnold Schwarzenegger, Sylvester Stallone and Chuck Norris.

Die Hard tells the story of a New York City policeman, John McClane, who has come to Los Angeles to spend time with his estranged wife and children in the hope they can all be reunited. But as he meets his wife Holly at her high-rise office McClane stumbles on a supposed terrorist plot. The ruthless gang is in fact planning to break into the vault and steal bonds worth millions. As they seize the building with its hostages, McClane manages to hide away and proceeds to scupper their plans with cunning and force. McClane acts alone on the inside but does have some support by way of a black policeman, Al Powell, on the outside.

Set on Christmas Eve this action-thriller is not only about wish fulfilment but being given a chance to prove one's worth, winning back the wife and keeping the family together. And there is a fairytale, gothic castle quality to this modern office skyscraper, in as much as McClane secretes himself in various rooms, passages, air vents and lift shafts. Moreover, this high tower lights up like a Christmas tree as the explosions rip through the building and fire erupts on the various floors.

On the whole critics on both sides of the Atlantic liked the movie precisely because it was over the top. Many pointed to the film's generic connections to disaster films such as *Towering Inferno* (1974) and combat survival movies such as *Rambo*, and most praised it for its special effects. Terrence Rafferty of the *New Yorker* summarised:

> *Die Hard* is a B-movie of gigantic proportions ... The most entertaining thing about this movie is the sheer joy it takes in destruction ... In a strange way this picture's mixture of sentimentality and violence defines Hollywood's version of the Christmas spirit: you get a lot of expensive toys and smash them all to pieces, because you know there are a lot more where they came from.[41]

However, film historian Peter Parshall was more interested in the film's generic connections with the classic Western. 'In many regards, *Die Hard's* story is an age old one: A hero conquers the villains ... John brings about justice single-handedly, trusting his own instincts rather than following procedure. Indeed, the film makes a running joke of John as cowboy hero.'[42] More pertinent to our study is Parshall's reading of the Christmas motifs. 'Christmas is used as a benchmark throughout the film, with the good guys shown to be pro-Christmas and pro-family and the bad guys anti-Christmas and hence anti-family.'[43] Initial images show John McClane clutching a giant teddy bear, a Christmas present for his children. Al Powell, the black policemen, is first seen buying snacks for his pregnant wife and singing a popular 1950s Christmas song 'Let It Snow!'. This of course is unlikely in Los Angeles at any time of the year. McClane's wife is given an appropriately seasonal name of Holly and is seen fending off advances from a colleague. Parshall argues that the film makes several suggestions that the corporate world is anti-family. Not only is Holly still working whilst the office party is in full swing, but the company is effectively keeping Holly and her husband away from their children. Indeed, the Nakatomi Chief celebrates his company's profits before he celebrates Christmas. The terrorists mock Christmas traditions of peace and goodwill by threatening the lives of the Nakatomi employees. Even the gang's technical expert Theo corrupts a well-known Christmas poem by adding his own twisted ending: ''Twas the night before Christmas and all through the house, not a creature was stirring ... except the four assholes coming in the rear in standard two-by-two cover formation'. Naturally the terrorists proceed to eliminate the crack police team. Parshall argues that McClane is defending both the Nakatomi employees and traditional societal values, as represented by the season of Christmas, from foreign invaders who not only pose a threat to American corporate life but are also stealing Christmas. Santa Claus is personified in the figure of John McClane who whistles 'Here Comes Santa Claus' when first entering the Nakatomi Tower and whose final words in the film are 'Merry Christmas'. Hans, on the other hand, is the Scrooge figure, the man who would kill to amass wealth, but ironically gets Holly and John together again and brings Christmas to Nakatomi Land, as the bearer bonds float down from the building like snow. As Parshall sums up, 'Greed has been replaced by the spirit of giving; love and laughter have overcome violence; and we have a white Christmas, even in L.A.'[44]

The sequel *Die Hard 2: Die Harder* is also set at Christmas. This time McClane goes to the airport in Washington to pick up his wife. The first thing to go wrong is that his car is towed away. McClane asks the policeman to show some Christmas spirit but this is obviously lacking as the cop insists on the car being forcibly removed. Shortly afterward our hero stumbles on a plot by anti-communist mercenaries to take over the airport and rescue a drug-trafficking South American dictator about to arrive on extradition and undergo trial for his offences. The villains are identified by the way they carry their weapons in Christmas presents. To add to the chaos the picturesque snow scene turns into a dangerous blizzard, making landing conditions treacherous. McClane complains, 'I can't fuckin' believe this! Another basement, another elevator – how can the same shit happen to the same guy twice?' McClane adds, 'just once I'd like a regular, normal Christmas, some eggnog, a fuckin' Christmas tree, a little turkey'. The film's poster turns the narrative's repetition into a selling feature with the strapline – 'They say lightning never strikes twice … They were wrong'. The villains continue to behave badly and contravene the spirit of Christmas by usurping an abandoned church and killing the old caretaker in the process. The film turns a number of reassuring images on their head to good effect. For example, the cavalry that supposedly comes to the rescue are dressed in white camouflage dress. They look like Christmas snowmen but in fact they are frauds, traitors to their unit, joining up with the mercenaries. Not surprisingly they pay for their transgression with their lives. For McClane, once again Christmas has gone horribly wrong – no wife, no kids, blizzards instead of snow, no Christmas spirit, terrorists and he is fighting for the life of his wife and himself. Although *Variety* complained the film lacked the inventiveness of the original, they praised it for its ability to once again assemble an ethnically well-mixed cast.[45] Certainly in both *Die Hard* films a black policeman, a black chauffeur, and a black airport technical manager aid McClane. There are also small parts for the Japanese Nakatomi Chief and Holly's Latino maid. The villains, on the other hand, range from Germans in the original to a South American general and black Commander in the sequel, but whether this does constitute an ethnically well-mixed cast is debatable, since the key players are white. Furthermore, it is McClane who is ultimately left to save his wife and the other passengers single-handed in the final showdown, once more salvaging Christmas and the American way of life.

Another violent 'R' rated action movie packed with explosions and special effects is *The Long Kiss Goodnight*, directed by Renny Harlin. With a track record that includes *True Lies*, *Cliffhanger* and *Die Hard 2*, and screen-writer Shane Black who made his name with *Lethal Weapon*, *The Last Boy Scout*, and *The Last Action Hero*, the film's narrative and style are somewhat predictable. The most original feature of this action-thriller was in making the lead a woman. Geena Davis plays amnesiac Samantha Caine who has forgotten her past as a CIA assassin and is living a normal life in a New England town. Her past comes back to haunt our protagonist when she is filmed taking part as Mrs Santa Claus in a local Christmas pageant. An old enemy seeks her out and her old skills are rekindled by a car accident precipitated by a deer crossing the road and hitting the vehicle. Relieving the animal of its suffering she expertly snaps the deer's neck. From this point on the action-adventure begins as she retraces her past with the aid of Mitch, a seedy but goodhearted private detective played by Samuel Jackson.

The British critics were not enamoured of the film nor by the way the action-genre seemed to be developing. They called the plot 'preposterous' and the $4 million spent on the screenplay as 'daylight robbery'. Davis's character was likened to 'Nikita' or 'Marnie', even called a 'Jane' Bond. Many felt the film set new benchmarks in terms of killing and carnage. Not many thought the film's style was tongue-in-cheek and not to be taken too seriously.[46]

Once again these films raised issues concerning representations of race. *New York Times* critic Michael Ross argued that the recent spate of black and white buddy films such as *48 Hours* (1982), *Beverly Hills Cop* (1985), *Lethal Weapon* trilogy (1987, 1989, 1992), *Shoot to Kill* (1988), *Die Hard* (1988), and *The Last Boy Scout* (1991), were motivated by box-office returns rather than artistic values.[47] Christopher Ames, on the other hand, examined these black–white buddy films in terms of their literary traditions and role reversal. 'These films judiciously avoid that black-as-brute stereotype, but at an intriguing cost. The reversal testifies, first of all, to the continued force of the stereotype, even though asserted through its careful absence. The respectability of the black male hero becomes paradoxically tied to his emasculation.'[48] In both *Lethal Weapon* and *Die Hard* it is the white cop who resorts to the violent solution while the black cop has to be re-educated to shoot-to-kill. Despite its seeming modernity in as much as the protagonist is female, the inter-ethnic buddy relationship in *The Long Kiss Goodnight*, between Samantha and Mitch, remains the same. Just as before, the ethnic co-operation should not be confused with racial harmony or seasonal goodwill but should once again be attributed to marketing strategy.

What the action-adventure genre manages to do successfully is invert traditional Christmas motifs and images to enhance the narrative. We have already seen how presents in these action-thrillers are not what they seem, often containing sinister objects such as weapons. In *Die Hard* Holly uses her maiden name of Gennaro for business purposes but this opens her up to other offers. Indeed, Holly accepts the gift of a gold Rolex watch from an admiring colleague. It is a symbol of her split from McClane, just as his wedding ring, which provides the film with one of its opening shots, is a symbol of his desire to remain married. The watch is also a sign of the bondage of Holly to her work, one which almost gets her killed when Hans clings on to her as he dangles from the window. Only after McClane releases the watch and eliminates the danger is she able to return to the safety of her husband's arms and married title of Holly McClane. In *The Long Kiss Goodnight* the present of a doll given to Caine's daughter is used to hide kerosene and cause an explosion. In this instance the weapon within the present is used in a positive manner to help Caine and her daughter escape from the villains. Caine provides another inverted symbol herself as she dresses up for the Christmas Parade. Not only is she fraudulently posing as Mrs Santa, she is not really the demure mother and teacher she appears to be but rather a trained assassin underneath. Similarly the churches in *Die Hard 2* and in *The Long Kiss Goodnight* provide no sanctuary for those within. Caine's daughter is kidnapped from church and another family threatened with a knife. Even the traditional Christmas tree and decorations purport to more sinister goings-on in the action-adventure film. In *Lethal Weapon* a Christmas tree business is a front for a cocaine operation that Riggs breaks up. In *Lethal Weapon*, *Die Hard*, and *The Long Kiss Goodnight*, rather than celebrating Christmas, as symbolized by the erection and decoration of the tree, these films appear to revel in the destruction of Christmas as trees and decorations are violently torn down and smashed.

Hollywood cinema of the 1980s and 1990s has provided audiences with a mixture of traditional and modern images of Christmas. Driven by the need to reach wider audiences both at home and abroad, not only have these Christmas stories remained secular but have attempted to become transgenerational in the case of the family film, and less gender-specific in terms of the action-thriller.

Not surprisingly in the family entertainment film, the narrative focus is on the family unit which even when disrupted is never really under serious threat. In the action-adventure film the family plays more of a symbolic role, especially when it is threatened. The family entertainment film often presents a utopian world on the surface but there are dystopian elements running underneath the seemingly harmless narrative revealing serious social concerns. Moreover, they tend to use a combination of realism and fantasy both in their story-telling and in their visual styles, sometimes with unsettling results as in the *Home Alone* films. The action-adventure film, on the other hand, presents a dystopian world and revels in placing the ideals of Christmas under attack. Of course the values of Christmas are restored by our protagonists but the anarchy provided by the characters, good and bad, the narrative disruption and colourful action is so appealing, it is no wonder the audience returned for more mayhem by way of the sequels.

The Christmas film is a remarkably sophisticated sub-genre that utilizes visual and musical iconography to great effect. The narrative within each of the genres scrutinized has provided us with insights into both the desires and fears of their respective audiences. Indeed, these films have proved surprisingly revealing in terms of social, economic and cultural problems latent in American society during the 1980s and 1990s. Whereas Christmas would appear to be a time for reassurance, the frequent use of violence in the extreme to solve problems in both the family entertainment film and action-adventure film is deeply disturbing. And thus over the last two decades Hollywood cinema has been found wanting in its ability to promote the essential Christmas message of 'Peace on Earth and Goodwill to All Men.'

Notes

1. *Motion Picture Almanac*, 59th and 69th edns (New York: Quigley Publishing, 1988; 1998).

2. *Die Hard 2* figures from the *Observer* (19 August 1990), *Jingle All the Way* figures from *Screen International* (25 October 1996).

3. Industry figures from R. Maltby and I. Craven, *Hollywood Cinema: An Introduction* (Oxford: Blackwell, 1995), pp 480–2.

4. David J. Fox , 'Honey, They Shrunk the Movie Audience', *Los Angeles Times*, Calendar (8 June 1993), section F, p 1.

5. Joseph Sartelle, 'Dreams and Nightmares in the Hollywood Blockbuster,' in G. Nowell-Smith (ed.), *The Oxford History of World Cinema* (Oxford: Oxford University Press, 1996), p 516.

6. Figures from Maltby and Craven, *Hollywood Cinema,* pp 480–2.

7. In 1983, despite *A Christmas Story* having no competition by way of Disney or any other family entertainment film it still did not manage to do well. In 1990, *Home Alone* was not only competing with (Disney) Buena Vista's *Three Men and a Little Lady*, but also Universal's *Kindergarten Kop* and Tri-Star's *Look Who's Talking Too* (see figures in *Screen International*, 11 January 1991). In 1992, *Home Alone 2* initially proved more popular than Disney's *Aladdin* (see figures in *Screen International*, 18 December 1992) but *Aladdin* went on to become the top-grossing film of 1992 earning $217.3 million in domestic gross (*Screen International*, 25 October 1996). In 1996, Disney's live action version of *101 Dalmations*, proved too strong for *Jingle All the Way* (see figures in *Screen International*, 20 December 1996).

8. Recently the Disney studio offered an animated version of an episode in the Old Testament with *Prince of Egypt* (1999). Martin Scorsese caused a stir with his production *The Last Temptation of Christ* (1988). Costing $30 million *King David* (1985) starring Richard

Gere proved a critical and box-office disaster. For a more reverent and popular translation of the New Testament to the screen one has to go back to 1977 and Franco Zeffirelli's television epic, *Jesus of Nazareth*.

9. The new MPAA system was introduced 1 November 1968 as follows:
'G' suitable for general audiences of all ages (later 'U'), 'M' (later 'PG') suitable for mature audiences, adults or those subject to parental guidance, 'R' restricted to adults, children under 16 must be accompanied by adult. 'X' no one under 16 (later 17) is admitted. In 1984, a new classification was added of 'PG-13' – special parental guidance for attendance of children under 13 years. And in 1990 the category 'NC-17' replaced the 'X'.

10. *Variety* (16 November 1983).

11. Andrew Sarris on the film's television premiere in *Village Voice* (31 December 1985).

12. Ian Christie, *Daily Express* (25 November 1984).

13. David Castell, *Daily Telegraph* (25 November 1984).

14. Interspersed in these films' soundtracks can be found well-known popular tunes such as: 'Jingle Bell Rock' sung by Bobby Helms, 'Sleigh Ride' sung by Darlene Love, 'The Most Wonderful Time of the Year' by Johnny Mathis, 'It's Beginning to Look a Lot like Christmas' sung by Vaughn Monroe, 'Let It Snow! Let It Snow! Let It Snow!' sung by Dean Martin or Vaughn Monroe, 'Santa Claus is Back in Town' sung by Elvis, 'Rockin' Around the Christmas Tree' sung by Ronnie Spector and Darlene Love, 'Run, Rudolph, Run' by Chuck Berry, and many more.

15. *Hollywood Reporter* (26 November 1990).

16. *Home Alone* became the second highest Thanksgiving grosser in history (*Back to the Future II* being in poll position at the time) *Screen International* (24 November 1990 and 1 December 1990).

17. Figures from Jim Hillier's *The New Hollywood* (London: Studio Vista, 1992), p 25.

18. *Variety* (19 November 1990).

19. Mary E. Mitchell, 'A Rambo Christmas for the Kids', *New York Times*, Editorial (23 December 1990).

20. Marsha Kinder, '*Home Alone* in the 90s,' in Cary Bazelegette and David Buckingham (eds), *In Front of the Children: Screen Entertainment and Young Audiences* (London: BFI, 1995) pp 80–1.

21. Fabian Worsham, 'Home Alone: American Dream/American Nightmare', *Film and Philosophy*, 1 (1994), p 81.

22. Ibid., p 83.

23. Ibid.

24. Shaun Usher, *Daily Mail* (7 December 1990).

25. Iain Johnstone, *Sunday Times* (9 December 1990).

26. Worsham, 'Home Alone: American Dream/American Nightmare', p 84.

27. Kinder, p 81.

28. Joe Levy, *Village Voice* (December 1992).

29. Neil Norman, 'Another Nice Little Earner', *Evening Standard* (10 December 1992).

30. 'Turkeys and Crackers', *Screen International* (25 October 1996), pp 14–16.

31. Jonathan Romney, 'Hell's Blonde Angel', *New Statesman and Society* (11 December 1992).

32. *Variety* (25 November 1990).

33. Philip French, *Observer* (8 December 1996).

34. Alexander Walker, 'A Thumping Bad Example From Arnie', *Evening Standard* (5 December 1996).

35. Adam Mars-Jones, *Independent* (5 December 1996).

36. Richard Donner quoted in *New York Times* (3 April 1987).

37. *Lethal Weapon* earned $6.8 million in debut week, see *New York Times* (11 March 1987) and remained box-office no.1 for 3 weeks earning $33.6 million, see *New York Times* (3 April 1987).

38. *Variety* (4 March 1987).

39. Alexander Walker, 'Rambos with Broken Hearts', *Evening Standard* (20 August 1987).

40. David Robinson, *The Times* (27 August 1987).

41. Terrence Rafferty, *New Yorker* (8 August 1988).

42. Peter F. Parshall, '*Die Hard* and the American Mythos,' *Journal of Popular Film and Television*, 18/4, (Winter 1991), p 136.

43. Ibid., p 137.

44. Ibid., p 145.

45. *Variety* (4 July 1990).

46. Nigel Andrews, *Financial Times* (28 November 1996); Tom Shone, *Sunday Times* (1 December 1996); Michael Owen, *Evening Standard* (29 November 1996); Steve Wright, *The Sun* (29 November 1996); Alexander Walker, *Evening Standard* (28 November 1996).

47. Michael E. Ross, 'Black and White Buddies: How Sincere Is the Harmony?', *New York Times* (14 June 1987).

48. Christopher Ames, 'Restoring the Black Man's Lethal Weapon: Race and Sexuality in Contemporary Cop Films', *Journal of Popular Film and Television* 20/3 (Fall 1992), p 59.

9

Christmas in French Cinema

Guy Austin

Christmas in France

The celebration of Christmas has a long tradition in France. It dates back at least to the year 496, when the French king Clovis was baptized at Christmas, along with three thousand of his soldiers.[1] In subsequent centuries, miracle and mystery plays representing Christ's birth, Christmas carols (known as *noëls*) and Nativity cribs became associated with the festival. More recently, Anglo-Saxon Christmas icons such as the Christmas tree and Father Christmas have been imported by the French, in the latter case not without some controversy. There remain, however, two principal characteristics which distinguish the French Christmas from the Anglo-American version. First, Christmas in France is not only a 'twin-peaked festival', but one in which New Year is a more important 'peak' than Christmas Eve or Christmas Day.[2] The latter is of course a religious festival, but it is New Year which is the primary occasion for gift-giving and general festivities. This is reflected in Claude Miller's film *Dites-lui que je l'aime* (*This Sweet Sickness*, 1977), a French adaptation of an American narrative. In the screen version the gift-giving scene is transposed from Christmas itself (in Patricia Highsmith's source novel) to New Year, just as the action is transposed from the United States to France.

A second, more important dichotomy exists in France between the religious and the materialistic conceptions of Christmas. This conflict is by no means unique to France, but in this case it is overlaid with certain tensions resulting from the longstanding French ambivalence towards American culture. At its crudest, this has resulted in the identification of the supposedly true meaning of Christmas – its religious, spiritual and moral values – as French, and its consumerist and non-Christian elements as American. This perception was probably at its height in the years immediately after the Second World War. Resentment at the apparent Americanization of French culture was fuelled by the Marshall Plan of 1947 – a huge aid package to war-torn France which also had the effect of allowing many American companies a foothold on French soil. In terms of Christmas, American capitalism seemed to be personified by the decidedly Anglo-Saxon figure of Santa Claus. The reaction of the French Catholic church – assuming the role of defender of national and religious values – reached a pitch of hysteria in the town of Dijon on Christmas Eve, 1951. As the French anthropologist Claude Lévi-Strauss reported in an essay inspired by the affair, 'A number of the clergy had for several months expressed disapproval of the increasing importance given by both families and the business sector to the figure of Father Christmas. They denounced a disturbing "paganization" of the Nativity that was diverting public spirit from the true Christian meaning of Christmas'.[3] This sudden 'paganization', with its attendant customs – such as large illuminated Christmas trees beside major roads, an abundance of Christmas wrapping paper and cards, and pleas for charity from the Salvation Army, 'customs which just a few years [previously] seemed so puerile and weird' to the French – was attributed to 'the influence and prestige of the USA'.[4] On 24 December 1951, matters came to a head when an effigy of Santa Claus was hung on the railings outside Dijon cathedral and then, as hundreds of Sunday school children looked on, was set alight. The burning of Father Christmas was approved by the local clergy and was even accompanied by a statement asserting that 'For Christians the festivity of Christmas must remain the annual celebration of the birth of the Saviour'.[5]

The irony of the situation was twofold, as Lévi-Strauss pointed out. First, the figure of Father Christmas was not a recent American invention, but in fact derived from ancient and extremely widespread myths and folk traditions, which included French avatars such as Croquemitaine and Père Fouettard.[6] Secondly, the burning of Santa Claus in effigy only succeeded in granting him a martyred grandeur, so that 'in wanting to put an end to Father Christmas, the clergymen of Dijon have only restored in all his glory ... a ritual figure they had intended to destroy'.[7] Nonetheless, the Dijon affair was not the last attack on Father Christmas in France. Probably the most controversial and popular French Christmas film of all, *Le Père Noël est une ordure* (*Santa Claus is a Louse*, 1982), undertakes a comic dismantling of everything that Father Christmas stands for, as we shall see below. And, in a real-life echo of the opening sequence from the film, a British newspaper recently reported that 'Chased from big department stores and hunted mercilessly by police for hanging around on the pavement, Santa Claus has become a threatened species in the French capital'.[8]

The French attitude to Father Christmas, and to the festival in general, is not however as unequivocal as might first appear. Even at the time of the Dijon affair, although the action of the Catholic clergy was supported by the Protestant Church, there was 'widespread disapproval' in the national press, and popular reaction to the issue revealed 'a rift between public opinion and the Church'.[9] Thirty years later, although the grotesque parody of Father Christmas in *Le Père Noël est une ordure* undoubtedly struck a chord with the cinema-going public and earned the film cult status, it also gave rise to concern, disgust and even censorship, as certain organizations within the film industry and the business community defended Father Christmas against attack. Both cases reflect the extent to which the meaning of Christmas in France remains open to negotiation and debate. The situation is complicated further by two distinct (though occasionally overlapping) strands in French representations of Christmas. As one might expect, most plays, songs, texts and films about the festival evoke diverse moral or religious values, including faith and wonder, a commitment to the family and the wider community, the practice of charity and gift-giving, the (temporary and authorized) reversal of social hierarchies, and so on. But a smaller number of works – of which *Le Père Noël est une ordure* is the most well known – adopt an ironic or parodic position, and seek to subvert received notions of Christmas.

The first cinematic representations of Christmas in France date from the early years of the century. These films competed with, and were often influenced by, more established Christmas spectacles such as puppet shows and pantomimes. Georges Méliès's Christmas fairytale *Rêve de Noël* (*Christmas Dream*, 1900) was probably inspired by a pantomime which ran in Paris three years previously, while the fantasy *Le Palais des mille et une nuits* (*The Palace of the Arabian Nights*, 1905) was based on an 1880 pantomime of *Aladdin*.[10] Another theatrical influence on early French cinema was the stage melodrama, and in particular the violent, crime-based variant known as *grand guignol*. Some of these brutal melodramas were set at Christmas for ironic effect, the most gruesome example being Auguste Linert's *A Christmas Story* (1890) in which 'a peasant girl, unable to find someone to take her in, kills the child she has just borne and throws its dismembered body to a farmer's pigs, while, in the distance, a group of neighbouring peasants sing Christmas carols on their way to midnight Mass'.[11] A slightly less grotesque, but equally violent and ironic Christmas narrative was filmed by Pathé as *Nuit de Noël* (*Christmas Eve Tragedy*, 1908).

Set on Christmas Eve, the film presented a tale of adultery and vengeance (rather than the family togetherness traditionally associated with the festival) and concluded with the wronged husband throwing his rival off a cliff. As Richard Abel notes, the blasphemous tone of the film was in keeping with the genre of *grand guignol* and indeed with the prevalent anti-clerical French mood of the time, but 'it seemed distinctly "foreign" in the United States, where one reviewer was disturbed enough at the film's morbidity to call for its censorship'.[12]

Not all French films of the early 1900s shared the *grand guignol* vision of Christmas. Although secular rather than religious, films such as Pathé's *Miracle de Noël* (*Christmas Miracle*, 1905) offered fairy-tales with a moral message (about giving and receiving) and presented themselves as '"wholesome" family entertainment'.[13] It is therefore possible to find contrasting representations of Christmas within films from one company (Pathé) or one genre (the melodrama). Moreover, 'the development, out of the *grand guignol* films, of an ironic voice of narration' contrasted with 'the moral voice characteristic of the domestic melodrama' and also of early American cinema.[14] Given the debates about the meaning of the festival, and the ambivalent French attitude to American popular culture (including cinema and also Christmas iconography), Abel's taxonomy of the 'moral voice' and the 'ironic voice' seems particulary apt for a discussion of the representation of Christmas in French film.

The Moral Voice

The Provençal Christmas: *Merlusse* (1935), *Le Château de ma mère* (1990)

The southern region of Provence has perhaps the richest heritage of Christmas customs in France, including carols written in the local language, Occitan. The two most important Provençal traditions are the decoration of the crib or *crèche*, and the Nativity plays known as *pastorales*. Particularly during the second half of the nineteenth century, these two customs reinforced each other, since each presented a similar range of character types derived from the shepherds and peasants who, according to the Bible story, worshipped the baby Jesus. From 1803 onwards, Christmas fairs at Aix and Marseilles revived 'the tradition of the fair that was in progress at Bethlehem when the Christ Child was born'.[15] Clay figures called *santons* were sold at the fairs and used for the decoration of cribs. Later, in 1844, the first Provençal *pastorale* was published in Marseilles. And when Provence came to be represented in French cinema – most notably in the films of Marcel Pagnol during the 1930s – it was often via stereotypical characters familiar from *santons* and *pastorales*, the most famous of which was the wondering peasant incarnated by the celebrated actor Fernandel. More generally, films depicting Provence have been described as 'wholly imbued with the consensual and unanimist atmosphere of Christmas'.[16] Hence the importance of 'collective events, usually of a festive nature', at which the local characters can congregate: examples include the wedding and cradle scenes in Pagnol's *Angèle* (1934) and *Regain* (*Rebirth*, 1937), and most notably the birth in a stable at the end of Jean-Paul Paulin's *La Nuit Merveilleuse* (*The Night of Marvels*, 1940), 'a film which precisely recreates the Nativity crib' in the context of occupied France.[17]

The nostalgia for collective values common to these films is again evident in Pagnol's short Christmas narrative *Merlusse* (1935). Although shot in the 1930s, the film is rather poignantly set in 1913, on the eve of the First World War. Its principal theme is the emergence of a communal festive spirit among a group of schoolboys of various nationalities who have to stay on at school in Marseilles over the Christmas holidays. Since the film was apparently conceived simply in order to test some new sound equipment, it is no surprise that the collective Christmas feeling is achieved through music, and especially through communal singing.[18] This first takes the rebellious form of an abusive song directed at the strict schoolmaster Merlusse by a gang of boys outside the gates. However, as Merlusse himself remarks (showing his deep but covert understanding of Christmas), during the pagan festival of the Saturnalia, slaves were indeed permitted to mock their masters. In the first half of the film Merlusse remains a target for the 'slaves': a dreaded disciplinarian, he is in many ways an archetypal Scrooge figure, resented by the schoolchildren for his cold and taciturn demeanour. The cue for his transformation is the ringing of bells at dawn on Christmas morning. Each boy wakes to find that the impoverished teacher has slipped a present into his slippers. Describing Merlusse as a real Father Christmas and 'baby Jesus's postman', the children each give him a gift in return, before singing a carol in his honour. The film ends with a second carol, this time sung by Merlusse, the headmaster and the deputy. Merlusse is not only rewarded spiritually (by the respect and affection of the children), but also materially, since his actions result in a long overdue promotion. In both cases it is through the medium of the *noël* that the triumph, and rewarding, of Merlusse's Christmas spirit is expressed.

If *Merlusse* is Pagnol's only Christmas film as such, *Le Château de ma mère* (*My Mother's Castle*, 1990), filmed by Yves Robert and based on Pagnol's memoirs, presents a concise compendium of Christmas customs. The film concerns several trips made by Pagnol's family from the city of Marseilles to the Provençal hills. The first of these excursions takes place at Christmas, which is evoked by references to snow, bears, the North

Pole, post office calendars and Canadian skaters in furs. On Christmas Eve the family dress the tree in their holiday cottage and sit down to a traditional festive meal consisting of 'the thirteen desserts'. Finally, they are joined by Uncle Jules, a rotund and amiable figure who manages to suggest not only Father Christmas (via his appearance and his gift-giving) but also – through his talk of midnight Mass, the crib and fourteenth-century carols – local religious customs. Secular and Catholic values are contrasted, however, when Jules prays that the Pagnol family may believe in God, for which Joseph Pagnol thanks him before restating his own atheistic convictions. The general tenor of the Christmas sequence is, then, one of diversity rather than consensus: hence the differing beliefs of Jules and Joseph, and the contrast between the urban Pagnols' festive spirit and the indifference towards Christmas shown by the peasant boy Lili. But what embraces the various characters, and indeed the film's rather episodic structure, is a sense of nostalgia for the early years of the century. As in *Merlusse*, this derives from the evocation of childhood and from the pre-war setting, but this time the latter element is rendered explicit. *Le Château de ma mère* concludes with a sudden change of tone, and recounts the deaths of Pagnol's mother, his brother Paul and his friend Lili. Although only Lili is killed in the First World War, the implication is that the spirit of childhood, of family security and of Christmas died in 1914.

Christmas and the Great War: *La Grande Illusion* (1937)

The greatest French film about the First World War, Jean Renoir's *La Grande Illusion* (*Grand Illusion*, 1937), uses Christmas as a more explicit moral symbol. Coming at the conclusion of the film, Christmas in *La Grande Illusion* summarises the beliefs expressed consistently throughout: pacifism, humanism, internationalism and class solidarity. Christmas in the trenches had already been represented in several popular novels and short stories published immediately after the war, including Alexandre Arnoux's *Le Cabaret* (1918), Gabriel-Tristan Franconi's *Un tel de l'armée française* (1918) and Pierre Chaine's *Les Mémoires d'un rat* (1923). In Renoir's film, the festival takes place not at the front but in a secluded domestic setting, on a farm to which the French prisoners of war Maréchal and Rosenthal have escaped. Although the farm is in Germany, it is a place where questions of national identity no longer matter. As such, it represents an oasis of peace and hope in the midst of the war, and it serves to crystallize the central dichotomy in the film between Renoir's own values of collectivity and inclusion, and the opposing, bellicose values of nationalism and exclusion. Elsa (Dita Parlo) has lost her husband and brothers in the war, but nonetheless she harbours the prisoners, tending Rosenthal's wounded foot and falling in love with Maréchal (Jean Gabin). The embryonic romance between Elsa and Maréchal is the culmination of a process by which the universal values of solidarity and love are seen to dissolve national or racial differences. Hence the comradeship between the gentile Maréchal and the Jew Rosenthal, and also between the French officer Boeldieu and the German prison commandant Rauffenstein. In the latter case, there is a certain class solidarity (between aristocrats), while language barriers are broken down (by a shared third language, English). On the farm, these themes are developed further: Maréchal is reminded of his own peasant upbringing; a romantic but symbolic exchange of languages takes place, whereby Maréchal speaks some German ('Lotte hat blaue augen') while Elsa learns a little French ('Le café est prêt'). On Christmas Eve, each wishes the other good night in the 'enemy' language.

Christmas is celebrated on the farm in an atmosphere which is almost defiantly optimistic and family-centred. Elsa's daughter Lotte is woken late on Christmas Eve to see the candles, the tree and the crib, while a gramophone plays festive music. The Christmas iconography here functions as a kind of shared third language which unites the participants (although it is not really part of Rosenthal's experience). This is particularly true of the baby Jesus, made (ironically by Rosenthal) out of a potato and placed in the crib. Before the popularization of Father Christmas later in the century, in both France and Germany it was the Christ child who was believed to distribute gifts to children.[19] When Lotte wants to eat the potato Jesus, she is picked up and hugged by Maréchal and a new family group is established as the camera focuses on Lotte, Maréchal and Elsa.[20] Rosenthal, meanwhile, is left to hover at the edge of the frame, sometimes in the shot and sometimes out of it: he remains on the margins of the family space and of the Christmas celebration. Although Rosenthal's position is therefore rather ambiguous, the Christmas sequence cements the romance between Elsa and Maréchal (they kiss for the first time) and provides a perspective beyond the end of the war (Maréchal later vows to return to Elsa and Lotte once the fighting is over). This hope is in fact foreclosed in the draft scenario: 'Maréchal and a companion … have escaped and reached Switzerland. Safely there, they agree to celebrate the next Christmas Eve together at Maxim's. The final scene occurs at Maxim's, where in the midst of the revelry marking the first Christmas after the war an empty table awaits two men who never appear'.[21] But in the filmed version, although it is tempered by realism, the hope evoked by the Christmas sequence remains. And thus Christmas in *La Grande Illusion* is an idealized moral symbol free from the pessimism of the original ending.

Family values: *L'Assassinat du Père Noël* (1941), *Les Parapluies de Cherbourg* (1964), *Juste avant la nuit* (1971), *Conte d'hiver* (1992)

The family is, then, a crucial element in both Renoir and Pagnol's evocations of Christmas. This is of course hardly surprising, since Christmas is 'the festival of the family as microcosm'.[22] If in Provençal cinema the family often functions as a microcosm of the local peasant community, in *La Grande Illusion* it symbolizes as we have seen the more universal values of pacifism and humanism. As well as being a primordial factor in Christmas celebrations,[23] family and fertility is a historically important issue in France, where particularly in the twentieth century great importance was attached to the birth rate, with various policies designed to increase the French population. The ideological status of the family was institutionalized during the Occupation, under Pétain's Vichy government, whose motto (replacing *Liberté, égalité, fraternité*) was *Travail, famille, patrie*.[24] It is consequently difficult to distinguish between the pro-family Christmas message and the reactionary political implications in Christian-Jacques's *L'Assassinat du Père Noël* (*The Killing of Father Christmas*, 1941), a film shot during the Occupation and set at Christmas in a remote French village. What can be said, however, is that the narrative – which concerns a number of crimes and suspicions that traumatize the snowbound village – emphasizes 'the unadvisability of going away' and 'the importance of stability within the community'.[25]

One might ascribe the same values (albeit shorn of any Pétainist political resonance) to Jacques Demy's *Les Parapluies de Cherbourg* (*The Umbrellas of Cherbourg*, 1964). Set at the time of the Algerian war, this musical eschews the customary optimism of the genre to present an extremely stylized but rather pessimistic view of young love. Geneviève (Catherine Deneuve) and Guy (Nino Castelnuevo) are in love, despite the disapproval of her mother. After Guy is called up to fight in Algeria, Geneviève discovers that she is pregnant by him. Some months later, hearing no news of Guy and suspecting the worst, she agrees to her mother's suggestion and marries the eligible jeweller Roland. Returning to Cherbourg a year later, Guy has to confront the loss of Geneviève (and his child) and the death of his own mother before he finally marries the latter's nurse, the maternal and long-suffering Madeleine. The transformation of values is clear: both protagonists reluctantly exchange passion for pragmatism. The romantic idealism of the first Act is, by the close of the third and final Act, felt as a threat to the hard-won family stability which Guy has secured. That family security is, moreover, symbolized by Christmas, the family festival par excellence.

Although the narrative covers six years, and is set in various seasons but predominantly in winter, Christmas is elided until the crucial final

The family at all costs: Guy (Nino Castelnuevo) reunited with his wife and son at the close of *Les Parapluies de Cherbourg* (1964). (Courtesy of Tartan Video, tel. 020 94 1400).

scene, which takes place at Guy's garage in December 1963. During Geneviève's pregnancy we see snow falling (as she reads Guy's final letter) and also the false snow (confetti) of the Easter carnival. In the first of these scenes, there is still a hope that Guy will return to marry Geneviève; in the second, all hope is gone and she is in despair. When the two finally meet up again, real snow is falling but the situation has changed. Geneviève is represented as an intruder whose arrival threatens the cosy domestic world of Guy, Madeleine, and their young son François. Having dressed the Christmas tree, Madeleine and François walk into town to see the window displays. Guy is thus alone, and vulnerable to the attentions of Geneviève, who calls in at the garage by chance on her way home to her husband in Paris. Glamorously dressed, and no longer a local, she is characterized as a Parisienne, and hence an implicit temptress or vamp.[26] Guy, however, is strong enough to resist temptation: he sacrifices the past to the present, refusing even to see his daughter by Geneviève. No sooner has Geneviève left than the music reaches a crescendo, the snow falls thicker than ever, and Guy's wife and son return. Rushing out on to the forecourt, Guy is reunited with them in a fever-pitched and almost neurotic celebration of family life. Christmas here is unequivocally associated with the defence of the family at all costs.

The family Christmas is portrayed in a rather more ambivalent light by Claude Chabrol in *Juste avant la nuit* (*The Vice* / *Just Before Nightfall*, 1971). The film belongs to Chabrol's 'Hélène cycle', a series of satires on the French bourgeoisie of the period. But as well being satirized, the bourgeois family is also to a certain extent idealized in these films. Like the first of the cycle, *La Femme infidèle* (*The Unfaithful Wife*, 1968), *Juste avant la nuit* concerns an apparently perfect marriage between a man called Charles (Michel Bouquet) and a woman called Hélène (Stéphane Audran). In both cases, family secrets concerning adultery and murder lurk beneath the glossy facade of bourgeois ease. We know from the outset of *Juste avant la nuit* that Charles is an adulterer and a murderer (he kills his mistress, Laura, in a violent sex game that goes wrong). The family scenes that follow, and in particular the Christmas celebrations, are therefore undercut by Charles's previous actions and by his secret sense of guilt. The festive atmosphere – including a champagne toast to the 'happy family' while the children play outside in the snow – is rendered doubly ironic by the presence of François, a family friend and the husband of the murdered Laura. But there is more to Chabrol's evocation of family than this simple irony at the expense of François and Hélène. Crucially, the family – in particular the relationship between Hélène, the children, and the au pair – is represented as relaxed and genuinely happy, especially in Charles's absence. In fact, the only fly in the ointment is Laura's murder and, more importantly, Charles's subsequent anguish. Once Charles confesses the affair and the murder to both François and Hélène, only to be exonerated from all blame and told to forget about it, the family is increasingly depicted as an ideal under threat but worth fighting to preserve. Because Charles refuses to forget his crime and wishes to give himself up to the police, the preservation of the family actually requires his own death. The film concludes with his assisted suicide at the hands of his wife (although one could also interpret this as murder) and the continuation of family life in his absence. In the final scene, set on a wintry beach, Charles's mother tells Hélène in a satisfied tone that the children are already beginning to forget him. The defence of the family that was expressed with such intensity at the end of *Les Parapluies de Cherbourg* has here been taken to a dispassionate and ironic extreme.

The premise of *Juste avant la nuit* is reversed in *Conte d'hiver* (*A Winter's Tale*, 1992), Eric Rohmer's Christmas tale of faith and wonder. Here the father is already absent and must be found in order to safeguard and complete the family. Five years have elapsed since Félicie (Charlotte Véry) enjoyed a summer romance with Charles (Frédéric Van Den Driessche). Although (due to a mistaken address) she has not heard from Charles since, she maintains an irrational belief that she will find him again and that her daughter Elise will thus meet her real father. The action takes place in the last two weeks of December, as Félicie vacillates between keeping her faith in Charles and choosing one of two potential suitors. Although it is clear that both men are suitable surrogate fathers for Elise, Félicie cannot bring herself to abandon her belief (ridiculed by those around her) that one day Charles will return to Paris. Her position is at one point likened to Pascal's wager (that the potential benefits of betting on God's existence outweigh the risks), a classic paradigm of Christian faith and the subject of Rohmer's earlier Christmas film, *Ma Nuit chez Maud* (*My Night With Maud*, 1969). The religious parallel becomes explicit when she prays beside the Nativity crib in Nevers cathedral that Charles may return to her. The symbol of the crib, although naturalistic and understated (like the film as a whole), is crucial: it associates Félicie's state of faith and wonder with that of the shepherds in the Bible account of Jesus's birth. The other major intertext for Félicie's story is Shakespeare's *A Winter's Tale*, which she goes to see towards the end of the film and which confirms her faith in miracles. The play also reinforces the themes of faith and wonder derived from the Nativity, most obviously in the climactic revelation when a statue appears to come to life.[27] When the miracle does come in *Conte d'hiver*, however, it is not at Christmas but at New Year. This allows Rohmer to confound audience expectations and to prolong suspense, but it also reflects the relative importance of the twin festivals in France. Christmas takes place but is given no special emphasis (in fact Félicie spends the day packing to go to Nevers). New Year by contrast is granted more significance (in this case, by Charles's miraculous appearance, his introduction to Félicie's mother, sister, and extended family, and the completion of the family unit). As in the Christmas sequences from *La Grande Illusion* and *Les Parapluies de Cherbourg*, the camera focuses on a family group of mother, father, and child, and one is again reminded that in the Christian festival 'the trinity of mother and father devoted to the birth of their child [is] the unambiguous centrepiece'.[28]

The cloning of Christmas: *La Cité des enfants perdus* (1995)

La Cité des enfants perdus (*City of Lost Children*, 1995) by Jeunet and Caro is the most spectacular French fantasy film of recent times, a synthetic fairy-tale which combines myths and monsters in a brilliant amalgam aimed at an early-teen audience. Surprisingly, however, the central references to Christmas and the film's implicit moral commentary on the nature of the festival have been ignored by critics and reviewers.[29] This is all the more surprising since the film features several characters dressed as Santa Claus and a rendition of 'Petit Papa Noël', the French equivalent of 'White Christmas'. The Christmas connection also provides a possible explanation of the film's obscure title (when the children are found, the setting is a harbour rather than a city).[30] Although puzzling to some reviewers, the title suggests a link with ancient and quasi-universal Christmas traditions.[31] For Christmas – like its autumnal sister Halloween – is a festival which, in its origins, simultaneously centres on children and placates the spirits of the dead. 'And the dead are the children'.[32] The 'city of lost children', in other words, symbolizes the realm of dead children and therefore one ancient meaning of Christmas itself.[33]

The plot of the film develops further the association of children and death which is found in the ancient myths from which Christmas is in part derived. The villain of the piece, Krank (Daniel Emilfork), is a bitter and grotesque genius who has grown old prematurely because of an inability to dream. Hence his need to kidnap children and consume their dreams. Krank is clearly a reworking of Saturn, 'devourer of his own children' and 'prototype for a number of similar figures' including Saint Nicholas and Father Christmas.[34] Krank even attempts to undergo the shift (from devourer of children to their benefactor) that over the centuries turned Saturn and his ilk into the benign figure of Santa Claus. But the results only terrify the kidnapped children as Krank, dressed as Father Christmas, mimes grotesquely to Tino Rossi's rendition of 'Petit Papa Noël'. First recorded by Rossi for the film *Destins* in 1946, the song has since sold over thirty million copies in France, and has become a cliché of the modern French Christmas.[35] But even this festive gambit fails in Krank's hands. The children can tell that he is not the real Father Christmas …

So where in *La Cité des enfants perdus* is the true festive spirit to be found? Certainly not in the various dystopian creation stories which, parodying the Nativity, populate the film with monsters, from Krank and his brothers (six identical clones and a brain in a jar, all created by a mad scientist) to the manipulative Siamese twin sisters called the Octopus and the army of cyborgs known as the Cyclops. Fighting against these evil forces are the children of the title and, in particular, a girl called Miette (Judith Vittet) and a man called One (Ron Perlman). In their search for the lost children, their symbolic family ties (One calls Miette his 'little sister' and at one point they are literally tied together) and even their appearance, they embody Christmas. Miette is always dressed in red and white; she comes down the chimney in the climactic dream sequence, and earlier, when reunited with One, asks him 'Who did you think it was – Father Christmas?' One is in a sense an honorary child, a dim-witted but big-hearted circus strongman who is searching for his adoptive 'little brother' Denrée. His name associates him with the uniqueness of the festival, in the face of cloning, replication, and the simulation of Christmas spirit by Krank. His slow and awestruck appearance also recalls Fernandel in Pagnol's Provençal films, and via him, the archetype of the wondering shepherd beside the crib. The traditional family values of Christmas are evoked by One's devotion to Denrée and Miette, and also by his goal to find a house and a wife (which is expressed in terms comparable to Guy's proposal to Madeleine in *Les Parapluies de Cherbourg*).

But *La Cité des enfants perdus* does not just allude to the modern French Christmas (via 'Petit Papa Noël'), the festive celebration of the family (One, Miette and Denrée), the Nativity (One as shepherd and the various birth narratives), and the Saturn myth (Krank). It also raises the question of the commodification of Christmas. The names of One and Denrée are already hints in this direction (*denrée* is French for 'commodity'), while the plot can be read as a battle between the unique (One, Miette, the kidnapped children, each with their own dream) and the multiple (the Siamese twins, the Cyclops who kidnap the children and the clones who serve them up for Krank). The film can in fact be interpreted as a moral commentary on the tension between the original, first Christmas (the birth of Christ, the 'true meaning' of the festival) and subsequent reproductions and simulations (the commodification and commercialization of Christmas). The latter would include not only Krank's miming to Tino Rossi's 'Petit Papa Noël' (a song that has been recorded by umpteen French artists) but also the theme of cloning which runs throughout the film (with the mad scientist, known as 'the Original', returning to destroy his unhappy progeny), and even the process of computer graphics which provides most of the special effects. The key is given in the opening sequence, which shows a child's dream being invaded by Krank. The dream begins as a stereotypical fairytale Christmas, with falling snow, old-fashioned toys and a delighted child in a warm, cosy room. When Father Christmas enters by means of the chimney, the idyll is complete. What signals that the dream is turning into a nightmare is the arrival of a second Santa, followed by a third, a fourth, a fifth, and so on. It is the multiplication – the cloning of something (someone) that is meant to be unique – that spells evil. Finally – the last of dozens of Santas – Krank appears, to send the child screaming out of his dream. Only at the end of the film will the situation be rectified, when Miette enters Denrée's dream (as Father Christmas) to defeat Krank. One could say that Denrée, like the boy in the first sequence, represents the spirit of Christmas (indeed the Christ child), kidnapped by the spirit of replication and commodification. It is only when he is ultimately rescued by his adoptive brother One and adoptive sister Miette that the moral significance of the festival is reasserted. Christmas has been brought back from the realm of the multiple to the realm of the One.

The Ironic Voice

Dismembering Christmas: *Le Père Noël est une ordure* (1982)

As we have already suggested, the most notorious and comprehensive cinematic assault on the French Christmas is Jean-Marie Poiré's frantic farce *Le Père Noël est une ordure* (*Santa Claus is a Louse*, 1982). The moral significance of the festival is gradually evacuated along with a host of accepted conventions and customs. True to its origins in the oppositional theatre known as *café-théâtre*, the film uses a blend of vituperative verbal comedy and slapstick to launch an all-out attack on its target. The attack begins with the title, which proved so controversial that it was changed in Belgium and Switzerland, while in France several cinemas blanked out the offending words 'une ordure' and one apparently added next to 'Le Père Noël' a sign reading 'Not the real one!'.[36] It proved impossible to find an American distributor for such an iconoclastic vision of Christmas, and numerous French companies – including the national railway (SNCF), Air France and the Morris advertising group – refused to publicize or screen the film. And yet, despite – or rather because of – what has been described as its 'ironic challenge to dominant cultural values' and its 'unsettling effect on the consumerist "establishment"',[37] *Le Père Noël est une ordure* has gained cult status in France. In July 1994 the readers of the French-language *Première* magazine voted it the top French film of all time and the third best film ever made, behind only *Gone With the Wind* and *Dances With Wolves*.[38]

Traditionally, at Christmas 'society functions according to a double rhythm of *heightened solidarity* and *exaggerated antagonism*, and these two aspects act together in balanced opposition'.[39] In *Le Père Noël est une ordure*, however, the balance is lost, the solidarity has disappeared and only the 'exaggerated antagonism' remains. This is all the more ironic given that the film is set in a Samaritans organization called 'SOS détresse' which is supposedly offering comfort and 'heightened solidarity' to the desperate on Christmas Eve. The charity workers Pierre (Thierry Lhermitte) and Thérèse (Anémone) are, however, incompetent, abusive and intimidated by turn, alienating their callers, refusing to answer the phone and provoking rather than preventing suicides. The Father Christmas of the title, meanwhile, also manages to invert the traditional qualities associated with his role: in reality an ex-con called Félix (Gérard Jugnot), this Santa steals rather than gives, assaults children, swears, drinks, advertises a strip show and denegrates the family by repeatedly fighting with his pregnant wife Josette (Marie-Anne Chazel).

As the film progresses, it is in particular the collective, inclusive model of Christmas which is tested and found wanting. Pierre, Thérèse, Félix and Josette are joined in the Samaritans' office by the Bulgarian neighbour Monsieur Preskovitch and the transvestite Katia. But there is no sense of 'heightened solidarity', rather a chaotic frenzy involving disparate individuals. The ideal of the inclusive Christmas (celebrated in *La Grande Illusion* and *Merlusse*) is at first evoked by the *réveillon* or Christmas Eve dinner, only to be destroyed by the treatment of the two outsiders, Preskovitch and Katia. The Bulgarian gives the Samaritans a sample of his local delicacy, but the sweets are disgusting and are spat out behind his back. The joke is repeated when Preskovitch again joins the party, this time to offer the diners a revolting parody of the traditional Yule log – *klug*, a cake that farts when cut open. At this point he is pushed out of the door by Pierre and told to return to his own country. Although at least managing to remain in the apartment, Katia is similarly excluded by Pierre, who resists his advances and ends up abusing him and shouting 'You're no friend of mine!' This rejection is the cue for Katia to invoke the moral values of Christmas in a superb speech about Pierre and Thérèse's exclusion of outsiders from their blinkered 'shitty moral universe'. But the serious note is short-lived. The moral voice which speaks briefly through Katia is swiftly submerged under the avalanche of gags at his expense, including verbal comedy (swearing), slapstick (Katia is soon after hit in the face with a door and also shot in the foot) and the general caricature of the transvestite as a hammy queen.

As the farce gathers pace and the comic violence increases, Thérèse reminds Josette that even wars stop on Christmas Eve. But the disputes, accidents, pratfalls, sexual insults and brawls escalate until a repairman is accidentally shot dead. The association of Christmas with life is thus inverted and the comedy assumes a blacker tone when Félix and Josette begin to cut up the dead body. Gift-giving has already been ridiculed when Pierre and Thérèse exchange ludicrous home-made presents (a huge knitted cardigan for him, a nude portrait with pig for her) and again when Pierre magnanimously offers Josette the oyster shells from the dinner table and an old waste paper bin. It is finally subjected to a grotesque parody in the film's climactic scene. In an ending added to the original play by the director Jean-Marie Poiré, the body parts are wrapped in Christmas paper and distributed by the cast, like so many presents, to the (meat-eating) animals in a zoo. Even here, the group fails to act concertedly (Katia innocently gives the 'presents' to giraffes and monkeys instead of lions and tigers), while the sequence serves not only to conclude but also to summarise the narrative, which has been a comprehensive and exuberant dismemberment of Christmas, bit by bit.

The death of the family: *La Vie est un long fleuve tranquille* (1988), *Elisa* (1994)

In *Juste avant la nuit*, the family Christmas is invested with several ironies, not the least of which is the fact that the continuation of the family is founded on the death of the father. Nonetheless, Chabrol's portrayal of the family is here (and elsewhere) at least as idealized as it is ironic. This cannot be said of the portrayal of the group in *Le Père Noël est une ordure* or of the two families in Etienne Chatiliez's comedy *La Vie est un long fleuve tranquille* (*Life is a Long Quiet River*, 1988). The latter is not a Christmas film as such, but the plot is anchored by a crucial Christmas sequence, and the family is the principal target for Chatiliez's nihilistic humour.

The film contrasts two families, the Groseilles (working-class slobs) and the Le Quesnoys (upper-class twits). Each family is the stuff of caricature, and both – but in particular the Le Quesnoys – are traumatized to learn that twelve years previously their youngest children were switched at birth. The baby-swap – which threatens family unity in both cases, and which ultimately leads to the dissolution of family structures – took place at Christmas. The ironic parallel with the Nativity is highlighted when, in her letter revealing the incident, the nurse Josette calls the simultaneous births 'a miracle'. What follows twelve years later is of course no utopian family narrative but an increasingly dystopian picture: on learning the truth about the babies, Madame Le Quesnoy (Hélène Vincent) begins to suffer from depression: she drinks, takes pills, and becomes a nervous wreck. The Le Quesnoy family values (admittedly already ridiculed as prissy and repressed) disintegrate as the children fraternize with the Groseilles and learn to drink, smoke and experiment with sex. Moreover, the two families are now represented as one amorphous group of youngsters, with no parental presence on either side. Far from cementing family bonds, the 'miracle' births at Christmas have ultimately resulted in the collapse of the family.

Christmas spells the death of the family more immediately in the melodrama *Elisa* (1994) by Jean Becker. Again, Christmas is associated with an ironic and dystopian birth narrative. In this case, the child concerned, Marie,[9] is aged about five when she is 'born'.[40] The pre-credit sequence details an astoundingly bleak family Christmas during which Marie's mother tries to stifle her daughter with a pillow before killing herself while their apartment burns around her. This outburst of violence is set in the context of a potentially happy family Christmas, suggested by the laughter and shouts of 'Joyeux Noël' from neighbouring apartments, the Christmas tree painted by Marie, the real tree illuminated by her mother, and even the festive record that plays during the attempt on Marie's life. At the end of the sequence, with her mother dead, Marie is rescued by firemen and is heard (in adult voice-over) declaring 'I was born with music one Christmas Eve'. Her (re)birth is thus equated with the death of her mother and the beginning of her new existence as a cynical and defensive orphan. In *Elisa* Christmas signifies only death and solitude.

Conclusion

Christmas in French cinema is multi-faceted, and includes celebrations of the archetypal family Christmas (*La Grande Illusion, Les Parapluies de Cherbourg*), reminders of longstanding local traditions (*Le Château de ma mère*), commentaries on the commodification of the festival (*La Cité des enfants perdus*) and wholesale evacuations of all that Christmas is meant to stand for (*Le Père Noël est une ordure*). The French ambivalence towards Christmas (in which the perceived 'Americanization' of the festival is surely a factor) ensures that there is no consensus about its meaning. Even as central a concept as the role of the family at Christmas is subject to diverse representations, with the moral certainties expressed by Pagnol, Renoir, Demy and Rohmer counterbalanced by the part-satirical, part-utopian commentary of Chabrol, and the raucous irony of Chatiliez. As Daniel Miller comments in his 'A Theory of Christmas', a 'sense of contradiction seems to pervade, as ambivalence, the experience of the festival today. We are used to thinking of Christmas as the time for both joy and suicides, of materialism and its repudiation, of family togetherness and family quarrelling'.[41]

The ambivalence within the family that Miller observes in the modern Christmas is encapsulated in one of the most recent French films to portray the festival, Sandrine Veysset's *Y aura-t-il de la neige à Noël?* (*Will it Snow for Christmas?*, 1997). Indeed 'joy and suicides' would be a useful summation of the contradictions which run throughout the film, which is both a brutal, ultra-realistic account of peasant agriculture in southern France and a fairytale about an earth-mother and her seven children.[42] If the 'family togetherness' is created by the mother, then the 'family quarrelling' focuses on the violent, manipulative figure of the father. The premise of Rohmer's *Conte d'hiver* is almost reversed here, since the Christmas miracle at the end of Veysset's film entails the disappearance of the father (he leaves to spend Christmas with his other, legitimate, family). While the demonization of the father is tempered by the mother's desire for him, it is in his absence that the family Christmas is celebrated. The portrayal of Christmas is, however, deeply ambivalent, since it is precisely at this time of the year that the tensions which are ever-present in the family's struggle for survival are most acute. The joy and warmth of the family unit reach their zenith at the Christmas Eve dinner (the *réveillon*), with songs and jokes, candles and laughter. But there is also a sense of despair in the scenes leading up to the *réveillon*, with the mother increasingly desperate in her battle to keep the children warm and fed (the father even denies them firewood the day before Christmas Eve). The despair is submerged in the *réveillon* scene, but reappears in the ambiguous ending, when the mother apparently tries to gas herself and her children (in a scene which can be interpreted as either a dream or reality).

Whatever the status of the gassing scene – and Veysset herself has said that it is intended to be ambiguous – the film concludes with a Christmas miracle, as the long-awaited snow begins to fall and the children run out into the night to play in it. Even here, however, the film's ambivalence continues: for how long have the family been saved?[43] How will they struggle through to next Christmas? The song which closes the film, moreover, suggests that the absent father is in some ways regretted by the mother. The film closes with a close-up on her face at the window while Salvatore Adano songs 'Tombe la neige', evoking bleak and lonely images of winter and addressing an absent lover ('The snow is falling/You won't come tonight'). Thus the film closes with a balance of family joy (the children playing in the snow) and family pain (the absence of a father who might have been part of this scene). Both within this film and across French cinema's representations of Christmas as a whole, 'a sense of contradiction seems to pervade, as ambivalence, the experience of the festival'.[44]

Notes

1. Daniel J. Foley, *Christmas the World Over. How the Season of Good Will is Observed and Enjoyed by Peoples Here and Everywhere* (Philadelphia, New York and London: Chilton Book Company 1963), p 42.

2. Daniel Miller, 'A Theory of Christmas', in Daniel Miller (ed) *Unwrapping Christmas* (Oxford: Clarendon Press, 1993), p 6.

3. Claude Lévi-Strauss, 'Father Christmas Executed', in Miller, pp 38–51.

4. Ibid, p 40.

5. Ibid, p 39.

6. Ibid, p 44.

7. Ibid, p 51.

8. Paul Webster, 'Parisian stores give Santa his cards', *The Guardian* (22 December 14 1998).

9. Lévi-Strauss, in Miller, p 39.

10. Richard Abel, *The Ciné Goes to Town: French Cinema 1896–1914* (Los Angeles and London: University of California Press, 1994), p 70, 175.

11. Ibid, p 502, n129.

12. Ibid, p 204.

13. Ibid, p 164.

14. Ibid, p 211.

15. Foley, p 43.

16. François de la Bretèque, 'Images of Provence: Ethnotypes and stereotypes of the south in French cinema', in Richard Dyer and Ginette Vincendeau (eds), *Popular European Cinema* (London: Routledge, 1992), pp. 58–71.

17. Ibid.

18. Marcel Pagnol, *Merlusse/Cigalon* (Monte Carlo: Editions Pastorelly, 1974), p 17.

19. Clement A. Miles, *Christmas in Ritual and Tradition, Christian and Pagan* (London: Unwin 1912), p 278. See also the story *Conte de Noël* by the Catholic novelist François Mauriac (Mauriac 1938).

20. A similar image of the crib is found in François Mauriac, 'Conte de Noél' (1938) in D.J. Colon (ed), *Anthologie de Contes Nouvelles Modernes* (London: Methuen 1968), pp 149–49.

21. Alexander Sesonske, *Jean Renoir: The French Films, 1924–1939* (Cambridge, Mass: Harvard University Press, 1980), p 283.

22. Miller, in Miller, p 29.

23. For an account of fertility rites in the Provençal Christmas, see Miles 1912: 255.

24. This translates as 'Work, family, homeland'.

25. Susan Haywood, *French National Cinema*, (London: Routledge, 1996), p 195.

26. Compare the archetypes of the devoted wife/mother and the seductive vamp from the city in Murnau's classic melodrama *Sunrise* (1927).

27. Note in particular two lines from this scene of the play (both of which we hear in the film): 'I like your silence; it the more shows off your wonder' and 'It is required you do awake your faith'.

28. Miller, in Miller, p 12. That is, assuming that one interprets Maréchal as a surrogate father for Lotte in *La Grande Illusion*.

29. See for example Audé 1995, which makes no mention of Christmas and asserts that there is a striking absence of Anglo-Saxon references in the film.

30. One should perhaps add that the French *cité* is more directly translated as 'community'.

31. Françoise Audé, '*La Cité des enfants perdue*: Le malade sans imaginaire', *Positif*, 412 (June 1995), pp 41–3.

32. Lévi-Strauss, in Miller, p 45.

33. Ibid.

34. Ibid, p 46.

35. Marion Vidal and Isabelle Champion, *Histoires des plus célèbres chanson du cinéema* (Paris: M.A. Editions 1990), p 234.

36. Alexandre Grenier, *Génération Père Noël* (Paris: Belfond 1994), p 270.

37. Sue Harris, '"Les Comiques font de la résistance": Dramatic Trends in Popular Film Comedy', *Australian Journal of French Studies*, XXXV/1 (January/April 1998), pp 87–100.

38. Grenier, p. 271.

39. Levi-Strauss, in Miller, p 47.

40. Her name is an ironic echo of the Mary of the Nativity.

41. Miller, in Miller, p 26.

42 There are deliberate echoes here of fairytales such as *Snow White and the Seven Dwarves*.

43 Vincent Ostria and Laurent Roth, 'Entretien avec Sandrine Veysset', *Cahiers du cinéma*, 508 (December 1996), 59–61.

44. Miller, in Miller, p 26.

10

Father Frost on 31 December: Christmas and New Year in Soviet and Russian Cinema[1]

Birgit Beumers

Are you the summer Santa?
Yes, Nadia, I'm the wizard from Maghreb.
What's the Maghreb?
The Maghreb is the land where the summer Santas live.
Is it a Soviet land?
Of course. All the summer Santas live in the Soviet Union.
And the winter ones?
They too.[2]

About Christmas, New Year and other Carnivals

As is perfectly clear to every child (and adult), each year Father Christmas faces the huge problem of delivering presents to all the children in the world during one single night. Even if he travels against the earth's rotation, he still has no more than 48 hours (taking into account that he would cross the dateline) to visit millions of children. That is why, in Russia, Father Christmas arrives only on 31 December, having, of course, by then turned into Father Frost. The following chapter is for those who are not satisfied with the above explanation.

A chapter on representations of *Christmas* in Soviet cinema could, in fact, be the shortest in this collection: suffice it to say that there were, at least officially, no Christmas celebrations in the atheist socialist state after its foundation in 1917. Yet even the perfect socialist state could not do without myths and celebrations. Moreover, the history of cinema in Russia began well before the Revolution and extends beyond the collapse of the USSR in 1991. First, therefore, we need to consider the traditions of Christmas in Russian culture and the place of Christmas in atheist Soviet Russia; even more urgently, we need to clarify the dates of various holidays and address the issue of calendars.

It was not until the time of Peter the Great that Russia adopted the Julian calendar in the process of Russia's Westernization. Until 1699 Russia had used the agricultural calendar according to which the New Year began on 1 September. The Gregorian (Western) calendar was adopted in Soviet Russia only as late as 31 January 1918. The difference between the Julian and Gregorian calendars (in the twentieth century) is thirteen days, so that New Year (1 January) falls on 13 January according to the New Style.

Before the 1917 Revolution Russian Christmas was celebrated on 25 December (7 January, New Style); the term 'Holy Days' (*sviatki*) was used to refer to the period between the birth and baptism of Christ (25 December to 6 January). The holiday of Christmas was officially abolished in Soviet Russia in 1918 after the October Revolution and was brought back as a public holiday only after the collapse of the Soviet Union in 1991. This does not mean to say, however, that families did not mark Christmas on 7 January in a private way in Soviet times. Now, in contemporary Russia, Christmas has regained its place as a religious holiday marked in church (on 7 January), but not associated with traditions of gift-giving and merry-making which remain firmly part of the New Year celebrations (during the night from 31 December to 1 January).

The atheist socialist regime initially abolished Christmas as a religious and public holiday, and with it New Year as an inappropriate festivity in a country shaken and starved by the Civil War. Yet the new regime soon perceived the public desire for a holiday with a festive atmosphere to provide some hope in bleak times and introduced the Soviet 'New Year' celebrations. The New Year is celebrated during the night of 31 December to 1 January around a decorated fir tree (*elka*), with Father Frost (*ded moroz*, literally 'Grandfather Frost') and the Snow Maiden (*snegurochka*), representing generosity and joy respectively; they also distribute presents to the children.[3] The figures of Father Frost and the Snow Maiden derive from pagan rites rather than religious traditions, and feature as such in Ostrovsky's play *The Snow Maiden* (*Snegurochka*, 1873) together with other pagan figures such as Spring (*vesna*) and Shrovetide (*maslenitsa*).

Christmas is, of course, characterized both in the West and in the East by the syncretism of pagan and Christian rituals. In the popular celebration of the festival, pagan rituals had remained stronger in Russian culture than in Western European cultures where the pagan celebrations of the Calends (first day of the month), Saturnalia (17–24 December) and the cult of the Iranian god of light Mithra (Deus sol invictus) were appropriated by the Roman church. It fixed the date on 25 December and adopted some of the pagan traditions for marking this holiday.[4] This preponderance of pagan rituals associated with Christmas made it relatively easy for the Soviet regime to appropriate the holiday and incorporate certain 'Soviet' rituals into the New Year celebrations.

January the 1st is referred to in Russian as New Year Night (*novogodniaia noch'*), or Carnival Night (*karnaval'naia noch'*), and it is on this evening that children receive their presents from Father Frost and the Snow Maiden under a decorated tree. This ritual on New Year's Eve remains intact in post-communist Russia (and has not been moved to Christmas proper). The folk ritual of merry-making and revelling, when groups of children would dress up, sing songs (*koliadovanie*) and collect money and donations for the poor in return for a blessing (*shchedrovanie*), had been abandoned during the Soviet period when there were, according to the official view, no needy people in the perfect communist state, but it was revived and absorbed in a revised 'Sovietized' form in the 1960s as a means of rewarding workers who had over-fulfilled the plan.[5]

If Christmas merges pagan and Christian ritual, then the Russian tradition has always dwelt more on the pagan and carnivalesque elements; the Soviet regime then adopted, as the Roman church had done several centuries earlier, those rituals that it deemed suitable to celebrate the New Year. It condensed all those rituals that had no religious significance into New Year: the ritual of giving presents and bringing the family together (Christmas) and the rituals of breaking social boundaries and masking (carnival proper). In Western European culture masking would remain associated with carnival (in February–March) while Russian carnival (*maslenitsa*) stood for the farewell to winter (and the beginning of fasting), accompanied in the Russian tradition by eating pancakes (farewell to rich food) which came in the shape of the sun (greeting of spring).

The invented Soviet holiday of New Year thus combines traditions that can also be found in the Dickensian Christmas: it emphasizes the folk and carnival rituals that serve to break social boundaries (Scrooge visits his employee Cratchit); it draws on the idea of inversion (spending after a whole year of thrift) in the sense that during New Year's Eve extraordinary things can happen, associated with magic and witchcraft

(Scrooge is visited by Marley's ghost). The theme of spending and generosity is insignificant in itself in a society such as the Soviet one which is not oriented toward materialism as opposed to the capitalist consumerism associated with Christmas in the Western world; special attention therefore needs to be paid to the presence or absence of gifts in the representation of New Year. The festival also dwells on the notion of the family: the entire family is brought together, which often leads to quarrels in modern society; there is, in a sense, often a subversive undertone in the perception of the family as an individualized and private sphere in a society where everything should be done for the collective, for society at large. But it remains the ideal night for lovers to make proposals. During the night from the old to the new year unknown energies are released which bring out in characters what is otherwise hidden; in the Bakhtinian sense, carnival evokes laughter to represent a victory over fear, which in this case means a transgression of social convention: characters do what they would otherwise be afraid of. They often adopt another role and wear disguises of various forms, including masks.

Christmas is a time of integration and of overcoming boundaries, of renewal and new hope; as such it is a festival of local, global and universal harmony. The cosmic dimension, symbolizing universal harmony and peace, features prominently in various rituals used to greet the New Year. It is noteworthy that during Soviet times the emphasis of the New Year celebrations in film was very much on the cosmic dimension, with all the political overtones that this carries from the communist belief in a world revolution.

The role of children in the Christmas celebrations is of great importance. Lévi-Strauss argues that children are perceived in the Christmas traditions as ghosts of the dead who return to make demands on the living; they are the voice of the outsiders, the poor, and the underprivileged. Children are the agents of the poor, they receive the gifts that repay the debts towards the dead, and this harmonious union of adults and children, the living and the dead, stresses the cosmic significance of the celebration. However, children as the main beneficiaries appear on screen only after the Soviet era.

In discussing the theme of 'Christmas' on the Soviet and Russian screen, we are thus looking at three festivals in three historic periods: Christmas as a religious holiday with folk rituals in the pre-Revolutionary period; New Year, celebrated with pagan rituals of merry-making and generosity toward others (by Father Frost and the Snow Maiden) as well as carnival rituals in the Soviet period and in contemporary Russia; and, least prominent, but nevertheless deserving some attention, the Old New Year marking the old-style beginning of the New Year both in Soviet and contemporary times. I have chosen to focus on the major New Year films rather than cover the representation of Christmas and New Year in ephemeral episodes in Soviet and Russian film as a whole.

Silent Night: Christmas before the Revolution

The films of the pre-Revolutionary period were often based on nineteenth-century literature rather than offering original plots. In 1913 Wladislaw Starewicz adapted Gogol's story 'Christmas Eve' (part of the cycle *Evenings on a Farm near Dikanka*, 1831–32) for the screen. The film contains elements of the supernatural in featuring, as the main characters, the witch Solokha and the devil. The events take place on Christmas Eve, when we see Solokha and the devil riding on a broom and trying to steal the moon. In the meantime, Solokha's son Vakula, the smith, visits Oksana, a beautiful Cossack girl, whom he wishes to marry. Yet she will only agree to the marriage if he brings her the Empress's shoes. Vakula conspires with the devil who whisks him off to the Palace in St. Petersburg, where Vakula meets the Empress's adviser Potemkin who hands Vakula the shoes, purportedly for his wife. Upon his return he offers Oksana the shoes, they marry, and live happily ever after with their son.

The plot is clearly informed by fairytale themes (the Cinderella theme of the shoe), but also by the themes of German Romanticism (the Faustian pact with the devil). As a fairytale, the story ends well. It is also rather comic overall, especially in the caricatured portrayal of individual characters, such as Solokha, who receives male customers to satisfy their erotic desires; since they arrive almost all at once, she hides them from each other in sacks. They are later disposed of by her son who tries to clear up the room, and thus they end up in different houses. The witch and the devil are, of course, figures from a pagan and supernatural tradition. They may be compared to the punitive figures of 'Zwarte Piet' and 'Knecht Ruprecht' in Dutch and German Christmas traditions, but in the film the traditionally wicked and evil figures emerge in a positive light. They are full of energy, which they use in a creative way: the devil transports Vakula to St. Petersburg on a broom, and the devil can shrink in size and hide in Vakula's pocket to assist him further. The trickery and foolery reduces the potential danger of the devil and the witch: the fear of an encounter with them is scaled down by showing them as subservient (the devil as a means of transport), or as trapped by their own ingenuity (Solokha putting her suitors in various sacks). The devil is playful, sitting on the roof to play with the sickle of the moon he has just stolen. The theft of the moon and the ride through the nocturnal skies also enhance, of course, the reference to the cosmic dimension contained in the concept of a global, universal Christmas. It is interesting to connect here the notion of Christmas as a holiday 'to bring "home" cosmological principles'[6] with the ride to the capital St. Petersburg to bring what is precious and desired as a gift from the city back to the village. The movement is centrifugal, away from the capital, from which gifts are generously scattered over the Empire, rather than the (selfishly) centripetal movement, which is typical of the Soviet period. The tension between the rich and the poor, the local and the global is resolved. There are no social boundaries, and generosity prevails: Vakula is not chased away from the Palace, and Potemkin gives away the Empress's shoes without hesitation.

The principal of inversion operates on the level of good and evil: Vakula comes across as a man with evil intention when he first visits Oksana; Oksana emerges as a girl obsessed with her looks (dress, hair, shoes). Vakula turns out to be a Father Frost figure (he delivers the gift) while Oksana regrets that she has asked for the shoes when Vakula has been missing for some time, and agrees to marry him irrespective of the shoes. Her materialism, her obsession with objects and gifts, and his evil appearance are inverted by the end, just as the witch and devil turn out to be positive. At the end of the film, as a result of the proposal during New Year's Eve, stands the traditional happy family with a son.

Christmas as shown in Starewicz's *Christmas Eve* is a festivity which inverts appearances, which makes people more generous than they are usually; however, pagan gods – the witch and the devil – dominate the scene and make this festivity a happy occasion. Other than the singers (*koliady*) passing by the houses there are no signs of Christian traditions, so that the film does not specifically develop the religious significance of the festival (the birth of Christ), but rather the folk belief and pagan rituals that lie at its root.

The Soviet New Year Party

In the 1920s the Soviet regime had begun to appropriate cultural rituals on all levels. Streets and cities were being renamed (Petrograd became Leningrad, etc); history was rewritten in such films as Eisenstein's *The Battleship Potemkin* which showed the failed 1905 Revolution as successful; and rituals were forged for holidays that were invented or appropriated (Day of the Army, Anniversary of the October Revolution). The 1930s also witnessed the first experiments with sound and colour. The musical comedy became the most prominent genre in Soviet cinema during the 1930s, and remained so until the 1950s and early 1960s. It was also the genre that most New Year films would adopt, especially seeing that, because of genre popularity, they would reach a larger audience than, say, a melodrama.

A fine example of the subversion of Christmas in one such musical comedy is the first Soviet colour film, made by Nikolai Ekk, entitled *Grunia Kornakova* (1936). The film is set in pre-Revolutionary Russia, where Grunia's father works as the caretaker at a porcelain factory. The film follows Grunia from her duties at home to her role as a revolutionary leader in the uprising by the exploited workforce of the factory. Instead of fireworks there is a fire which destroys the factory and allows the factory owner to replace the wooden wing of the factory with a new brick building, paid for with the insurance money; thirty-nine people, among them Grunia's father, are killed in the fire.

In the first frames of the film Grunia is decorating a Christmas tree: the emphasis is on home and happiness; a family reunion takes place with the arrival of Grunia's uncle. Yet the family's political and social standing is only too obvious: Grunia's father is a caretaker and still at work, while her brother is in prison for revolutionary activities and thus also absent from the gathering. The focus on the home and happiness in the seclusion of the family and on presents (dress material for Grunia and a snuff box for her father), paves the way for a critique of such seclusion.

Christmas is celebrated on three social levels: at a society ball in St. Petersburg, where couples dance in a ballroom; the preparations at Grunia's home; and the working class slaving at work, exploited by the factory owner who is himself at the ball in St. Petersburg. There is no breaking of social boundaries, no carnival spirit in this Soviet view of pre-Revolutionary society. In the eyes of socialism, capitalist society offered no relaxation from class divisions, and the happy seclusion of the family is shown to be a mere illusion of peace which crumbles away during the course of the film.

Certain stereotypes feature in *Grunia Kornakova*. The breaking of a piece of china normally means luck; for Grunia the breaking of the vase specially made for the factory owner brings misery: the Kornakovs are sacked and Grunia's mother is sent away. There is no inversion, but a subversion of the traditional motifs associated with Christmas. The family unit is not brought together, but destroyed at Christmas (father Kornakov dies); social classes do not mix, but the divide becomes even larger; the devil (the figure of the manager Solomon) does no good, but harm (he tries to rape Grunia); and the broken vase brings no luck, but misery and suffering.

There is no magic force in operation during the night, but it is in man's hands to act and create the inversion: Grunia, who has a good revolutionary pedigree (her brother is a revolutionary), leads the women's protest against the exploitation of the workers and reveals the fraud on the insurance regarding the cause of the fire. The traditions of the holiday are subverted to demonstrate the backwardness of folk beliefs and their dangerous ability to stifle and paralyse the revolutionary energy of the people: if Grunia had not been torn away from her Christmas tree by the fire and the tragic loss of her father, she would never have become a revolutionary, she would never have fought for the cause of the social good of the workers.

As such, *Grunia Kornakova* is very much a film of the 1930s, made at the height of Stalin's regime of terror and at the beginning of the purges. The view of the Christmas tree in the first frames of the film seems to lay the blame for the delay of social progress at the feet of the Christmas and New Year celebrations which are perceived as bourgeois traditions of the last century that have no room in Stalin's Russia.

As I mentioned in the introductory paragraphs, children hardly feature at all in any New Year films made before 1991, but an exception is Ivan Lukinsky's film *Chuk and Gek* (*Chuk i Gek*, 1953) based on the children's writer Arkady Gaidar's (1904–41) story of the same title. Here, the brothers Chuk and Gek travel with their mother to Siberia to see their father who is there on a geological expedition. When they arrive, all the geologists have left the expedition's base station on a special mission, due back just in time for New Year's Eve. In fact, the mother and children arrive there despite the father's instructions: he had sent a telegram telling them not to come, but the boys had thrown the telegram away while they were playing and had not told their mother. The underlying message therefore is that the family is united at Christmas by mistake. The family takes second place after social duty. It is also interesting that the movement in the film is centripetal: it goes from Moscow to Siberia and back to Moscow for the chimes of the Kremlin tower at midnight on 31 December. The emphasis is on Moscow as the centre of both political and everyday life. Indeed, the image also echoes the pre-eminence of Moscow anywhere in the Soviet state, where all timetables indicated arrival and departure times according to Moscow rather than local times.

It was not until after Stalin's death in the period of the Thaw that the first films were made especially for the New Year and about the festivities of New Year. Father Frost and the Snow Maiden feature only ephemerally in these New Year films. The best-known and most celebrated of all New Year films is Eldar Riazanov's *Carnival Night* (*Karnaval'naia noch'*, 1956), a musical comedy with the debut performance of Liudmila Gurchenko, in the role of Lena Krylova, which would establish her as a star of Soviet cinema for decades to come.

Lena Krylova is in charge of the New Year party to be held at a House of Culture in Moscow; the director is on leave and has left Serafim Ogurtsov in control. Lena is courted by Grisha Koltsov who is also preparing the show. In fact, the names already give away almost the entire story: Seraphim (the angel) Ogurtsov (*ogurets* means gherkin) makes a fool

Carnival Night. Scene from the film.

of himself, while the 'winged' Krylova (*kryl'ia* are wings) rescues the show and receives a proposal (symbolically a ring) from the 'ringed' Koltsov (*kol'tso* means ring).

Lena is devoted to the organization of the ball, but Ogurtsov wishes to see the event as a serious and official ceremony, especially since he is expecting the arrival of a Soviet official. Consequently he takes Lena's plans to pieces: a Soviet man should not hide behind a mask, so no masks were to be worn, no roles to be played; the ballerina performing *Swan Lake* should cover up her legs; the jazz music performed by a quartet should be performed by a 'mass quartet'; the orchestra which, in his view, played inappropriate music should be replaced by the orchestra from the neighbouring Veterans' Club; the librarian could play the piano and sing (but add to the line 'I am alone, all on my own' the words 'with my collective'), and the accountant could recite a fable he has not recited since he finished school forty years ago. Ogurtsov's requests echo, in fact, the silly and incomprehensible requests Party and State bureaucrats would often make regarding any cultural or artistic activity. Here, however, the enemy (the bureaucrat) is captured in his essence as he is in reality and parodied. Such a parody is possible thanks to the setting of the film on the night in which everything is inverted, everything is permissible, and everything is carnivalized. Thus the view this film offers of New Year and its carnival celebrations is almost diametrically opposed to the view upheld by Ekk in his 1936 film. This in itself reflects not only the liberalism associated with the carnival night of New Year, but also the liberal climate during the Thaw in the late 1950s when criticism of bureaucracy and of the personal abuse of social positions was encouraged by the Party.

The film also has the traditional love intrigue in the relationship between Lena and Grisha, and between the elderly couple of the accountant and the librarian. Yet on both occasions, their duty to the event comes before the personal. Lena is not united with Grisha in a dance until the show is over. Eventually, their happiness is a more permanent result than the New Year's Party and the temporary victory over bureaucracy; in fact, their happiness triumphs despite and because of the stifling interference of bureaucracy as represented by Ogurtsov.

Disguises feature prominently: Grisha disguises himself as an old man and poses as his own uncle to speak well of himself to Lena; the clowns, on the other hand, take off their guises when Ogurtsov insists that they must be serious and speak as themselves rather than as clowns. The speech Ogurtsov wishes to make is taken from his pocket by the magician, and Ogurtsov pulls out some magic props – pigeons, scarves and flowers – instead. The professor who is supposed to deliver a speech is made so drunk that he appears on stage as a clown. Clowns are deprived of their disguise, while the bureaucrats are turned into clowns. The members of the orchestra originally hired appear in the guise of old men to pose as the orchestra of the Veterans' Club. The inversion of social roles, of ages, and of the serious and comic is complete. In a classless society, breaking social boundaries cannot be a major concern; however, even the integration of the waitresses is achieved by their part in the performance of dance and song. In fact, music and dance as well as disguises and masks are the prime sources for the carnival atmosphere created in the film.

Carnival Night is a classic of Soviet cinema on the theme of New Year, both because of the songs (the most popular being 'Five Minutes') and the atmosphere of carnival it creates, but also for its implied parody of Soviet bureaucracy and officialdom that wants to see everything according to plan in the one night of the year when carnival should reign. The New Year's Eve is also defined here as the most suitable time for declarations of love and proposals. The declaration of feelings at the conclusion of a year instils hope for the future and for the new relationship (or a fresh start) in the next year. These characteristics are more in tune with Western traditions of the New Year than with Christmas and family reunion.

Grisha's proposal to Lena is made in public; feelings are not part of the private sphere in the Soviet society of the 1950s. In fact, Grisha records his declaration of love on a record which Lena accidentally plays on the transmission system for the entire House of Culture during the preparations for the party. The proposals in Riazanov's next film set on New Year's Eve move away from the public sphere into the setting of the home.

Irony of Fate, or Have a Good Sauna! (*Ironiia sud'by, ili s legkim parom*, 1975) focuses on the proposals made on a New Year's Eve in Moscow and Leningrad: that of Zhenia to Galia (in Moscow) and Ippolit to Nadia (in Leningrad). The connection between the two proposals is the 'completely unusual story which can only and exclusively happen upon New Year's Eve', as the intertitle at the beginning of the film explains. The film also contains, just like *Carnival Night*, a parodic reference to the stereotyped architecture in Soviet cities: the cartoon-like intertitles point out that all houses look alike, all the flats possess the same layout, all the furniture is standardized so that everybody can feel at home in any Soviet town.

Zhenia tells his old school friends that he is getting engaged to Galia while they are on their traditional New Year's Eve visit to the bathhouse and, as is the Russian custom, they have to drink to this event. Gradually they get more and more drunk, before they accompany one of their circle, Pavel, to the airport; here they have a few more drinks with dinner. Eventually, they are so drunk that they cannot remember which of them was travelling to Leningrad, and they put Zhenia on the plane instead of Pavel. Zhenia next finds himself somehow in a taxi that takes him to his house: Third Construction Street number 25, flat 12. He opens the door with his key (standard locks), and enters a flat that is furnished like his (with standard furniture), although in a somewhat disorderly way, but, after all, he has only just moved in. Zhenia lies down to sleep off his hangover when Nadia comes back. While they argue over whose flat this is, Zhenia discovers that he is in Leningrad, not Moscow. Nadia's fiancé Ippolit arrives, and does not believe this unbelievable story that is, nevertheless, the truth; neither does Zhenia's fiancée Galia back in Moscow. Eventually, a relationship develops between Nadia and Zhenia as both lose their original partners. Their emotions are largely expressed through songs which they sing to each other on the guitar, so the music-hall atmosphere of *Carnival Night* is replaced by a more individualized and lyrical use of music in this film. The next day Zhenia leaves, and Nadia follows him to Moscow (the centre); thus Riazanov asserts also the centripetal movement so typical of Soviet films.

The New Year's Eve in *Irony of Fate*, then, is a night during which genuine feelings emerge. Again, it is the ideal night for proposals, but both women, Nadia and Galia, want to meet the New Year at home rather than at some party or in a restaurant. Zhenia is quite the opposite of his true self during the Leningrad visit: the shy and brisk surgeon is socially inept in everyday life, but in Nadia's flat he is inventive, sensitive, caring, domestic (he makes coffee, helps Nadia zip up her boots, washes the dishes). He is bold and energetic, and takes the initiative when he suggests he will leave later on 1 January rather than on the first flight. For Riazanov the fate of Galia and Ippolit is secondary to the relationship between Nadia and Zhenia.

There are a number of traditional signs of New Year festivity: Nadia breaks a plate which is a sign of luck: Zhenia poses as Ippolit for the sake of keeping up appearances in front of Nadia's colleagues, and temporarily plays a role. There is even a hint of witchcraft in the bunch of birch twigs (*venik*) which Zhenia carries in his briefcase – it is the 'brush' he used in the bathhouse, but it is also associated with witchcraft; he returns to Nadia's flat because he has left his briefcase with the twigs behind, and later Nadia brings it to Moscow: it is the object that gives her a reason for coming, that puts her under Moscow's spell. Nadia says at one point that things will fall into place once New Year is over, but effectively she takes fate into her own hands. Leningrad features in the film as the mirror image of Moscow, the inversion of everyday normality, where true feelings emerge. These true feelings can then be taken back into normality (Moscow).

True feelings are also at the heart of another film about family relationships during the Old New Year festivities (celebrated on 13 January) in Oleg Efremov's film *Old New Year* (*Staryi novyi god*, 1980, a television film based on Mikhail Roshchin's play (1967) of the same title and a stage production for the Moscow Arts Theatre directed by Efremov in 1973). Here, the working-class family of the Sebeikins and the intelligentsia family of the Poluorlovs exemplify the principle of the crossing of social (class) boundaries: the men of both families end up in the bathhouse (where *Irony of Fate* began). The Old New Year is, in both families, perceived as a holiday, even if it is not a public holiday. There is, seemingly, even a process of giving and taking: while the Poluorlovs throw out their furniture, the Sebeikins keep receiving deliveries of new furniture and kitchen equipment, having just moved into a new flat. In both families, the table is laid and drinks offered, and both use the occasion to tell everybody the truth about life in general and what they really think of each other, which inevitably leads to a quarrel. As such, the film represents the traditional family setting for New Year, where the closeness in the family unit leads to an argument. Meanwhile, the younger generation meets the Old New Year merrily on the staircase. The party celebrated by society at large (the inhabitants of the house meeting on the staircase) is successful, while the withdrawal from society (the Sebeikins and

Poluorlovs) leads to disputes. Thus, *Old New Year* relies on the standard pattern of the Society reading of New Year as a public, not private holiday, where gifts are inappropriate since they are a burden and reduce the space in the flat; most importantly, objects deflect from the real concerns with the meaning of life. *Old New Year* is very much a traditional 'Society' view of the New Year, subversive only in the insistence that the celebration should happen on 13 January. It is clearly a film of the early 1970s rather than the 1980s; the date of the theatre production is, in this case, more telling than the date of the film's release.

The standard repertoire of films televised on New Year's Day includes two films made specially for television, both mainly concerned with the carnivalesque and magic side of the New Year: *This Merry Planet* (*Eta veselaia planeta*, directed by Yuri Saakov and Yuri Tsvetkov, 1973) and *The Wizards* (*Charodei*, directed by Konstantin Bromberg, 1982).

In *This Merry Planet* a UFO with the extraterrestials X and Y and their female commander is spotted through a telescope by a man dressed up as a magician who is about to leave for a New Year party. The magician creates a link with the cosmos, and the ensuing party brings together not only gardeners and academics, but also humans and extraterrestials, breaking both social and spatial boundaries, and enlarging the celebrations to encompass not only the globe, but the entire universe. The three aliens wander around and hide in a Christmas tree where their glass helmets look like Christmas baubles. One after the other, they venture into the hall where the party is being held, and their true identity is mistaken for a disguise; at the same time, an inventor dressed up as an alien is believed to be the alien who landed with the UFO which was sighted by the magician. Misunderstanding, disguise and carnival are thus at the core of this celebration. The aliens participate in the games: pulling a cord, dancing, singing; none of these activities makes any sense to them, but they find them enjoyable. Even the rigid woman commander is moved to tears when she is made 'queen of the ball'. The mass celebrations of the New Year allow for the creation of a music-hall setting. Truth is mistaken for a joke, the extraterrestials are believed to be humans; misunderstandings results in the revelation of genuine feeling (the human inventor courts the alien commander). Eventually, the aliens try to take the elderly bank manager back on board the UFO so that he can see the truth and testify to who the real aliens are; yet he wants nothing more than to stay where he is, since he has just discovered his feelings for a fat lady at the party. The UFO leaves, but he is left behind to ask whether anybody really believed that any of this was true. The fairytale theme returns together with the magic dimensions already seen in Starewicz's *Christmas Eve*, while the cosmic dimension in a Soviet film of the early 1970s must be linked to the global theme of Christmas, and to the preoccupation of the Soviet regime with the topic of conquests in space following the successful American missions to the moon.

The theme of believing in the magic of Christmas, and in the extraordinary powers of that night (and the power of Father Frost), is one that resounds in *The Wizards*, too. This film is based on the work of the sci-fi writers, the Strugatsky brothers. Ivan, who works in a factory in Moscow, is taking leave over the New Year holidays since his girlfriend Alena is coming from Kitezhgrad,[7] the city which has recently been 'raised from the water', where she is a witch in the service-sector. Ivan's manager does not believe a word of the story and thinks that Ivan is making excuses; but Ivan is only telling the truth.

In Kitezhgrad, Alena is employed at the NUINU (an acronym which might be translated as 'so-then-what'), the Universal Scientific Institute for Unusual Services. Her boss, Kira Shemakhanskaia (Shemakha being the capital of Shirvana and residence of the shah from the ninth until the sixteenth century), has been asked to marry Ivan Kivrin, the scientific director, but she keeps turning down his proposal. Just before the New Year, the latest invention of the Institute is ready for presentation: a magic wand that will make any wish come true. Shemakhanskaia proposes to hold a New Year's Ball in honour of this invention, and present it to a high commission which is to be invited from Moscow. Kivrin is swiftly sent to Moscow to make the necessary arrangements. Alena prepares to leave for her Christmas with Ivan in Moscow with the same flight as Kivrin. Sataneev, the accountant, wants to oust Shemakhanskaia and seizes the opportunity: he kindles her jealousy by telling her that Alena will marry Ivan (Kivrin), and that they have left for Moscow together. Shemakhanskaia bewitches Alena and turns the pleasant woman into a spiteful beast who will succumb, though, to Sataneev's advances. Alena can only be woken if she kisses Ivan, an act only too reminiscent of the Grimms' *Sleeping Beauty*.

Magic is now needed: two wizards from NUINU expedite Ivan from Moscow to Kitezhgrad; they operate a magic table (the Grimms' Tischlein-Deck-Dich) to entertain Ivan and his little sister once they arrive; they teach him to walk through walls, they can reduce themselves in size to miniature figures, just like the devil in Starewicz's film. Yet all this magic does not have any impact on human relationships: when Ivan wishes with the magic wand for Alena to be in the room, all he gets are objects – and a cow – with the name Alena ... Relationships are in the hands of humans only. In the meantime, Sataneev endeavours to retrieve his youth (the Faust theme) with the help of the magic wand. At the New Year's Party the magic wand fails to fulfil his wish and propels him instead through the chimney. When Ivan rescues him from there, Alena kisses Ivan and becomes her true self again. Kivrin appears in the guise of

Father Frost and proposes to Shemakhanskaia. Two happy couples stand at the end of the film: Kivrin and Shemakhanskaia, Ivan and Alena. Ivan's little sister creates the Christmas tree and organizes the dinner with the magic wand.

For the first time in Soviet cinema a child is portrayed as an active supporter and maker of a merry Christmas, but not as its main beneficiary. This role would only be discovered in the 1990s. The theme of the devil and the witch, of magic acts and rejuvenation, link the New Year celebration in *The Wizards* more to the pre-Revolutionary *Christmas Eve* than to any films of the Soviet period. The emphasis is on the extraordinary powers with which humans are endowed during this season, and pagan and folk beliefs (especially the reference to Kitezh). The inversion from good to evil transpires in the bewitched Alena, but also in the witch who refuses to do the 'Tischlein-Deck-Dich' laying of the table for Ivan, and only does so upon the instructions of the wizards. The film is traditionally Soviet in its use of dance and music, the carnival atmosphere of the party, and in the emphasis on New Year as the night for the foundation of relationships in the two engagements.

The Wizards is unconventional in its emphasis on myth and in the centrifugal movement that propels Ivan and the commission to the mythical city. It is significant that Ivan and his sister should then become the driving forces that establish happiness under the Christmas tree: Ivan by kissing Alena and dispelling the curse, and his sister by operating the magic wand. Instead of celebrating Christmas in private, Ivan devotes his holidays to the good of society and makes others, including himself, happy through his actions.

In Soviet films New Year was almost always interpreted with some socialist overtones. The reference to folk traditions was perceived with suspicion concerning their backwardness (*Grunia Kornakova*). New Year was seen as a serious rather than carnival event, since carnival represented a threat to stability (as expressed by Ogurtsov in *Carnival Night*) with its unpredictability and inversion. It was mischievously assessed as a private and individual celebration rather than a public and collective one (*Carnival Night, This Merry Planet, The Wizards*). Children were peripheral to the films, which focus instead on renewal of the family and new relationships being formed (*Carnival Night, Irony of Fate, The Wizards*). The two television films with their magical and surreal world (*This Merry Planet* and *The Wizards*) were films *for* children, rather than *with* children.

Another aspect worth noting is that in a non-consumer-oriented society presents were largely absent in the films made during the Soviet period. Grunia is given some dress material, but she is celebrating Christmas pre-Revolutionary Russia, and the present does not bring her happiness. For some characters in *Old New Year* possessions are a burden, and the bronze statue the Poluorlovs receive from their guests is an exquisite example of a useless item. Similarly the expensive perfume and shaver Ippolit and Nadia present to each other do not bring them happiness. The watch Kivrin offers to Shemakhanskaia is rejected as superfluous. Gifts in Soviet films about the New Year do not make those who receive them happy; this function of the gift will change only in the films of the 1990s.

In 1991 the Soviet Union collapsed, and the Orthodox service celebrating Christmas rose to prominence again. Christmas would return to the church, and to Russian households as a religious holiday rather than one associated with generosity and merry-making, consumerism and excessive consumption of food and drink. Father Frost and the Snow Maiden were perpetuated in their function as gift-givers on New Year's Eve.

The New Year had featured as a theme in movies throughout the Soviet period, but the holiday itself was not used to release new films specially for the occasion. With commercial film production rising in the 1990s, the gap in the market for Christmas films (especially at a time when the majority of new Russian films portrayed life in rather bleak terms) was soon discovered and exploited. Movies were produced to be released on video and television to cater for the demands of audiences on public holidays, such as the New Year.

Gift-giving and merry-making in post-Soviet Russia

The first film made in the new Russia about New Year was a debut film shot by a student of the Moscow Film School (VGIK), which is experimental rather than symptomatic of the new patterns and conventions that would emerge notably after 1996.

Natalia Piankova's *Happy New Year, Moscow* (*S novym godom Moskva*, 1993) is shot in black and white and deals with the relationships of people in a communal flat in Moscow. The script was developed together with the actors, fellow students of Piankova.[8] Ilya Glezer, a child of the intelligentsia now reduced to the job of caretaker, is visited by his sister Masha from St. Petersburg. Masha is clearly affluent: she shops in foreign currency stores, wears fashionable and expensive clothes, and her present for Ilya is in the form of $100 – at a time when hard currency was still an extremely rare possession for ordinary Russians. Her visit to Ilya's flat is also a return to the past: she wants to be again as she was then, before she left for St. Petersburg, where she has established herself as a painter, selling her works to foreign customers. She puts on her old clothes left in a drawer in the flat, makes the flat homely, and begins to decorate the tree and lay the table. All the time, she expects the return to the flat of her ex-boyfriend Sasha Krasnov. Her family celebration is temporarily disrupted first by the arrival of the girl Liusia, who lives in Ilya's room, and then by the neighbours: the hockey-player Misha has returned from a trip abroad and has brought his wife Galia some Western luxuries, and Galia immediately begins to give away some of her things to the people around while keeping the Western goodies to herself. She sheds her old life, but her act of giving is a disposal of things she needs no more, while Masha has brought a present specially for Ilya and also for Sasha, who eventually arrives and with whom she wants to rekindle their affair. Masha ignores the fact that Sasha is bisexual, being in a relationship with both Liusia and Ilya. Sasha swiftly leaves with Liusia, pushing Masha to one side. New Year as a happy reunion has failed in its attempt to restore relations as they once were in the past.

Piankova observes her characters from a distance. The camera is positioned statically, an amateurish device which enables Piankova, however, to refrain from assessing her characters in any way. She condemns none of the characters' actions or moral positions and does not focus specifically on their main characteristics which would normally dominate the plot, but here seem ephemeral: the Glezers' Jewishness, Masha's possession of foreign currency, Ilya's drug addiction, Sasha's bisexuality, Liusia's nakedness, the neighbours' obsession with Western luxuries. As one critic has observed, the film is almost void of any reflection.[9]

Piankova's film is auteur cinema; it is not a comedy, and not made for entertainment. At the same time, it is a most thoughtful reflection on the crippling attempts to make New Year a happy gathering, including a critique of materialism and consumerism. As such, it is exceptional among Russian New Year films.

The production of commercial films for New Year began in 1996. The most important move here came from the first television channel ORT where the General Producer Konstantin Ernst initiated, together with Dmitri Fiks and Leonid Parfenev, the production of *Old Songs about the Main Thing*. The first series was broadcast on 31 December 1995, followed by two more parts in 1996 and 1997. The first show was based on the theme of collective farm life (*kolkhoz*) in the summer, with scenes from the most famous collective farm musicals and songs of the 1950s performed by popular artists. The second programme moved forward into the 1960s with a focus on the theme of the city in winter. The third programme was centred around the theme of foreign lands with songs of the 1970s. The show is an attempt to recapitulate the history of Soviet popular music through memorable film clips. It is interesting to note here a common concern of this programme with that of other new Russian films about the New Year: they both draw on musical traditions and on the conventions of the Soviet holiday rather than starting afresh on their treatment of the subject.

The four films discussed in this section are symptomatic of the commercialization of the New Year holiday. They were released on video in the weeks immediately preceding the festivity in their respective years of production, and have all, with the exception of *New Year Story*, become part of the typical television programme for 31 December and 1 January. *New Year Story* is included in this discussion because of its diffuse and unbelievable plot, which parodies the genre of the traditional New Year film.[10]

Alexander Rogozhkin's film *Operation 'Happy New Year'* (*Operatsiia's novym godom'*, 1996) could, in many ways, hardly be more conventional in its treatment of the New Year celebrations. Rogozhkin cast for the film the stars of contemporary comedy: Alexei Buldakov who had already played General Ivolgin in Rogozhkin's *Peculiarities of the National Hunt*, and the comic actor Leonid Yarmolnik.

The film is set in a hospital ward on New Year's Eve. The characters' (or patients') respective histories bring them, and the spectator, to the traumatology department: a writer of erotic novels practises with his typist-mistress the experience of intercourse while he insists on having his hands, each finger separately, tied to the bed. His mistress, a heavy Russian beauty, pulls him down with her weight during the sexual act, and as a consequence he ends up in hospital with all his fingers broken. As his hands are being set in plaster cast, Army General Ivolgin has his New Year television address recorded; when he steps down from the stage, he slips and breaks his leg. There could be no more banal way of breaking a leg for a general, so he disguises the exact nature of the accident under the veil of a military secret once he arrives at the ward. A New Russian businessman (Yarmolnik) is hunted through fields by two mafia hitmen and, as he flees from the gunfire, runs into a piece of military equipment and sustains a painful injury to his genitals; moreover, his jaws became rigid in the position of his scream. Both conditions are treated successfully, but he remains unable to speak until a doctor adjusts his jaws, and unable to walk for several days.

All possible groups, or classes – (pseudo)-intellectual, military, and business – of the new Russian society are brought together in the ward, where they join the patients already there, including an actor and a 'fatally ill' patient, and, of course, the hospital staff. Furthermore, a policeman brings in a thief whom he has arrested, but who has swallowed the policeman's medal which the policeman wishes the doctors to retrieve for him. Class separation becomes impossible: the thief is chained to the policeman, doctors borrow patients' telephones, and even a top security door can be opened by anyone. Social boundaries are broken, while all the patients are dressed in gowns and masked with various parts of plaster casts.

The solidarity of everybody in the ward reaches its peak when all carry out an operation on the 'fatally ill' patient which leaves a scar in the shape of 'Happy New Year' on his spine; it is performed to the instructions of the General who reads from an American sci-fi journal. The operation is successful and the patient can walk; it is the compassion that the patients show towards him which proves to be the cure he needed. At the end of the film, all the patients form a group portrait and sing Russian folk songs in chorus beside the Christmas tree.

This film enhances the unity of diverse social groups; the power of compassion to make the patient walk; the friendship and mutual under-standing that can develop between the police and the person who breaks the law (the thief, the patients who stole the Christmas tree). In this sense, it is a complete inversion of reality, where the General issues commands and pays no attention to the instructor with whom he later dances during the party, where the mafia hitmen are so foolish as to fall into their own trap (they inadvertently become victims of their own grenade attack and end up in a plaster cast, receiving a drip dispensing vodka), and where drunken doctors perform miracles.

The General organizes the party with all the strategic precision of a military manoeuvre: he arranges for a tree to be stolen, food to be bought, and the women from the other wing to be invited. The General repre-sents power, and in his physical appearance he is a cross-section between Brezhnev and General Lebed.[11] He organizes the feast, conducts the choir, and supervises the operation. Without military power harmony is impossible. Rogozhkin's film thus celebrates the return to a past where an authority commands, to the golden past of Soviet times that also forms the core of the television show *Old Songs about the Main Thing*.

Operation 'Happy New Year' is successful in making everybody laugh at the absurd plot of the film and the comic scenes which it presents. At the same time, the film reverts to the classical tradition of musical comedy with its emphasis on well-known tunes and dances. Most important is the celebration of the Russian's dearest toy on this occasion: booze, be it vodka, champagne or beer. And of that there is plenty in the ward.

In 1995 the Gorky Studio in Moscow launched, under the leadership of the studio's director Sergei Livnev, a project which was designed to release films to coincide with public holidays. The film *New Year Story* (*Novogodniaia istoriia*) was their contribution to the spate of New Year films; it was released in 1997, directed by Alexander Baranov and produced by Sergei Livnev and Bakhyt Kilibaev of the Gorky Studio.

The film is an interesting mixture of various New Year traditions and cinematic conventions. It begins with a pseudo-documentary extract about the 1945 Yalta conference and the commitment of Churchill, Roosevelt and Stalin to collaborate on the anti-cosmic defence programme, designed to offer resistance against invasions from other planets. For this purpose, the three nations set up the unit 3XOmega. In the Moscow of 1996 3XOmega locates a cosmic force in the Gorky Studio where a New Year show is being recorded. Here one of the hired actors in the guise of Father Frost is singled out because his red coat shows different ornaments from the others, and in reply to the question as to 'where he comes from' he answers, truthfully, that he comes from Lapland, which is misunderstood to mean the vodka label 'Laplandia', thus he is mistaken for an advertising agent. As a consequence his Snow Maiden Ania, a working girl, has to leave the stage, too. After the programme Father Frost – who turns out to be real – animates the male puppet of the 'happy couple' in wedding clothes that serves to decorate the stage so that Ania has a dance partner; furthermore, he offers to fulfil any wish of hers. The studio's security guards overhear this conversation and rush on to the stage to consult about the nature of the wish they would like to come true; they reject money, women, and the Russian economy as areas that they can sort out themselves: why ask for miracles if we just need to work? The difficulty lies in the correct formulation of the wish. As they try to do this, 3XOmega attempts to destroy the cosmic force in the building; this requires concentrated energy, granted by President Yeltsin, and then at his request by German Chancellor Kohl and American President Clinton, who switch off the lights in their countries to boost the energy of the lethal weapon. It cannot, however, destroy Father Frost, who splits instead into different centres of energy. No wish can be formulated, and it seems that Russia does not need anything; the wish is given away to the animated bridegroom, who wishes for his bride to come to life too, since the greatest happiness is to be a human being. The artificial couple are united in happiness, and so is Ania, who during the chase has fallen in love with one of the security guards. The orphan boy Vania who squats in the studio and had been a thorn in the flesh of the guards makes friends with his main opponent and they decide to go off together to the Father Frost Party at the Kremlin (for which Father Frost has left tickets in his stocking). The American officer on 3XOmega is now the next target: it transpires that he is part of another cosmic force, and he is destroyed as he tries to escape in a helicopter.

The plot is complex to the point of being incoherent in places, and borders on the ridiculous in the use of stereotypes. The film makes several points about New Year: children (the boy Vania) do not believe in Father Christmas, but President Yeltsin does (he refuses to request energy for further fire, just in case this is the real Father Frost). The political

The Sympathy Seeker. Nastia (Elena Shevchenko) with one of her pupils.

dimension is crudely generalized: the American officer aims to destroy the Russian Father Frost, but fortunately he is found out and eliminated. The Russian attitude to a wish is also significant: there is nothing to wish for that could not be achieved by the people, and the assertion that life itself is the greatest value cannot be taken for anything but a political message to the people: be content with what you have and work hard to achieve anything further. These messages appear not only as ridiculous, but also are Soviet rather than Russian: the leader of the country has a childlike belief in supernatural powers, while children see things for what they are – Vania says he does not believe in the tale of the wish coming true, and wants to be transposed into the cinema, only to find himself in the midst of the reels of one of Soviet Russia's greatest spy movies (*Seventeen Moments of Spring*); the message of work rather than hope also reflects the socialist ethos rather than that of contemporary Russian society.

The clichés and stereotypes are extremely overdone in the film, but they are not effectively exposed to parody. In fact, conventions of magic forces at work, the link with extraterrestrials, and the happy reunion of two couples at the end of the film conform too much to traditional patterns to allow for the parody to be explored. The film is a detective story at best, but not a comedy. It remained peripheral to the films offered for New Year in 1997. By far the two most popular New Year films of the 1990s are *The Sympathy Seeker* (*Sirota kazanskaia*, 1997) and *Poor Sasha* (*Bednaia Sasha*, 1997).

The Sympathy Seeker is star actor Vladimir Mashkov's debut as a filmmaker and based on a script by Oleg Antonov, a playwright and screenwriter with whom Mashkov had previously worked in the theatre. Mashkov engaged veteran stage actors for his film, and with Elena Shevchenko and Nikolai Fomenko recruited the most popular young actors. The Russian title of the film is a phrase used for children who have no relatives left, a 'Kazan Orphan'. Nastia, a village schoolteacher, is such an orphan; she would prefer to stay at home with her fiancé Kolia to meet the New Year rather than go to a party – like so many of her Soviet predecessors, she prefers the home to society parties – since she wants to tell Kolia that she is pregnant. Nastia has published in the newspaper a letter that her late mother wrote to her father (but never sent) in the hope that her father will make contact with her. As a consequence three potential fathers called Pavel arrive: a magician (Valentin Gaft), a cosmonaut (Lev Durov) and a cook (Oleg Tabakov). They are all alone and have no home. They all bring the same huge toy dog for Nastia as a present, absolutely unaware that their daughter, if she turns out to be her, would be twenty-nine years old. None of them is really Nastia's father, and they realise this in the morning when they find the photo album Nastia had pretended she could not find so she would not upset the harmony of the New Year Night. They all leave, quietly, but Nastia stops their train: for her, their wish to have a child, to give their vagrant lives a meaning, is so important that she agrees to play that part even beyond New Year and accept her three 'fathers'. Mashkov here uses the overtly religious symbol of the trinity of the father-figure.

In the course of the evening the three fathers prepare the meal, decorate the tree, and mend the television set. The cosmonaut Pavel simulates a flight into space and thus creates a link with the universe, a device typical of Soviet New Year films. He also creates the connection to Moscow via the satellite 'dish' which he installs to receive a US channel that switches over, thanks to the impact of the champagne cork, just in time for the Moscow chimes: even in the village, Moscow is the centre.

With its emphasis on the cosmic dimension, the centripetal movement to Moscow, the religious symbol of the trinity and the emphasis on the family, the film remains well within the conventions of Soviet representations of New Year parties. Ultimately there is nothing exciting or new in this interpretation of the New Year.

A different case is that of *Poor Sasha*, a hit among the New Year films, made by Tigran Keosayan who has directed several children's films in the past. He too relies on the performance of a star actor, Alexander Zbruev, along with some veteran stars of Soviet cinema. But what is original here is the genre – a mixture of comedy and detective story, ultimately defying social and material boundaries and uniting the girl Sasha, her mother Olga and the thief Berezkin (Alexander Zbruev) in a happy family.

Berezkin is a computer expert who is serving a term in prison for robbing a bank (after taking money that belonged to him). He is called away from prison, dressed up as Father Frost, to crack the code of a door behind which a minister has been accidentally locked up. Having solved this task, he is given a holiday over the New Year. He returns to Moscow, buys presents for his wife and friends, and gives money to a beggar boy, who steals his entire purse. He returns home, only to find that his wife has sold the flat so that he sets off the burglar alarm; his wife has left him and is going to emigrate to Israel: suddenly, Berezkin is without money, without presents, and without a wife. He meets a beggar (Aristarkh) in the street who is disguised as Father Frost, and together they plan to break into the flat of a banker and empty the safe; the banker, Olga, has a twelve-year-old daughter, Sasha, whom she is leaving alone over New Year because of her business. Sasha catches the thief Berezkin and forces him to rob her mother's bank so that her mother will have more time for her. As they carry out this plan, it turns out that Olga's companion Kolia has cheated Olga and, having been discovered by her, has now decided to fake a robbery and kill Olga. But Berezkin thwarts their plans, and rescues both Olga and Sasha.

The thief Berezkin is really a good man, and so is the beggar Aristarkh: appearances are misleading. Furthermore, nobody believes the truth when it is told. The film also features the standard reunion of couples: both Aristarkh and Sasha's tutor Amalia, and Olga and Berezkin find happiness during that night. But most important is another feature of this film: for the first time a child is in control. Sasha is the driving force of the plot, and she suggests to her mother that she takes the part of the woman Berezkin sees in his dreams at the end of the film.

The film is the first which affirms the power of children, and the fact that children are, or at least should be, at the centre of the New Year celebrations. This does not, however, exclude the family happiness matrix for an elderly couple and the young family. Harmony and unity cut across age, class and social status. The concern is with emotion rather than material well-being, and this is now a reaction against the new consumer-orientation of Russian society rather than a phenomenon dictated by socialist ideology.

Russian film-makers, then, adopt various approaches to the New Year and its treatment in Soviet films. Rogozhkin dwells on the carnival elements and the union of diverse social classes that have emerged in the New Russia while he attributes paramount importance to a powerful leader (the General) to realize the dream of a harmonious Russian society.

He thus indulges in fond memories of the golden past of Soviet times with his emphasis on the leadership and authority that are necessary for a successful and enjoyable celebration of the New Year. Similarly, in *New Year Story* political power (the president) defends the myth of Father Frost, and a political and social appeal to the people to work for their own happiness (while the president believes in Father Frost) is attached to the festivity, which should remain free of political overtones. Thus, both Rogozhkin and Baranov 'Sovietize' the holiday. The cosmic dimension, so important in Soviet New Year films, is exposed to laughter in the ridiculous plot of *New Year Story*, but also in the silly simulation of a flight into space which never took place in *The Sympathy Seeker*. The focus is on contemporary everyday life rather than an escape into other worlds.

Only the last two films discussed are free of political overtones and concern themselves with New Year as a time for the family and children, and for relaxation from the chores of everyday life. Both films depict people whose main task it is to make others happy, and thereby themselves too: Sasha unites Olga with Berezkin, and is herself happy to have a mother and a father; Nastia brings back the three homeless Pavels and gives them a task in life (to look after their 'daughter' and their grandchild), making herself happy in so doing. The emphasis on generosity not in the material sense, but on the level of help and support, is new for Russian cinema and represents a reaction against the consumerism of the 'New Russians', and a reinforcement of the human and spiritual values that have always been at the root of Russian culture. Russian cinema no longer views the New Year as a carnival, or as a festivity where magic and supernatural powers come into force. Rather, New Year is turned into a family celebration, which unites families but always includes children (Nastia in *The Sympathy Seeker* is pregnant, the boy Vania in *New Year Story* benefits from Father Frost, and Sasha in *Poor Sasha* controls the action). At last, children have occupied their true place in the festivity.

Overall we can trace a parallel in the treatment of Christmas on screen and the current ideological and social developments in Russian history. In the pre-Revolution period we have seen a festivity dominated by pagan rites: at Christmas dreams of personal happiness come true in a fairytale way with the help of supernatural forces.

In the first half of the Soviet era under Stalin, family happiness and celebrations in isolation from the community were shown in a negative light as they contradicted the collective spirit: Grunia is held back in her social commitment by domestic life, and for Chuk's and Gek's father the priority lies with his work in which the visit of his family interferes. The film-musicals of the post-Stalin era emphasize the carnival spirit of the New Year: social hierarchies can be overcome, disguises allow people to discover their true self, global and universal harmony can be achieved. It is the ideal moment for proposals and for the foundation of new relationships, pointing into the future. This sets the second half of the Soviet period against the first, when the future was considered to have been achieved in the present, so that time was static.

Post-Soviet films represent New Year as a festivity endowed with an exceptional carnival spirit: everybody is equal, which is synonymous with a return to the socialist equality of the 'golden Soviet past'. While early post-Soviet films ridicule and parody stereotypes, the last two films discussed here show the concern with the future of the family now including children, thus bringing the concept of the festivity closer to its American and European counterpart.

Notes

1. I should like to thank the Arts Faculty Research Fund of the University of Bristol for providing the reindeer for me to go to Russia, and Ksenia Iasneva for helping me locate Christmas trees on the screen.

2. Dialogue from Nikita Mikhalkov's *Burnt by the Sun* (1994), where Mitia introduces himself to the little girl Nadia.

3. See Christel Lane, *The Rites of Rulers*, Cambridge: Cambridge University Press, 1981, p 137.

4. See Daniel Miller, 'A Theory of Christmas' (pp 3–35), and Claude Lévi-Strauss, 'Father Christmas Executed' (pp 38–51), in Daniel Miller (ed.), *Unwrapping Christmas*, Oxford: Clarendon Press, 1993.

5. See Lane, *The Rites of Rulers*, p 137.

6. Miller, p 29.

7. Kitezh is a mythical city sunk in a lake.

8. See an interview with Natalia Piankova and Ilya Narodovoy by Alla Gerber, 'Plemia mladoe i ... znakomoe,' *Iskusstvo kino*, 10 (1993), pp 13–17.

9. Alexander Arkhangelsky, 'Nu chto, dosashkalis'?', *Iskusstvo kino* 10 (1993), pp 9–12.

10. For a discussion of *Poor Sasha*, *The Sympathy Seeker*, and *New Year Story* see also Lidia Maslova, 'O prazdnichnom torte, denezhnem krogovorote i russkom Gollivude', *Iskusstvo kino* 4 (1998), pp 88–94.

11. See Kirill Razlogov, 'Vpered v proshloe,' *Iskusstvo kino* 3 (1997), p 36.

11

Satirizing the Spanish Christmas: *Plácido* (Luis García Berlanga 1961)

Peter William Evans

Like most Western countries, Spain celebrates Christmas as a time for family reunions, gifts, over-indulgence in food and drink – *mazapanes* (marzipan), *turrón* (various types of originally almond-based sweets), *besugo* (sea-bream), and other seasonal delicacies – revelries of various sorts and, decreasingly, for religious reaffirmation marked by *villancicos* (carols) and Midnight Mass. Unlike some places, such as the United Kingdom and the United States, though, these festivities are not crammed around the few days leading up from Christmas Day to New Year's Eve. Christmas in Spain stretches as far as Twelfth Night, or Epiphany, and in traditional Spanish households presents are not given until 6 January, in memory of the gifts offered to the infant Jesus by the *Reyes Magos* or Three Wise Men. Traditionally, too, Father Christmas or Santa Claus is not the figure who distributes gifts. This essentially Northern European tradition, increasingly making inroads in Spain – to the point where in some places the hybridization of the feast is almost complete – has its counterpart in the role played by the Three Wise Men, Melchor, Gaspar and Baltasar. In Spanish towns and cities everywhere a procession or *cabalgata* organized by the local community sees the Three Wise Men – in traditional attire – arrive in time to begin the distribution of gifts. In Spanish department stores they take up their position to hear the requests of excited children. Slowly but surely, though, Father Christmas has been steadily encroaching on the Wise Men's territory, encouraged of course by all retailers, a situation that now often means not one but two spending sprees, one to coincide with the aged patriarch's Christmas Eve chimney visits and another with the royal Easterners' later arrival.

The *Christmas Carol* sentimentality of the feast is captured in one of the most commercially successful Spanish films of all time, *La gran familia* (Fernández Palacios 1962), which came out only a year after the release of *Plácido*, Berlanga's jaundiced Christmas narrative, a film that in typical Berlanga fashion takes a sceptical look at seasonal cheer. Where *Plácido* is dystopian, *La gran familia*, made by a director at ease in the conservative ideological climate of Francoism, unproblematically promotes a utopian idea of the family in a film where the festive atmosphere and the special-ness of the festivity are made all the more poignant through absence. One of the numerous children in the film's idealized family is kidnapped by a childless couple, an incident that highlights not only the despair of a family coming to terms with the nightmare of a kidnapped child, but also the special agony of such a loss at what is perhaps the most family-orien-tated moment of the year, Christmas. The sugary treatment of the family in *La gran familia*, a ringing endorsement of the dominant attitudes of the day, provides a striking contrast to *Plácido*'s acerbic, unidealized approach to the same subject. The later film seems also somehow to want to redeem the sexually active single woman played by Amparo Soler Leal, transforming her into the selfless, docile Madonna of sexual fidelity and maternal refuge in *La gran familia*.

Mainstream, commercially produced Christmas films, then, stress family values in a country that has always, regardless of political regimes, prioritized the importance of family life. Films made outside the main-stream, by more dissenting directors such as Berlanga, use Christmas as an opportunity for questioning the centrality of the family and the ideology that sustains it. A more recent film, *Amantes* (Aranda 1990), approaches the topic even more darkly than *Plácido*. There Victoria Abril plays a 'noirish' *femme fatale* – contrasted with the more conventional woman played by Maribel Verdú – whose Christmas-decorated home *mise-en-scène* highlights secular more than spiritual drives. In *Plácido*, too, Christmas offers its director an opportunity to expose the venality of a festivity increasingly losing its significance as a spiritual, family-centred time of renewal and charity.

On *Plácido* Berlanga teamed up once again with Rafael Azcona, an author and scriptwriter with a host of major film credits to his name (Riambau and Torreiro 1998). The mutual interests of these two land-mark figures in the history of Spanish cinema (Cañeque and Grau 1993; Perales 1997) became apparent on their first joint assignment, a pilot film for a Spanish TV series, *Se vende un tranvía* (*Tram for Sale*, 1957). An eye for comedy drew the two men together: Azcona first came to prominence in his work from 1951 onwards on *La Codorniz*, a satirical magazine gently mocking the prejudices of the Franco regime, in power at the time, of course, since the end of the Civil War in 1939. Azcona's taste for comedy and satire led him at first to work with Marco Ferreri, a partnership that resulted in the making of two key comedies from this period, *El pisito* (*The Little Flat*, 1955), and *El cochecito* (*The Little Car*, 1960), before going on to make with Berlanga some of the major films of recent Spanish cinema history: *Plácido*, *El verdugo* (*The Executioner*, 1963), *Vivan los novios* (*A Toast to the Bride and Bridegroom*, 1969), *Tamaño natural* (*Life Size*, 1973), *La escopeta nacional* (*National Rifle*, 1978), *La vaquilla* (*The Heifer*, 1984) and many others both with Berlanga and other directors.

The comic instinct shared by the two men places them firmly in what is often referred to as a tradition of 'dark comedy' in Spain (Perales 1997: 57–8), a description that Berlanga has sometimes resisted: the sixteenth- and seventeenth-century picaresque novel, with its unflinching treatment of low life, the eschatalogical, grotesque humour of the seventeenth-century satirist Quevedo, the monstrous wit of Goya, the *esperpentos* of the early twentieth-century dramatist and novelist Valle-Inclán, with their comic fun-fair mirror distortions of everyday realities, as well as, of

Berlanga's 60s Spanish Christmas: little faith, less hope and no charity

course, the savage but also forgiving temperament that characterizes the films of Luis Buñuel.

The traces of this native tradition are clear in Berlanga. But, looking beyond Spain, and especially from the point of view of film history, the voices of René Clair and the Italian Neo-Realist directors (especially Fellini), as well as, from Hollywood, Frank Capra, Preston Sturges and Billy Wilder, are clearly heard. In addition to the film's narrative, group-centred and location-shooting structures, the music by Asins Arbó very much recalls in melodies and orchestration the work of Nino Rota. As in the films, too, of Sturges and Wilder, city-based comedy provides the basis for *Plácido*, where class, family and other areas of group dynamics assume more than cursory importance.

In *The Anatomy of Criticism* (1957), Northrop Frye distinguishes between city or court comedy and 'green world' comedy. The distinction between the two is also made in practice by Spanish writers, for instance in the work of comic dramatists like Tirso de Molina or essayists like Antonio de Guevara. Frye's discussion, which is really aimed at making connections between Shakespearean comedy and the Classical tradition, defines the city as a space ruled by the reality principle, where characters are governed by the social law, and the country as a realm of liberated desires where individuals run wild defying prohibition. The portrayal of the sleazy consumerism and commercial-world narcissism of, say, *The Apartment* (Wilder, 1960) resembles *Plácido*'s focus on the egotistical group of bogus philanthropists whose act of Christmas charity serves little purpose other than to assuage their own guilt-complexes in the very act of inflating even more their already bloated self-importance. *The Apartment*'s target is the dehumanized world of American corporate culture; *Plácido*'s, a reactionary ideology's use of charity as a denial of radical reforms in the country. In each case the film concentrates not simply on a central couple (the roles played by Jack Lemmon and Shirley MacLaine in *The Apartment*, Castro Sendra 'Cassen' and Elvira Quintanilla in *Plácido*), but on the group. Both films offer a microcosm of their irresponsible societies, a key feature of which is the group's refusal of solidarity.

The setting of *Plácido* against a Christmas background – all the events take place on Christmas Eve – makes this failure of community spirit all the darker. More recently these sentiments have spilled over into current debates about nationalism in Spain, something that in Berlanga's eyes threatens the collective identity and community of spirit of the country as a whole. Nationalism, an ideal of which Berlanga has always been more than a little sceptical, creates no genuine bonds of human sympathy. In Democratic Spain as much as in the Franco years it continues to strike like a cancer, though at different targets, against the body politic as a whole:

De España me preocupa su 'fragmentación'. No me gustan nada los nacionalismos y vamos a llegar a la ridícula situación de que uno se separe de su cuñado y pida su territorio ... Lo que se respira en todas mis películas es que yo me siento incómodo en esta sociedad; tanto en la época de Franco como ahora mismo. (García Berlanga, quoted in Echeverría 1994: 224) (I am worried by Spain's 'fragmentation'. I dislike nationalism and we are going to arrive at the ridiculous situation where one becomes separated from one's brother-in-law and claims his territory ... What you find in all my films is my uneasy relationship with this society; as much in the Franco period as now.)

Significantly, in this respect, the film's title is a third choice. Two earlier titles were discarded after difficulties with the censors (Zumalde Arregi 1997: 502). The original *Siente a un pobre a su mesa* (*Take a Poor Person Home to Dinner*), and its first revision, *Los bienaventurados* (*The Lucky Ones*), place the emphasis not, as in the third version, *Plácido*, on an individual, but on the group. The first attempts are conceptual, stressing the importance of community; they are also ironic, the first highlighting the group's dubious intentions, the second ambiguous enough to allow the audience to question which group, the charitable, Plácido's family, or the poor, is more accurately described by the term. The final choice, *Plácido*, reduces the scope for subversion, privileging a member of the group, as if forcing the film to highlight individual eccentricities and patterns of behaviour as opposed to social constructions of identity and collective social responsibility. This is the equivalent of the censors' insistence that *Calle Mayor* (Bardem, 1956) should carry a prologue distancing the events of the film from contemporary Spanish realities. And yet the choice of the name 'Plácido' manages to retain a measure of irony since this character, and almost everyone else who gets caught up in the Christmas charity event, though not the poor beneficiaries of the event themselves, are the very antithesis of placidity. The frenzied activity of the characters as the project gets under way, emphasized by the restless, feverish movements of the camera and the orchestration of group movement in and out of the frame from one space into another, subverts the traditional while highlighting the commercial or spurious attributes of Christmas. A film about Christmas, this narrative concentrates not on togetherness, renewal of family unity or on acts of generosity and spiritual regeneration, but on the self-seeking ambitions of a privileged class.

Plácido is a film of two interrelated narratives: the first depicts the efforts of Plácido himself to pay off a monthly instalment on his motor-cycle/car, an indispensable vehicle for earning his living; the second concerns the charity event in which he too becomes involved and, as a result, is in danger of missing the deadline for the payment of the instalment. This event is organized by a group of well-to-do bourgeois (the events take place in Burgos, famed for its religiosity, general reactionariness and support of Franco), who arrange various activities, including a procession through the city, the auctioning of one of the visiting film starlets as the Christmas dinner guest of one of the families, and the invitation to the target group of paupers to dine with members of the wealthy families.

The Plácido Narrative

Although the film presents itself more as a pageant, a wide-angled survey of a whole community, it does privilege one of the characters, here – as is often the case in Berlanga films – someone whose importance, though somewhat complicated in view of the enforced changes, is underlined by the film's eventual choice of title. The isolation of Plácido in narrative terms establishes him as the most focused version of the audience's *alter ego*. His quest for money to pay off the instalment on the vehicle, his unavoidable involvement in the charity event – especially in relation to his unashamed exploitation by Quintillana (José Luis López Vázquez), a leading figure in the project – and his struggle to help secure the material well-being of his family, all mark him out as a prioritized character. In part, the comedy of the Plácido narrative derives from the frustrations to which the project of uniting the family in what for Spaniards is the most important night in the year, the 'Nochebuena' (Christmas Eve), is endlessly subjected.

In keeping with its exposure of the alienation of working people or the dispossessed from mainstream rituals and festivities, the film follows a Bakhtinian pattern in celebrating the marginal at the expense of the centre or of privilege. The focus here, though, avoids excessive concentration on individual psychology. Whereas often in comedy – in marriage as much as in courtship narratives – the emphasis lies on self-discovery through the dynamics of human relationships, the inspiration behind Plácido's comic drive stems more from his role as guide to the stultified society's flawed domain of privilege. His role is expository, his own situation reproducing the bleak realities of the picaresque tradition: under the control of powerful men – the bankers and lawyers unmoved by his predicament – he is married to a woman whose job as a Ladies' lavatory attendant graphically affirms the lowliness of a social status beneath which there is only one rung, that occupied by the penniless guests of the charity freaks. Most of Plácido's family affairs seem to be conducted – to the surprise of some of its patrons – in the Ladies' lavatory, a situation that highlights both the personal shame of Plácido (though he himself seems sanguine enough about this state of affairs) and the wider social malaise of the times, a barbed comment on the so-called economic miracle trumpeted by the Franco government in the 1960s. In keeping, too, with the picaresque tradition, Plácido's exposure of the bombast and self-delusions of the centre, as well as his contact with the charity event's guests of honour, result in little empathy with the plight of the poor and no reflection on the motivation of their benefactors.

Plácido is ruled by self-interest, an attitude hardened by the standards of the day, a moment in Spanish history defined more by the letter than by the spirit of a faith the regime endorsed with such obvious relish. The characteristic care and attention given to detail is noticeable here, as elsewhere, in the film's response, another characteristically Berlangian motif, to state-sponsored approval of the Catholic Church. At the railway station, as the organizing committee prepares to welcome the film stars who are expected to promote the charity event, the film packs in a series of interrelated references. While the crowd gathers, the talk is of the anticipated appearance of Carmen Sevilla, one of the major stars at this time of the Spanish cinema, especially musicals. But, naturally, she fails to appear. Her failure provides an ironic perspective to the words spoken by a member of the welcoming committee whose remark 'agradecemos al séptimo arte' (we are grateful to members of the seventh art) seems to gesture towards the perceived ineptitude and betrayals of mainstream cinema during this period – an industry already attacked by 'auteurists' like Bardem and Berlanga himself and others at the Conversaciones de Salamanca in 1955, a conference on the state of Spanish cinema – when few dared challenge on screen the orthodoxies of the day.

The equation of Carmen Sevilla and the 'seventh art', or the definition of Spanish cinema of the time as a largely commercial, escapist form of entertainment, stresses this film's frustrations at the enforced direction that, with some notable exceptions, Spanish cinema was taking at that time. But this cinema is a form of betrayal, one that does not keep its own promises, a cinema characterized by absence – symbolized by Carmen Sevilla's failure to appear – and, much like its mirror-image audience, here portrayed as the charity's organizing committee – only inspired by its own self-importance, something brilliantly caught in the detail of the remark by the slighted leading actor when he pompously exclaims 'esto es un ultraje a mi categoría artística' (this is an outrage against my artistic status).

All these self-conscious elements are mixed up with an even clearer but nevertheless necessarily understated critique of political and religious attitudes. Still at the station, a sign in the background reads 'En la España nueva no se blasfema' (in the new Spain there is no room for blasphemy), while in the foreground two policemen lead a handcuffed wretch to his uncertain but predictably unpleasant fate in a Franco cell. The criss-crossing of muted subversive undercurrents is a marked feature in the film, here through the superimposed effects of *mise-en-scène*, dialogue, cultural allusion and narrative, elsewhere through its remarkably skilful orchestration of group movement. In this respect, an early shot that sees a religious funeral procession interrupted along its journey by a military band repeats a dominant theme of the film, the regulation of a country's moral and spiritual health by the predicates of fascism.

The Group

Like the films of Capra and René Clair, Berlanga's usually prefer a canvas wide enough to accommodate many levels of social as well as private patterns of human behaviour. The tone, though, differs slightly. The populism of Capra, and the poetic realism of Clair, are eschewed here in favour of the harsher treatment of a Wilder, a Sturges or even a Buñuel. Three groups come under the film's critical gaze: paupers, charity organizers, and Plácido's family and friends. As in *Viridiana* (Buñuel, 1961) a film very near in spirit and time to the making of *Plácido*, and one that also questions a reactionary government's trust in charity rather than economic or social reform as the cure for social ills, there is no false sentiment expended on the representation of the poor. Some of the characters singled out for a Christmas treat (for instance, the Luis Ciges character) waste little time in tucking into their unexpected slap-up meal. Others, like the elderly couple Pascual and La Concheta, are used by the film to reiterate its theme of social transgression. Ill, frail, ashen-faced, this couple might be expected to conform to a sentimental stereotype of docile senior citizenship showing gratitude for caring treatment from their sponsors. Instead, the film, with daring humour, uses them as another strategy through which to ridicule the pieties of the day, in this instance the regime's championing at all cost of marriage and family life. Before the Christmas meal is over, the ironically named Pascual (or Paschal lamb) falls fatally ill, but before he dies everyone realizes he and La Concheta have failed to regularize their relationship. To the horror above all of their bourgeois hosts, they are discovered to be unwed. Members of the charity project crowd around the unfortunate Pascual, eagerly encouraging him to propose to his life-long partner, only to be rebuffed at every turn. Each time he is asked whether he wishes to marry her in his dying moments, he answers, unable to utter any words, with a horizontal movement of his head, negatively. Finally, undoubtedly exercised as much by the thought of infringement of a social law as by anxiety over the destination of his blackened soul, one of the stouter matronly women on the organizing committee takes matters in hand by stationing herself behind Pascual so that when he is asked, for the umpteenth time, as he is on the point of expiry, whether he wishes to marry La Concheta, she is handily placed to move his head vertically, thus in yet another dubious act of charity safeguarding in a single gesture the sacred tenets of Church and State.

The film's point, clearly expressed in this comic detail, is that charity springs not from a genuine desire to improve the social conditions of the poor, to restructure society in a way that would benefit all levels, to create mechanisms for self-determination and dignified, respectful economically viable state reforms, but from a controlling ideology. The woman manipulating the wretched Pascual's head is an ideological puppeteer, Pascual no more than her helpless victim. The Christmas carol sung by a child at the film's closure restates the failure of a charity conceived by ideologues: 'Madre, a la puerta hay un niño/tiritando está de frío;/dile que entre y se calentará/porque en esta tierra ya no hay caridad/ni nunca la ha habido ni nunca la habrá' (Mother, there's a child at the door shivering with cold/ tell him to come in and get warm/because there's no charity here/there never has been and there never will be). True charity, a genuine concern for the plight of individuals, is alien to the Francoist ideologies.

The film reserves its bleakest satire for the charity event organizers. Sometimes posed with stiff formality in deep focus shots to convey the rigidities and constraints of their shared group values sometimes presented in long takes as the characters rush animatedly in and out of various interrelated spaces in shots suggesting the group's essentially futile, sheep-like obedience, few among the group rebel against the status quo. Perhaps only Marilú (Amparo Soler Leal), who at least recognizes in Christmas an occasion for festivity, for the release of the libido, even if her lover turns out to be a feckless swain more concerned at protecting his own reputation than gratifying his carnal desires, attempts to take full advantage of the seasonal mood. Martita, too, obviously weary of the unmanly, over-jealous attentions of her opportunistic *novio* (fiancé) Quintanilla, yearns for a more thrilling kind of romance, one promised by the dashing actor whose split trousers she has symbolically been helping to repair. But the theme of sexuality, and above all its repression in Franco's Spain, is given its most elaborate and most symbolic treatment in the Christmas dinner motif.

The equation of festive eating and sex, and the group's sublimation of the latter through promotion of the former, draws attention to the film's exploration of wider cultural issues. Reflection on Freud's meditations on identity and related questions on food and desire may help clarify the film's interest in the group. In 'Group Psychology and the Analysis of the Ego' (Freud 1985), Freud's discussion of identification eventually distinguishes between narcissistic and anaclitic forms of attachment. With one or two exceptions, especially in the treatment of the transgressive Marilú character, those who belong to the charity event's organizing group seem welded to one another in what, in Freud's terms, could be defined as a narcissistic-object choice, where the group as a whole seek love-objects modeled on their own egos. Elsewhere, in 'Three Essays on the Theory of Sexuality' (Freud 1981), Freud further argues that there is a close relationship between sexuality and eating, something that derives from the early life of the child where sexual activity is related to self-preservation. Sexuality and eating are intimately linked in *Plácido*, but whereas Christmas does indeed offer Marilú, and to a lesser extent Martita, an opportunity to exemplify the connection, it only serves in the case of almost everyone else in the group as the audience's clue to sublimation and sexual repression. One of the characters, for instance, is more concerned about changing the tablecloth as soon as she learns a neighbour is about to make a call, than about almost anything else.

Christmas, a northern European festivity of Saturnalian origins, has become both sanitized and trivialized under the influence of a sanctimonious political and social creed. In drawing the contours of the dominant group's identity, the film seems to be reformulating Freud's remarks on the ambivalence of identification. The group is held together through ideology, identifies itself as a group this way, and seems to have regressed to an almost cannibalistic state where the poor, invited to feast on Christmas fare, become themselves the morsels devoured by a group whose narcissism and instincts of self-preservation through this act of cannibalism remain undiscovered and unacknowledged.

When *Plácido* was screened two decades later on Spanish TV the *El País* reviewer (Basteiner 1983) welcomed this change from the usual Christmas fare of films like *El Judas* (Ignacio Iquino, 1952) and Hollywood sacred biopics. Berlanga's 1960s Ghost of a Christmas Past, with its *Dolce Vita*-style exposure of the false piety and self-centred altruism of an earlier moment in Spanish history, is a reminder to 1980s audiences, and beyond, of the struggle like-minded film-makers had in resisting the mainstream practice and ideological pressures of the national film industry of the time. In its hectic narrative pace, feverish group-centred activities and, perhaps above all, in its characters' ceaseless release of torrential verbiage, this bittersweet film brilliantly pokes fun at what Ángel Fernández Santos has described as the absurdities, frustrations and inanities of life in Spain in the 1960s (Fernández Santos 1976: 62). Christmas here becomes a metaphor for a trivialized society's unanswered call for redemption from the repressive measures of a powerful regime. Instead of a miraculous birth to herald social regeneration, the film offers us a death: the symbolic demise of Pascual, the ironically named emblem of the old order's continuing hold over a victimized population.

Works Cited

Basteiner, M.A. (1983), 'La postal navideña de Berlanga', *El País* (23 December).

Cañeque, Carlos and Maite Grau (1930), *¡Bienvenido Mr Berlanga!* (Barcelona, Ediciones Destino).

Echeverría, Rosa María (1994), 'Luis García Berlanga', *Blanco y Negro* (6 February), pp 224–7.

Férnandez Santos, Ángel (1976), '*Plácido* de Berlanga: un hormiguero español', *Cuadernos para el diálogo* (31 July), p 62.

Freud, Sigmund, 1981 (1918), 'Three Essays on the Theory of Sexuality', *On Sexuality*, Pelican Freud Library, vol. 7 (Harmondsworth, Penguin Books), pp 261–84.

_____, 1985 (1919), 'Group Psychology and the Analysis of the Ego', in *Civilization, Society and Religion*, Pelican Freud Library, vol. 12 (Harmondsworth, Penguin Books), pp 91–78.

Frye, Northrop (1957), *Anatomy of Criticism: Four Essays* (Princeton, NJ, Princeton University Press).

Heredero, Carlos, Julio Pérez Perucha and Esteve Riambau (1998), *Diccionario del cine español: Dirigido por José Luis Borau* (Madrid, Alianza).

Perales, Francisco (1997), *Luis García Berlanga* (Madrid, Cátedra).

Riambau, Esteve and Casimiro Torreiro (1998), *Guionistas en el cine español; quimeras, picarescas y pluriempleo* (Madrid, Cátedra).

Zumalde Arregi, Imanol (1997), '*Plácido*', in Julio Pérez Perucha (ed.), *Antología crítica del cine español 1906–1995* (Madrid, Cátedra), pp 501–4.

Filmography

The Assassination of Father Christmas (*L'Assassinat du Père Noël*), France 1941, Continental Films.
Sc. Pierre Véry and Charles Spaak; d. Christian Jaque; ph. François Carron and Armand Thirard; m. Henry Verdun.
Renée Faure; Marie-Hélène Dasté; Hélène Manson; Marcelle Rexiane; Marcelle Monthil; Mona Dol.

Black Christmas (aka *Silent Night, Evil Night*), Canada 1974, EMI/Film Funding/Vision IV.
Sc. Roy Moore; d. Robert Clark.
Olivia Hussey; Keir Dullea; Margot Kidder; Andre Martin; John Saxon; Marian Waldman; Art Hindle.

Carnival Night (Karnaval'naia noch'), USSR 1956, Mosfilm.
Sc. Boris Laskin; d. Eldar Riazanov and Vladimir Poliakov; ph. Arkadi Koltsaty; m. Anatoli Lepin.
Liudmila Gurchenko; Igor Ilyinsky; Yuri Belov; Georgi Kulikov; Sergei Filippov.

The Cheaters, US 1945, Republic Pictures.
Sc. Frances Hyland; d. Joseph Kane; ph. Reggie Lanning; m. Walter Scharf.
Joseph Schildkraut; Billie Burke; Eugene Pallette; Ona Munson; Raymond Walburn; Ruth Terry; Anne Gillis; David Holt.

A Christmas Carol, US 1938, MGM.
Sc. Hugo Butler; d. Edwin L. Marin; ph. Sydney Wagner; m. Franz Waxman.

Reginald Owen; Gene Lockhart; Kathleen Lockhart; Terry Kilburn; Leo G. Carroll; Lynne Carver; Barry Mackay.

A Christmas Carol, GB 1984, Entertainment Partners.
Sc. Roger O. Hirson; d. Clive Donner; ph. Tony Imi; m. Nick Bicat.
George C. Scott; Frank Finlay; Angela Pleasence; Edward Woodward; Michael Carter; David Warner; Susannah York; Anthony Walters.

Christmas Eve (*Noch' pered rozhdestvom*)**,** Russia 1913, Khanzhonkov Films.
Sc. Wladyslaw Starewicz; d. Wladyslaw Starewicz; ph. Wladyslaw Starewicz.
Ivan Mozzhukhin; Olga Obolenskaia; Lidia Tridenskaia; P. Lopukhin.

Christmas in Connecticut, US 1945, Warner Bros.
Sc. Lionel Hauser and Adele Commandini; d. Peter Godfrey; ph. Carl Guthrie; m. Fredrick Hollander.
Barbara Stanwyck; Dennis Morgan; Sydney Greenstreet; Reginald Gardiner; S.Z. Sakall; Robert Shayne; Una O'Connor; Frank Jenks.

A Christmas Story, US 1983, MGM/UA.
Sc. Jean Shepherd, Leigh Brown and Bob Clark; d. Bob Clark; ph. Reginald H. Morris; m. Carl Zitter and Paul Zea.
Peter Billingsley; Melinda Dillon; Darrren McGavin; Ian Petronella.

Christmas Under Fire, GB 1940, CFU. GPO Film Unit.
Sc. Harry Watt and Quentin Reynolds; d. Harry Watt.
Quentin Reynolds (narrator).

Chuk and Gek (*Chuk i Gek*), USSR 1953, Gorky Film Studio.
Sc. Viktor Shklovsky; d. Ivan Lukinsky; ph. Grair Garibian. m. Anatoli Lepin.
Yura Chugunov; Andrei Chilikin; Vera Vasilieva; Dmitri Pavlov.

La Cité des enfants perdus (*City of Lost Children*), France 1995, Claudie Ossard Productions/Constellation/Lumiere/Studio Canal Plus/France 3/Elias Querejas/Tele Munchen.
Sc. Gilles Adrien, Jean-Pierre Jeunet and Marco Caro; d. Jean-Pierre Jeunet.
Ron Perlman; Dominique Pinon; Judith Vittet; Daniel Emilfork.

Conte d'hiver (*A Winter's Tale*), France 1992, Les Films du Losange.
Sc. Eric Rohmer; d. Eric Rohmer.
Rosette; Marie Riviere; Charlotte Véry; Frédéric Van Den Driessche.

A Diary for Timothy, GB 1945, CFU.
Sc. E.M. Forster; d. Humphrey Jennings.
Michael Redgrave (narrator).

Die Hard, US 1988, Fox/Gordon Company/Silver Pictures.
Sc. Jeb Stuart and Steven E. de Souza; d. John McTiernan; ph. Jan de Bont; m. Michael Kamen.
Bruce Willis; Bonnie Bedelia; Reginald Veljohnson; Paul Gleason; De'Voreaux White; Alan Rickman.

Die Hard 2, US 1990, Fox/Gordon Co./Silver Pictures.
Sc. Edward de Souza and Doug Richardson; d. Renny Harlin; ph. Oliver Wood.
Bruce Willis; Bonnie Bedelia; William Atherton; Reginald Veljohnson; Franco Nero; William Sadler; John Amos.

Don't Open 'til Christmas, GB 1983, 21st Century.
Sc. Derek Ford and Al McGoohan; d. Edmund Purdom.
Edmund Purdom; Alan Lake; Gerry Sundquist; Belinda Mayne; Mark Jones.

Elisa, France 1994, Canal Plus/Films Christian Fechner/BNP Images/TF1.
Sc. Jean Becker; d. Jean Becker.
Gerard Depardieu; Vanessa Paradis.

Ernest Saves Christmas, US 1988, Warner/Touchstone/Silver Screen Partners III.
Sc. B. Kline and Ed Turner; d. John Cherry; ph. Peter Stein; m. Mark Snow.
Jim Varney; Douglas Seale; Oliver Clark; Noelle Parker; Gailard Sartain; Billie Bird; Bill Byrge; Robert Lesser; Key Howard.

The Grand Illusion (La Grande Illusion), France 1937, Réalisations d'Art Cinématographique Sc. C. Gourdji, Jean Renoir and Charles spaak; d. Jean Renoir; ph. Christian Matras; m. Joseph Kasma.
Jean Gabin; Dita Parlo; Pierre Fresnay; Eric von Stroheim; Julien Carette; Marcel Dalio; Georges Péclet; Werner Florian.

Gremlins, US 1984, Warner/Amblin.
Sc. Chris Columbus; d. Joe Dante; ph. John Hora; m. Jerry Goldsmith.
Zach Galligan; Phoebe Cates; Hoyt Axton; Polly Holliday; Keye Luke; Scott Brady; Edward Andrews.

Grunia Kornakova, USSR 1936, Mezhrabpomfilm.
Sc. Nikolai Ekk and Regina Yanushkevich; d. Nikolai Ekk; ph. Fedor Prokhorov; m. Yakov Stolliar.
Valentina Ivasheva; Nikolai Ekk; Z. Kashkareva.

Happy New Year, Moscow (*S novym godom, Moskva*), Russia 1993, ARS-90, VGIK.
Sc. Natalia Piankova and Yulia Damsker; d. Natalia Piankova; ph. Alexander Kariuk; m. Vadim Piankov.
Maria Gangus; Ilya Narodovoi; Vadim Piankov; Yulia Damsker.

Holiday Inn, US 1942, Paramount.
Sc. Claude Binyon and Elmer Rice; d. Mark Sandrich; ph. David Abel; m/ly. Robert Emmett Dolan/Irving Berlin.
Bing Crosby; Fred Astaire; Majorie Reynolds; Virginia Dale; Walter Abel.

The Holly and the Ivy, GB 1952, British Lion/London.
Sc. Anatole de Grunwald; d. George More O'Ferrall; ph. Ted Scaife; m. Malcolm Arnold.
Ralph Richardson; Celia Johnson; Margaret Leighton; Denholm Elliott; John Gregson; Hugh Williams; Margaret Halstan; Maureen Delany; William Hartnell; Robert Flemyng; Roland Culver.

Home Alone 2, Lost in New York, US 1992, Twentieth Century Fox/John Hughes.
Sc. John Hughes; d. Chris Columbus; ph. Julio Macat; m. John Williams.
Macaulay Caulkin; Joe Pesci; Daniel Stern; Catherine O'Hara; John Heard; Devin Ratray; Hillary Wolf; Brenda Fricker; Tim Curry.

Hope and Glory, GB 1987, Columbia/Goldcrest/Nelson.
Sc. John Boorman; d. John Boorman; ph. Philippe Rousselot; m. Peter Martin.
Sarah Miles; Susan Wooldridge; Ian Bannen; David Hayman; Derrick O'Connor; Sebastian Rice-Edwards; Sammi Davis.

How the Grinch Stole Christmas, US 1966, CBS-TV.
Sc. Dr Seuss; d. Chuck Jones.
Boris Karloff (narrator)

I'll Be Seeing You, US 1944, Selznick International.
Sc. Marion Parsonnet; d. William Deterele; ph. Tony Gaudio; m. Daniele Amfitheatrof.
Ginger Rogers; Joseph Cotten; Shirley Temple; Spring Byington; Tom Tully; Chill Wills.

In Which We Serve, GB 1942, Rank/Two Cities.
Sc. Noël Coward; d. Noël Coward and David Lean; ph. Ronald Neame; m. Noël Coward.
Noël Coward; Bernard Miles; John Mills; Richard Attenborough; Celia Johnson; Kay Walsh; Joyce Carey; Michael Wilding; Penelope Dudley Ward; Kathleen Harrison; Philip Friend; George Carney; Geoffrey Hibbert; James Donald.

Irony of Fate, or Have a Good Sauna! (Ironiia sud'by, ili s legkim parom), USSR 1975, Mosfilm.
Sc. Emil Braginsky and Eldar Riazanov; d. Eldar Riazanov; ph. Vladimir Nakhabtsev; m. Mikael Tariverdiev; songs; Alla Pugacheva and Sergei Nikitin.
Andrei Miagkov; Barbara Brylska; Yuri Yakovlev; Alexander Shirvindt.

It's a Wonderful Life, US 1946, RKO/Liberty.
Sc. Frances Goodrich, Albert Hackett and Frank Capra; d. Frank Capra; ph. Joseph Walker and Joseph Brioc; m. Dimitri Tiomkin.
James Stewart; Henry Travers; Donna Reed; Lionel Barrymore; Thomas Mitchell; Beulah Bondi; Frank Faylen; Ward Bond; Gloria Grahame; H.B. Warner; Frank Albertson; Samuel S. Hinds; Mary Treen.

Jingle All the Way, US 1996, Twentieth Century Fox, 1492 Productions.
Sc. Randy Kornfield; d. Brian Levant; ph. Victor J. Kemper; m. David Newman, Steve Boyum.
Arnold Schwarzenegger; Sinbad; Jake Lloyd; Phil Hartman; Rita Wilson; Robert Conrad; Martin Mull; James Belushi.

Just before nightfall (Juste avant la nuit), France/Italy 1971, Films la Boétie.Columbia/Cinemar.
Sc. Claude Chabrol; d. Claude Chabrol; ph. Jean Rabier; m. Pierre Jansen.
Stéphan Audran; Michel Bouquet; François Périer; Anna Douking; Dominique Zordi; Marina Nichi.

Lethal Weapon, US 1987, Warner/Richard Donner/Joel Silver.
Sc. Shane Black; d. Richard Donner; ph. Stephen Goldblatt; m. Michael Kamen and Eric Clapton.
Mel Gibson; Danny Glover; Gary Busey; Mitchell Ryan; Tom Atkins; Darlene Love.

The Long Kiss Goodnight, US 1996, Entertainment/New Line/Forge/Steve Tisch (Renny Harlin, Stephane Austin, Shane Black).
Sc. Shane Black; d. Renny Harlin; ph. Guillermo Navarro; m. Alan Silvestri.
Geena Davis; Samuel L. Jackson; Patrick Malahide; Craig Bierko; Brian Cox; David Morse; G.D. Spradlin; Yvonne Cimla.

The Man Who Came to Dinner, US 1942, Warner Bros.
Sc. Julius J. and Philip G. Epstein; d. William Keighley; ph. Tony Gaudio; m. Fredrick Hollander.
Bette Davis; Monty Woolley; Ann Sheridan; Jimmy Durante; Reginald Gardiner; Billie Burke; Richard Travis; Grant Mitchell; Ruth Vivian.

Meet Me in St. Louis, US 1944, MGM.
Sc. Irving Brechter and Frank Finklehoff; d. Vincente Minnelli; ph.
George Folsey; md. Georgie Stroll.
Judy Garland; Margaret O'Brien; Mary Astor; Lucille Bremner; Leon
Ames; Tom Drake; Majorie Main; Harry Davenport.

Merlusse, France 1935, Société des Films Marcel Pagnol
Sc. Marcel Pagnol; d. Marcel Pagnol; ph. Albert Assouad and Roger
Ledru; m. Vincent Scolto Henri Poupon; André Pollack; Thommery;
André Robert; Jean Castan; Fernand Bruno; John Dubrou; Robert Chaux.

Mickey's Christmas Carol, US 1983, Disney.
d. Burney Mattinson.
with the voices of: Alan Young (Scrooge McDuck); Clarence Nash
(Donald Duck); Wayne Allwine (Mickey Mouse).

Miracle on 34th Street, US 1947, Twentieth Century-Fox.
D. George Seaton; ph. Charles Clarke and Lloyd Ahern; m. Cyril
Mockridge.
Edmund Gwenn; Maureen O'Hara; John Payne; Natalie Wood; Gene
Lockhart; Porter Hall; William Frawley; Jerome Cowan; Thelma Ritter.

Miracle on 34th Street, US 1994, Twentieth Century Fox.
Sc. George Seaton and John Hughes; d. Les Mayfield; ph. Julio Macat; m.
Bruce Boughton.
Richard Attenborough; Elizabeth Perkins; Dylan McDermott; Mara
Wilson; Joss Ackland; Robert Prosky; J.T. Walsh; James Remar; William
Windom.

The Muppet Christmas Carol, US 1992, Buena Vista/Disney/Henson.
Sc. Jerry Juhl; d. Brian Henson; ph. John Fenner; m. Miles Goodman.
Michael Caine; Steven MacKintosh; Meredith Brown; Robin Weaver;
Kermit the Frog; Miss Piggy; The Great Gonzo; Fozzie Bear.

My Mother's Castle (Le Château de ma mère), France 1990, Gaumont/
Gueville/TFI.
Sc. Jerome Tonnere and Yves Robert; d. Yves Robert; ph. Robert
Alazraki; m. Vladimir Cosma.
Phillippe Caubre; Nathalie Roussel; Didier Pain; Therese Liotard; Julien
Ciamaca; Victorien Delmare; Pierre Darras (narrator).

New Year Story (Novogodniaia istoriia), Russia, 1997, Gorky Studio (S.
Livnev and B. Kilibaev).
Sc. Arkady Kazantsev; d. Alexander Baranov; ph. Dmitri Perednia.
Leonid Kuravlev; Anna Yanovskaia; Ivan Martynov; Alexander Karpov.

The Nightmare Before Christmas, US 1993, Buena Vista/Touchstone.
Sc. Caroline Thompson, Michael McDowell, Tim Burton; d. Henry Selick; m/ly. Danny Elfman.
Voices of Danny Elfman; Chris Sarandon; Catherine O'Hara; William Hickey; Glenn Shadix; Paul Reubens.

Old New Year (*Staryi novyi god*), USSR 1980, Mosfilm (Gosteleradio).
Sc. Mikhail Roshchin; d. Oleg Efremov and Naum Ardashnikov; ph. Naum Ardashnikov and Grigori Shpakler; m. Sergei Nikitin.
Viacheslav Nevinny; Alexander Kaliagin; Ksenia Minina; Irina Miroshnichenko; Nastia Nemoliayeva.

Operation 'Happy New Year' (*Operatsiia 's novym godom'*), Russia 1996, STV, TV-6 and Nikola Film (T. Voronovich, I. Kalenov and S. Selianov).
Sc. Alexander Rogozhkin; d. Alexander Rogozhkin; ph. Andrei Zhegalov; m. Vladislav Panchenko.
Alexei Buldakov; Sergei Makovetsky; Leonid Yarmolnik; Semen Strugachev; Sergei Russkin.

The Umbrellas of Cherbourg (*Les Parapluies de Cherbourg*), France/W. Germany 1964, Parc/Madeleine/Beta.
Sc. Jacques Demy; d. Jacques Demy; ph. Jean Rabier; m. Michel Legrand and Jacques Demy.
Catherine Deneuve; Anne Vernon; Nino Castelnuevo.

Plácido, Spain 1961, Jet Films.
Sc. Luis García Berlanga, Rafael Azcona and José Luis Font; d. Luis García Berlanga; ph. Francisco Sempre; m. Manuel Asins Arbó.
Castro Sendra 'Cassen'; José Luis López Vázquez; Elvira Quintanilla; Manuel Alexandre; María Carmen Yepes; Amelia de la Torre; Amparo Soler Leal; Luis Ciges.

Poor Sasha (*Bednaia Sasha*), Russia 1997, Goldvision, TV-6 (T. Voronovich, D. Keosayan).
Sc. Sergei Beloshnikov and Vladimir Bragin; d. Tigran Keosayan; ph. Yuri Liubshin; m. Artemi Artemiev.
Alexander Zbruev; Yulia Chernova; Vera Glagolieva; Olga Volkova; Valeri Garkalin; Boris Sichkin; Armen Dzhigarkhanian.

Remember the Night, US 1940, Paramount.
Sc. Preston Sturges; d. Mitchell Leisen; ph. Ted Tetzlaff; m. Fredrick Hollander.
Barbara Stanwyck; Fred MacMurray; Beulah Bondi; Elizabeth Patterson; Sterling Holloway.

Santa Claus, GB 1985, Rank.
Sc. David Newman; d. Jeannot Szwarc; ph. Arthur Ibbertson; m. Henry Mancini.
David Huddleston; Dudley Moore; John Lithgow; Judy Cornwell; Christian Fitzpatrick; Burgess Meredith.

Santa Claus Conquers the Martians, US 1964, Embassy.
Sc. Glenville Mareth; d. Nicholas Webster; ph. David Quaid.
John Call; Leonard Hicks; Pia Zadora.

The Santa Clause, US 1994, Disney.
Sc. Leonard Benvenuti and Steve Rudnick; d. John Pasquin; ph. Walt Lloyd; m. Michael Conventino.
Tim Allen; Judge Reinhold; Wendy Crewson; Eric Lloyd; Peter Boyle.

Scrooge, GB 1935, Twickenham.
Sc. Seymour Hicks and H. Fowley Mear; d. Henry Edwards; ph. Sidney Blythe and William Luff.
Seymour Hicks; Donald Calthrop; Athene Seyler; Oscar Asche; Barbara Everest; Maurice Evans; C.V. France; Marie Ney.

Scrooge, GB 1951, Renown.
Sc. Noel Langley; d. Brian Desmond Hurst; ph. C. Pennington-Richards; m. Richard Adinsell.
Alastair Sim; Mervyn Johns; Kathleen Harrison; Jack Warner; Michael Hordern; Hermione Baddeley; George Cole; Miles Malleson.

Scrooge, GB 1970, Cinema Centre/Waterbury.
W/m/ly. Leslie Bricusse; d. Ronald Neame; ph. Oswald Morris.
Albert Finney; Michael Medwin; Alec Guinness; Edith Evans; Kenneth Moore; David Collings; Laurence Naismith; Kay Walsh.

Scrooged, US 1988, Paramount/Mirage.
Sc. Mitch Glazer and Michael O'Donoghue; d. Richard Donner; ph. Michael Chapman; m. Danny Elfman.
Bill Murray; Karen Allen; John Forsythe; Robert Mitchum; John Houseman; Lee Majors.

Silent Night, Deadly Night, US 1984, Tri Star.
Sc. Michael Hickey; d. Charles E. Sellier; ph. Henning Schellerup.
Lilyan Chauvin; Robert Brian Wilson; Britt Leach; Linnea Quigley.

Silent Partner, Canada 1978, Carolco.
Sc. Curtis Hanson; d. Daryl Duke; ph. Stephen Katz; m. Oscar Peterson.
Christopher Plummer; Elliott Gould; Susannah York; Celine Lomez; Michael Kirby.

The Sympathy Seeker (Sirota kazanskaia), Russia, 1997, NTV-Profit.
Sc. Oleg Antonov; d. Vladimir Mashkov; ph. Nikolai Nemoliayev; m. Sergei Bondarenko.
Elena Shevchenko; Nikolai Fomenko; Valentin Gaft; Lev Durov; Oleg Tabakov; Misha Filipchuk.

Tales from the Crypt, GB 1972, Metromedia/Amicus.
Sc. Milton Subotsky; d. Freddie Francis; ph. Norman Warwick; m. Douglas Gamley.
Ralph Richardson; Geoffrey Bayldon; Peter Cushing; Joan Collins; Ian Hendry; Robin Phillips; Richard Greene; Barbara Murray; Roy Dotrice; Nigel Patrick; Patrick Magee; Chloe Franks.

36: 15 – Code Père Noel, France 1989, LM/Deal/Garance.
Sc. Rene Manzor; d. Rene Manzor; ph. Michel Gaffier.
Alain Musy; Brigitte Fossey; Louis Ducreux; Patrick Florsheim.

This Happy Breed, GB 1944, Two Cities.
Sc. David Lean, Ronald Neame, Anthony Havelock-Allen and Noel Coward; d. David Lean; ph. Ronald Neame; m. Noel Coward.
Robert Newton; Celia Johnson; Stanley Holloway; John Mills; Kay Walsh; Amy Veness; Alison Leggatt.

This Merry Planet (Eta veselaia planeta), USSR 1973, Mosfilm (Gosteleradio).
Sc. Dmitri Ivanov, Vladimir Trifonov and Yuri Saakov; d. Yuri Saakov and Yuri Tsvetkov; ph. Konstantin Petrichenko; m. David Tukhmanov.
Saveli Kramarov; Leonid Kuravlev; Alexander Vokach; Ekaterina Vasilieva.

To All a Goodnight, US 1980, IRC/IWDC/4 Features.
Sc. Alex Rebar; d. David Hess; ph. B. Godsey.
Jennifer Runyon; Forest Swanson; Linda Gentile.

Tunisian Victory, GB/US 1944, Army Film and Photographic Unit/ American and Allied Film Services.
Sc. James Lansdale Hodson and Anthony Veiller; d. Hugh Stewart and Frank Capra; comm. Leo Genn, Anthony Veiller, Bernard Miles and Burgess Meredith.

Turkey Time, GB 1933, Gaumont.
Sc. Ben Travers; d. Tom Walls; ph. Charles Van Enger.
Tom Walls; Ben Travers; Robertson Hare; Dorothy Hyson; Mary Brough; Norma Varden.

Life is a Long Quiet River (La Vie est un long fleuve tranquille), France 1988, Telema/MK2/FR3 Films.
Sc. Etienne Chatiliez and Florence Quentin; d. Etienne Chatiliez.
Benoit Magimel; Hélène Vincent; Andre Wilms.

White Christmas, US 1954, Paramount.
Sc. Norman Krasna and Melvin Frank; d. Michael Curtiz; ph. Loyal Griggs; m/ly. Irving Berlin.
Bing Crosby; Danny Kaye; Rosemary Clooney; Vera-Ellen; Dean Jagger.

The Wizards (*Charodei*), USSR, 1982, Odessa Film Studio (Gosteleradio).
Sc. Strugatsky Brothers; d. Konstantin Bromberg; ph. Konstantin Apriatin; m. Evgeni Krylatov.
Alexandra Yakovleva; Alexander Abdulov; Valentin Gaft; Ekaterina Vasilieva; Valeri Zolotukhin; Emmanuel Vitorgan.

Will It Snow For Christmas? (*Y aura-t-il de la neige à Noël?*), France 1997, Ognon Productions.
Sc. Sandrine Veysset; d. Sandrine Veysset.
Dominique Reymond; Daniel Duval.

You Better Watch Out, US 1980, Pressman.
Sc. Lewis Jackson; d. Lewis Jackson; ph. R. Aronovich.
Brandon Maggart; Dianne Hull; Scott McKay.

Index of cast, crew, characters and film locations

(Character names shown in *italic*)
Note, author names are given in the general index

General Index

action genre, 155–161
A Christmas Carol
  book, xi, 3, 8, 9–14
  film adaptations, 3–4, 5, 14–16, 18, 20, 24, 34, 39
  influence on/appearance in other films, 60, 112, 120, 136, 137, 169, 212
  musical adaptations, 24–25
  novelty/other productions, 14, 24–25, 29, 30, 31
aliens, 5, 197, 205
Aldwych farce, 97–105
American Christmas, 39, 54, 81–82, 112, 116, 126, 138, 162
Americanism and the American Way, 50, 127, 150, 214
angels, use of, 41, 45, 75, 111, 138
Anglo-American forces, 84, 85
animation, 30, 33, 141
audience
  levels, 59, 74, 144, 157
  expectations, 80, 93, 145, 162, 175
  targeting, 70, 76, 81, 147, 154, 157

Beveridge Report, The, 22–23
blockbuster syndrome, 26, 144
box-office failure/success, 39, 45, 59, 70, 101, 133, 144, 149, 153, 157
Britain
  Christmas in, 84, see also *Victorian Christmas*
  representations of, 87

British films, 16–18, 77–95, 97, 100, 118, 139

café-théatre, 178
capitalism, 20, 46, 52, 122, 166, 188, 191
'Capra-corn', 39, 50
carnival, 187–188, 194, 197
carols, use of
  in films, 17, 19, 24, 45, 61, 73–74, 84–87, 103, 108, 112, 139, 169, 219
  in society, 2, 3, 13, 165, 168, 211
Catholic church, the, 2, 74, 166–167, 170, 217
celebration of Christmas, 1–3, 79, 84, 93, 165, 171, 186
charity, 19, 28, 32, 33, 152, 154, 166, 167, 214, 216, 218
children
  films for, 31, 146–155, 175, 199, 206, 208
  use of in films, 23, 63, 69, 73, 80–81, 84–86, 103, 161, 180, 192, 200
Christmas cards, 13, 67, 81, 82, 88, 138
Christmas decorations, 88, 95, 108, 138, 139, 161
'Christmas film' formula, 60, 64, 157–158
Christmas iconography, 145, 158, 168, 170
Christmas tree, use of
  in society, 2, 3, 165, 166, 187
  in films, 67, 71, 73, 80, 83, 85, 108, 139, 145, 147, 150, 155, 161, 171, 180, 192, 199